# BLACK CAT

## ON THE RUN

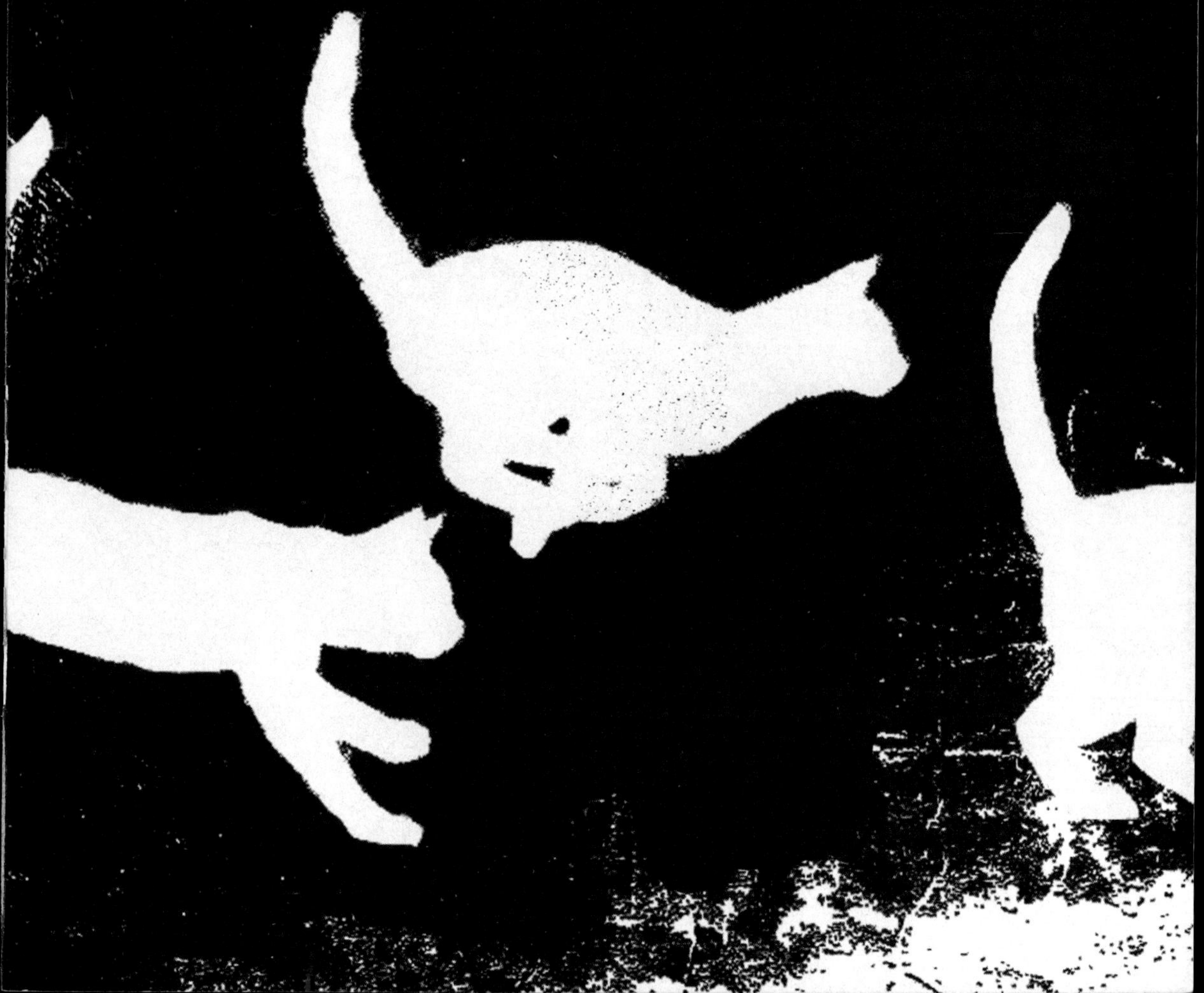

BH[C

### The Black Cat's Crew's Haul to Date*:

- One Old Master's Painting of Christ Crucified with Two Thieves (The Frick Collection)
- One Original Deed to the Island of Manhattan (Sanctum Sanctorum)
- One Authentic Manuscript of Hypothetical Science: *The Papers of Phineas Randall* (4 Yancy St.) †
- One Heart of Johnny Storm (*Ibid.*) ‡

*Felicia Hardy's mentor – the crew's – the Black Fox, has assured her, Dr. Boris Korpse and Bruno Grainger that their growing inventory serves a larger scheme: robbing the extradimensional vault of the New York Thieves Guild.

†This heist was a challenge. A requisition for an evening of personal time has been submitted and approved.

‡Incidental acquisition.

collection editor **JENNIFER GRÜNWALD** ♦ assistant managing editor **MAIA LOY**
assistant managing editor **LISA MONTALBANO** ♦ editor, special projects **MARK D. BEAZLEY**
vp production & special projects **JEFF YOUNGQUIST** ♦ book designer **JAY BOWEN**
svp print, sales & marketing **DAVID GABRIEL** ♦ editor in chief **C.B. CEBULSKI**

**BLACK CAT VOL. 2: ON THE RUN.** Contains material originally published in magazine form as BLACK CAT (2019) #6-10. First printing 2020. ISBN 978-1-302-91921-4. Published by MARVEL WORLDWIDE, INC., a subsidiary of MARVEL ENTERTAINMENT, LLC. OFFICE OF PUBLICATION: 1290 Avenue of the Americas, New York, NY 10104. © 2020 MARVEL No similarity between any of the names, characters, persons, and/or institutions in this magazine with those of any living or dead person or institution is intended, and any such similarity which may exist is purely coincidental. **Printed in Canada.** KEVIN FEIGE, Chief Creative Officer; DAN BUCKLEY, President, Marvel Entertainment; JOHN NEE, Publisher; JOE QUESADA, EVP & Creative Director; TOM BREVOORT, SVP of Publishing; DAVID BOGART, Associate Publisher & SVP of Talent Affairs; Publishing & Partnership; DAVID GABRIEL, VP of Print & Digital Publishing; JEFF YOUNGQUIST, VP of Production & Special Projects; DAN CARR, Executive Director of Publishing Technology; ALEX MORALES, Director of Publishing Operations; DAN EDINGTON, Managing Editor; SUSAN CRESPI, Production Manager; STAN LEE, Chairman Emeritus. For information regarding advertising in Marvel Comics or on Marvel.com, please contact Vit DeBellis, Custom Solutions & Integrated Advertising Manager, at vdebellis@marvel.com. For Marvel subscription inquiries, please call 888-511-5480. **Manufactured between 7/10/2020 and 8/11/2020 by SOLISCO PRINTERS, SCOTT, QC, CANADA.**

10 9 8 7 6 5 4 3 2 1

# KCAT
## ON THE RUN

| | |
|---|---|
| writer | **JED MacKAY** |
| artists | **MIKE DOWLING** (#6), **TRAVEL FOREMAN** (#7), **DIKE RUAN** (#8), **ANNIE WU** (#8) & **KRIS ANKA** (#9-10) |
| color artist | **BRIAN REBER** |
| letterer | **FERRAN DELGADO** |
| cover art | **J. SCOTT CAMPBELL** & **SABINE RICH** (#6-8 & #10) & **EDGAR DELGADO** (#9) |
| assistant editors | **KATHLEEN WISNESKI** & **LINDSEY COHICK** |
| editor | **NICK LOWE** |

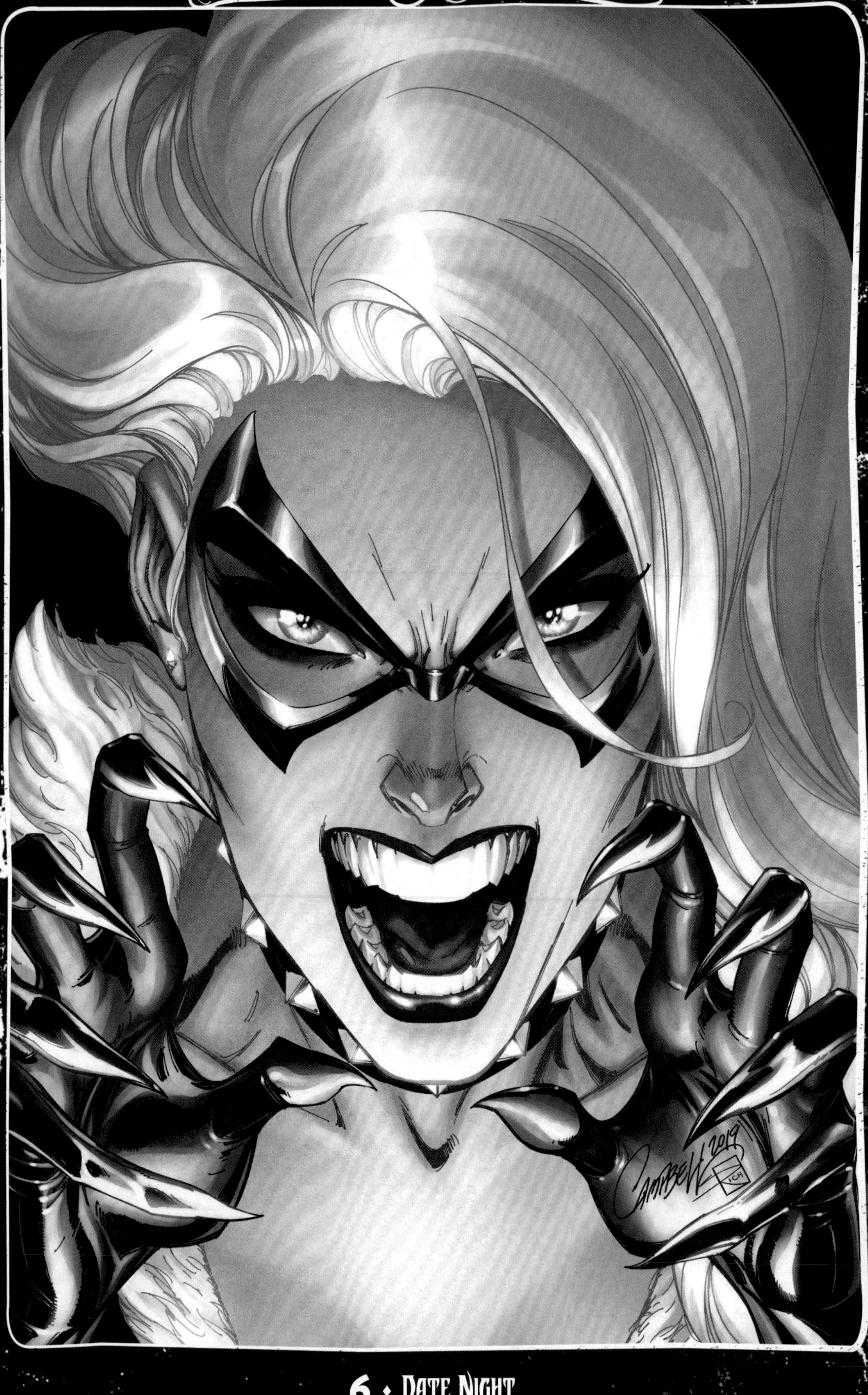

## 6 • Date Night

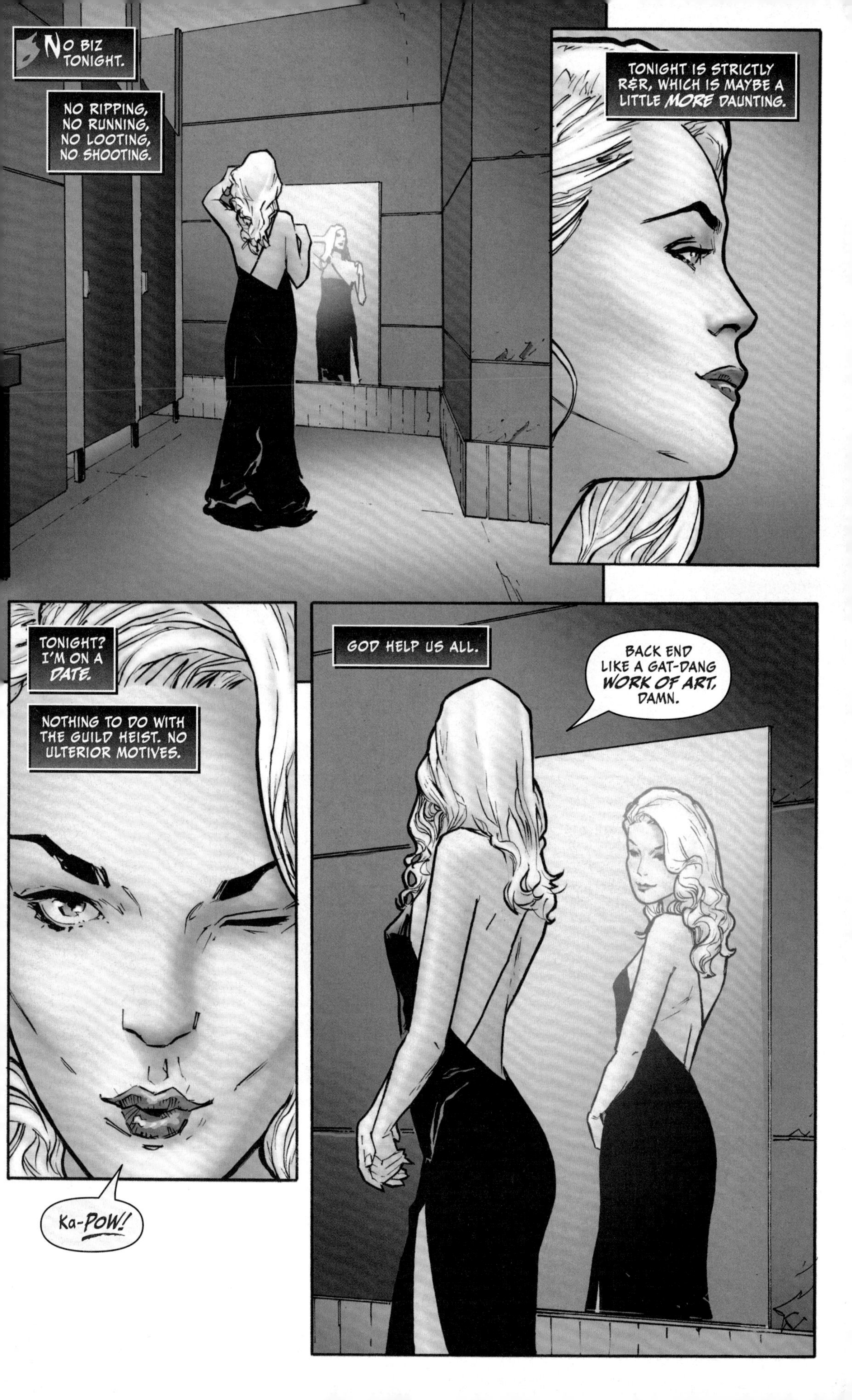
NO BIZ TONIGHT.
NO RIPPING, NO RUNNING, NO LOOTING, NO SHOOTING.
TONIGHT IS STRICTLY R&R, WHICH IS MAYBE A LITTLE MORE DAUNTING.
TONIGHT? I'M ON A DATE.
NOTHING TO DO WITH THE GUILD HEIST. NO ULTERIOR MOTIVES.
Ka-POW!
GOD HELP US ALL.
BACK END LIKE A GAT-DANG WORK OF ART. DAMN.

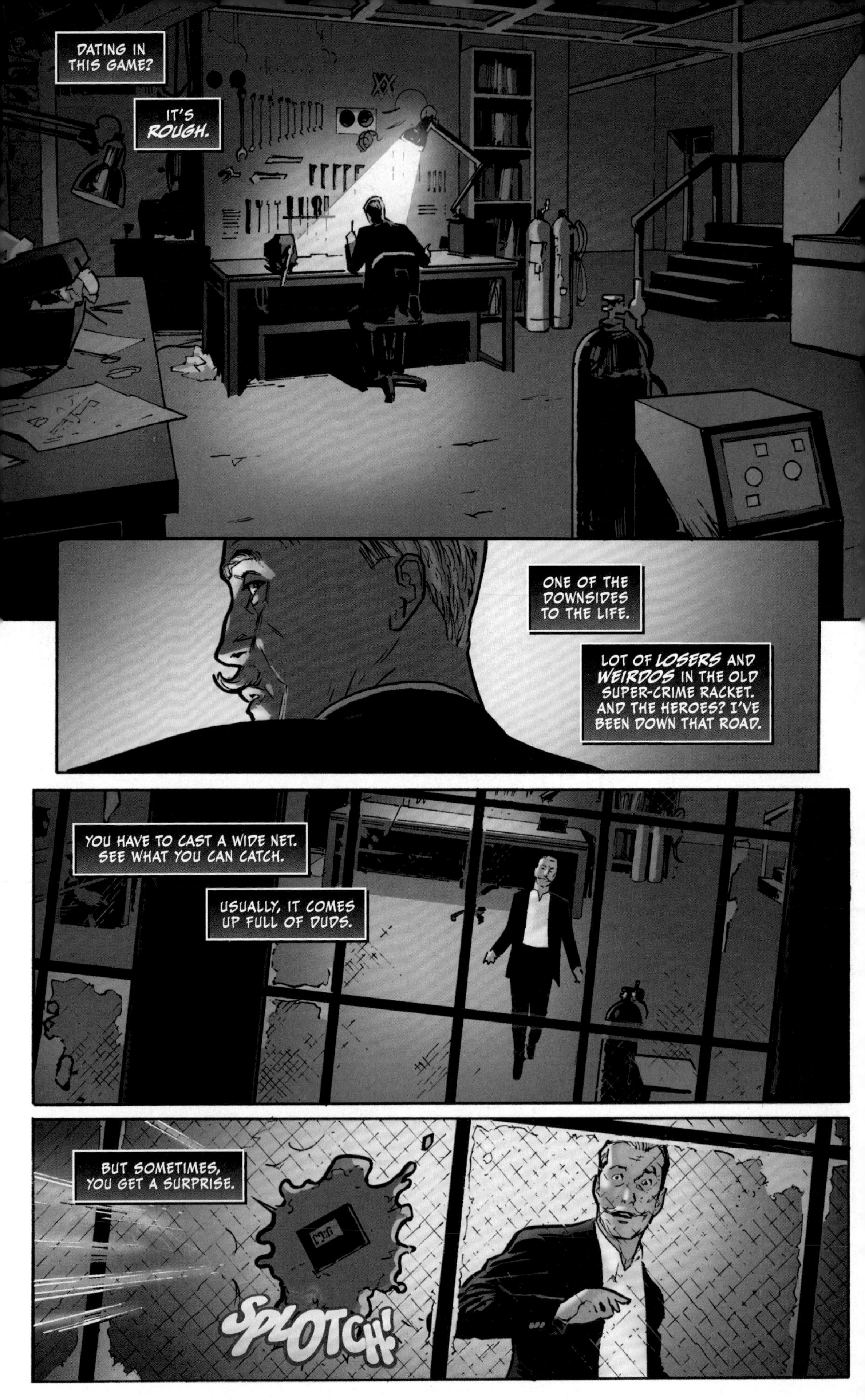
DATING IN THIS GAME?
IT'S *ROUGH.*
ONE OF THE DOWNSIDES TO THE LIFE.
LOT OF *LOSERS* AND *WEIRDOS* IN THE OLD SUPER-CRIME RACKET. AND THE HEROES? I'VE BEEN DOWN THAT ROAD.
YOU HAVE TO CAST A WIDE NET. SEE WHAT YOU CAN CATCH.
USUALLY, IT COMES UP FULL OF DUDS.
BUT SOMETIMES, YOU GET A SURPRISE.
SPLOTCH!

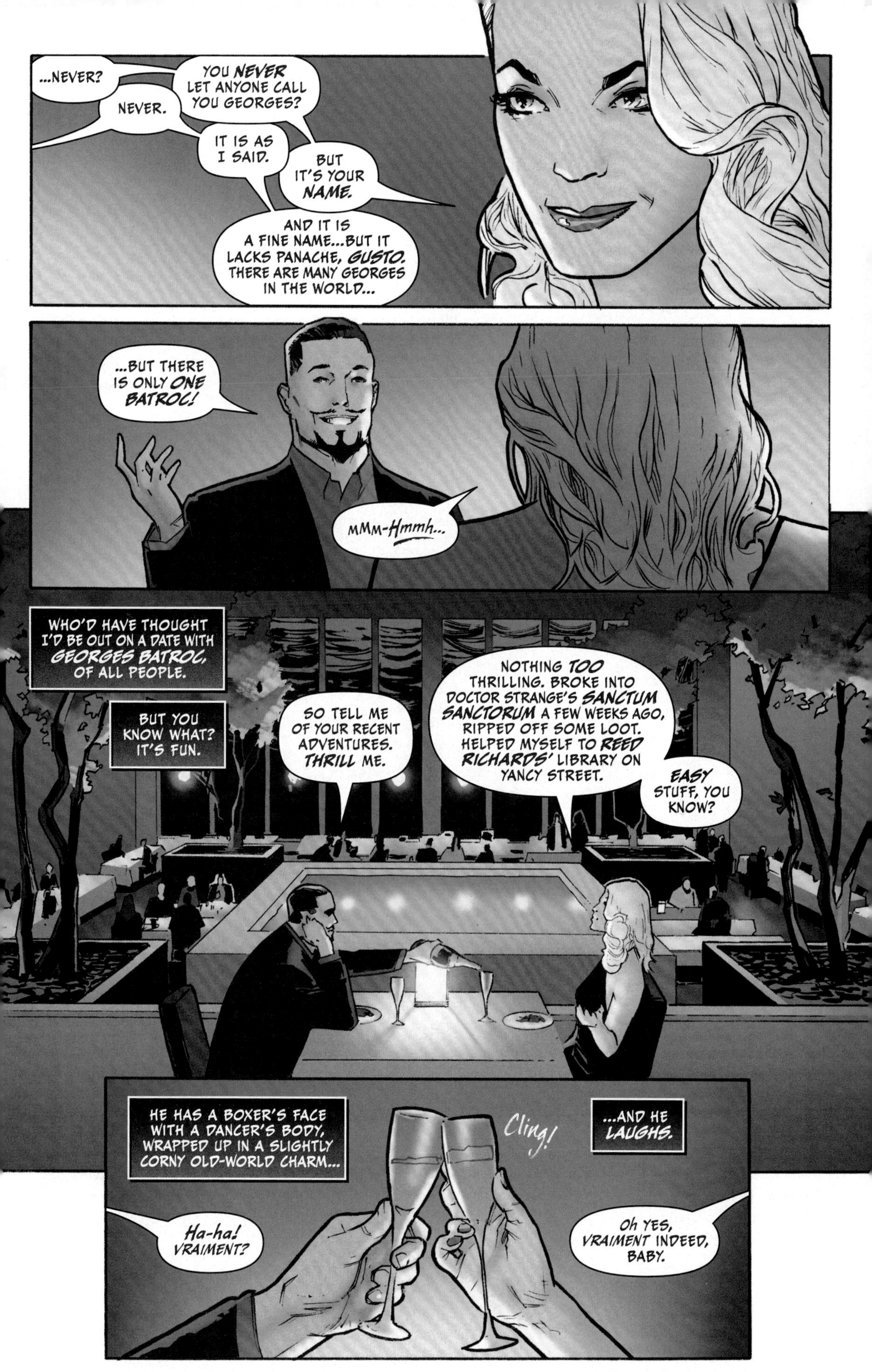
...NEVER?
YOU NEVER LET ANYONE CALL YOU GEORGES?
NEVER.
IT IS AS I SAID.
BUT IT'S YOUR NAME.
AND IT IS A FINE NAME...BUT IT LACKS PANACHE, GUSTO. THERE ARE MANY GEORGES IN THE WORLD...
...BUT THERE IS ONLY ONE BATROC!
MMM-Hmmh...
WHO'D HAVE THOUGHT I'D BE OUT ON A DATE WITH GEORGES BATROC, OF ALL PEOPLE.
BUT YOU KNOW WHAT? IT'S FUN.
SO TELL ME OF YOUR RECENT ADVENTURES. THRILL ME.
NOTHING TOO THRILLING. BROKE INTO DOCTOR STRANGE'S SANCTUM SANCTORUM A FEW WEEKS AGO, RIPPED OFF SOME LOOT. HELPED MYSELF TO REED RICHARDS' LIBRARY ON YANCY STREET.
EASY STUFF, YOU KNOW?
HE HAS A BOXER'S FACE WITH A DANCER'S BODY, WRAPPED UP IN A SLIGHTLY CORNY OLD-WORLD CHARM...
Cling!
...AND HE LAUGHS.
Ha-ha! VRAIMENT?
Oh YES, VRAIMENT INDEED, BABY.

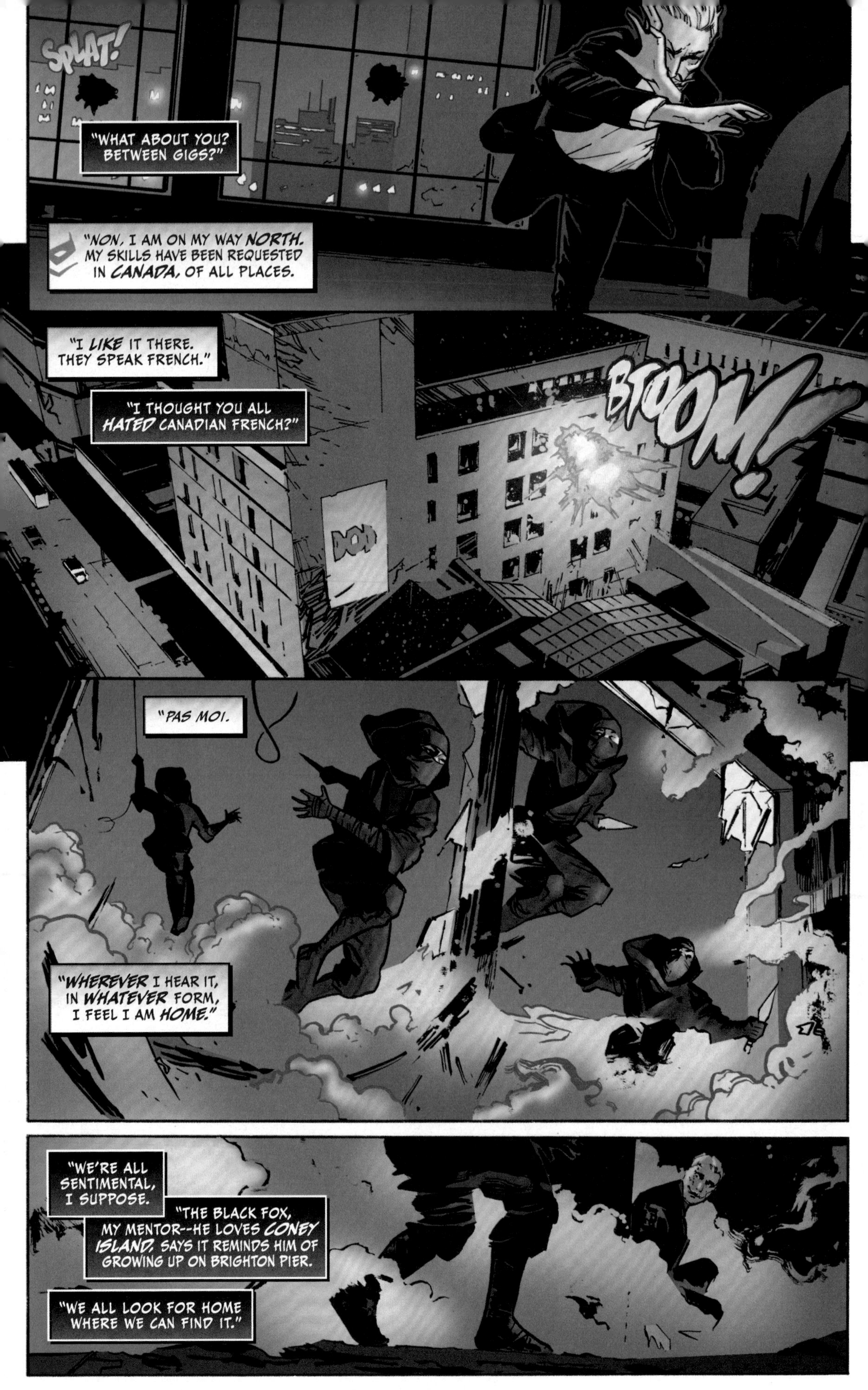
SPLAT!
"WHAT ABOUT YOU? BETWEEN GIGS?"
"NON, I AM ON MY WAY NORTH. MY SKILLS HAVE BEEN REQUESTED IN CANADA, OF ALL PLACES.
"I LIKE IT THERE. THEY SPEAK FRENCH."
"I THOUGHT YOU ALL HATED CANADIAN FRENCH?"
BTOOM!
"PAS MOI.
"WHEREVER I HEAR IT, IN WHATEVER FORM, I FEEL I AM HOME."
"WE'RE ALL SENTIMENTAL, I SUPPOSE.
"THE BLACK FOX, MY MENTOR--HE LOVES CONEY ISLAND. SAYS IT REMINDS HIM OF GROWING UP ON BRIGHTON PIER.
"WE ALL LOOK FOR HOME WHERE WE CAN FIND IT."

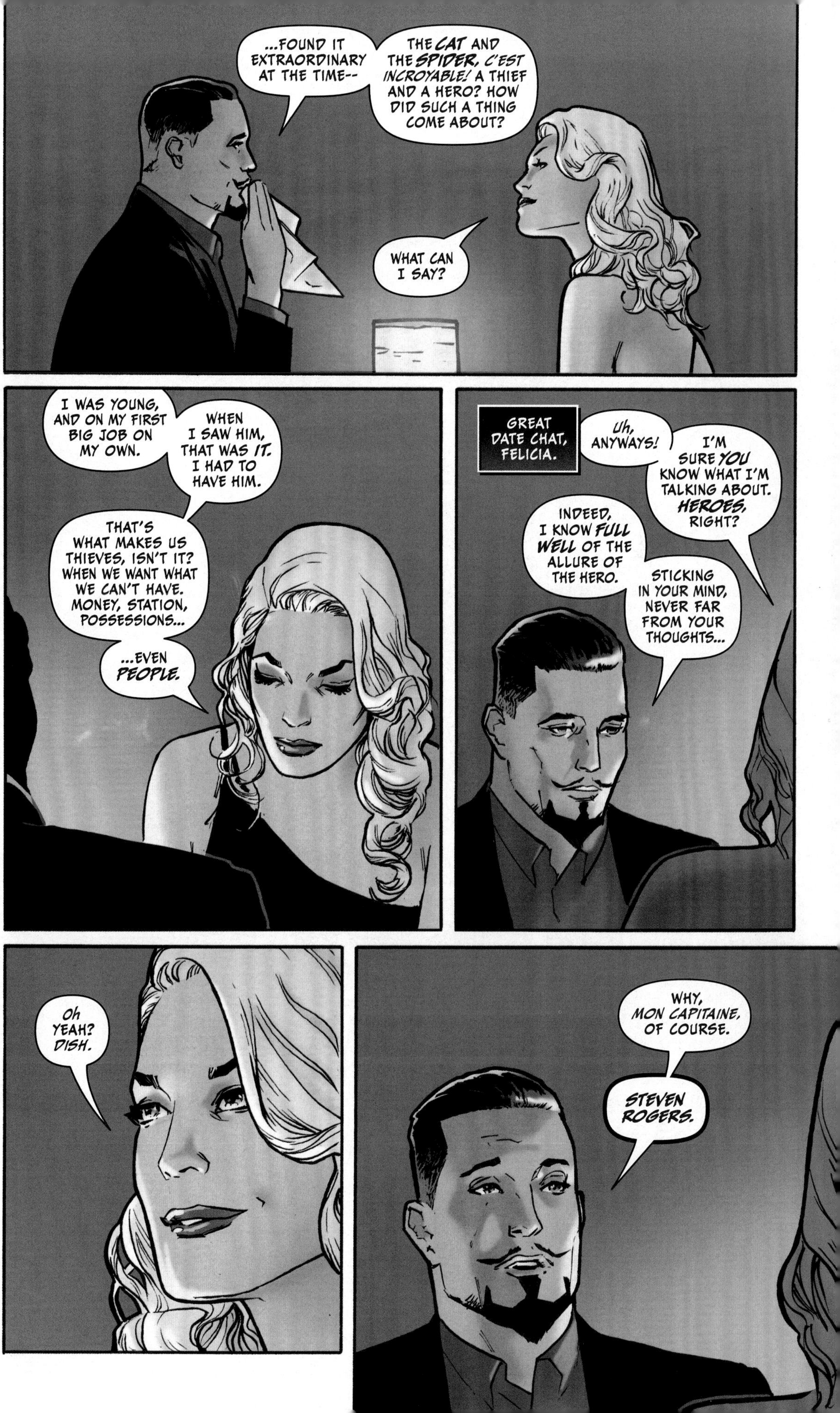
...FOUND IT EXTRAORDINARY AT THE TIME--
THE CAT AND THE SPIDER, C'EST INCROYABLE! A THIEF AND A HERO? HOW DID SUCH A THING COME ABOUT?
WHAT CAN I SAY?
I WAS YOUNG, AND ON MY FIRST BIG JOB ON MY OWN.
WHEN I SAW HIM, THAT WAS IT. I HAD TO HAVE HIM.
THAT'S WHAT MAKES US THIEVES, ISN'T IT? WHEN WE WANT WHAT WE CAN'T HAVE. MONEY, STATION, POSSESSIONS...
...EVEN PEOPLE.
GREAT DATE CHAT, FELICIA.
Uh, ANYWAYS!
I'M SURE YOU KNOW WHAT I'M TALKING ABOUT. HEROES, RIGHT?
INDEED, I KNOW FULL WELL OF THE ALLURE OF THE HERO.
STICKING IN YOUR MIND, NEVER FAR FROM YOUR THOUGHTS...
Oh YEAH? DISH.
WHY, MON CAPITAINE, OF COURSE.
STEVEN ROGERS.

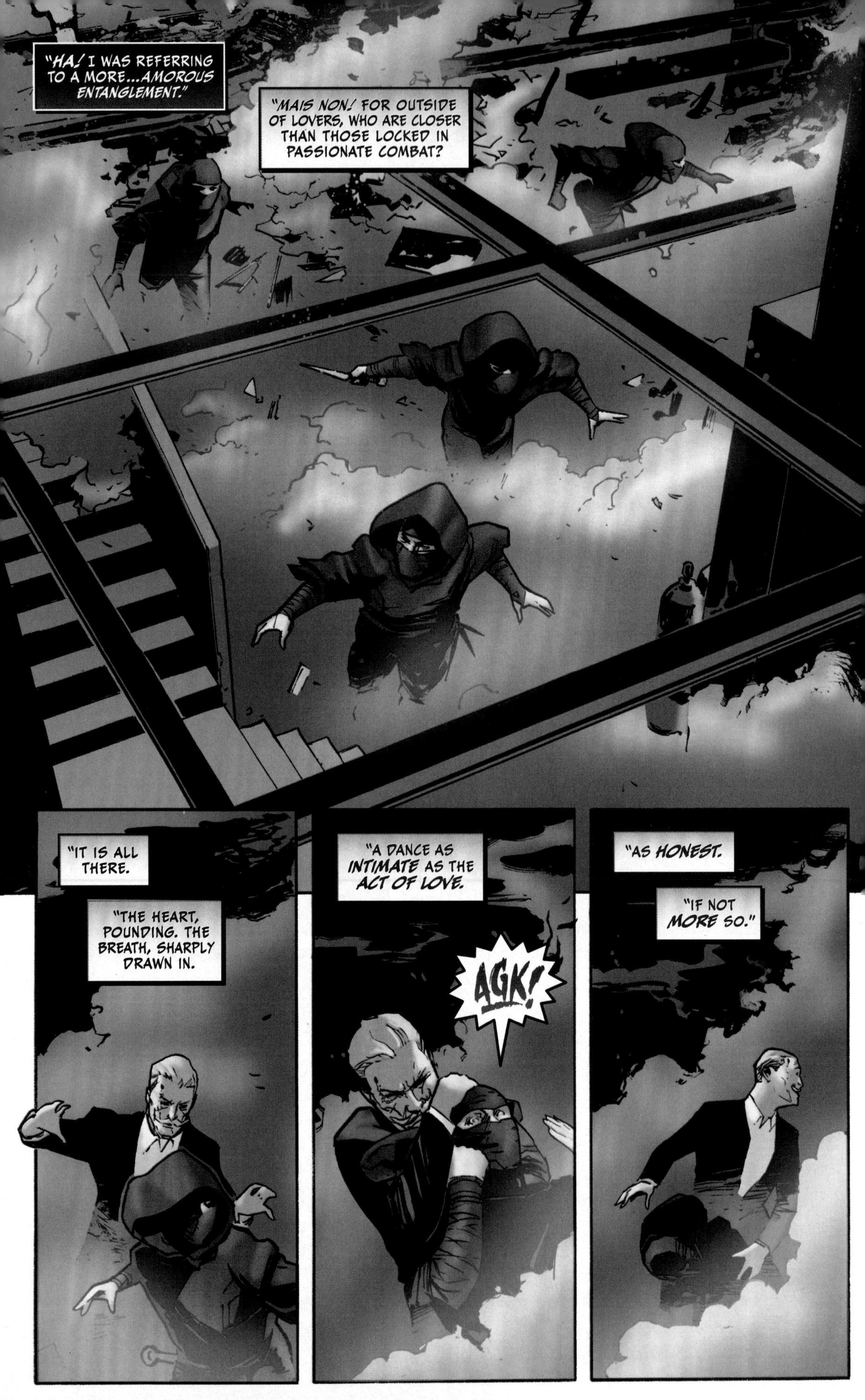
"HA! I WAS REFERRING TO A MORE...AMOROUS ENTANGLEMENT."
"MAIS NON! FOR OUTSIDE OF LOVERS, WHO ARE CLOSER THAN THOSE LOCKED IN PASSIONATE COMBAT?
"IT IS ALL THERE.
"THE HEART, POUNDING. THE BREATH, SHARPLY DRAWN IN.
"A DANCE AS INTIMATE AS THE ACT OF LOVE.
AGK!
"AS HONEST.
"IF NOT MORE SO."

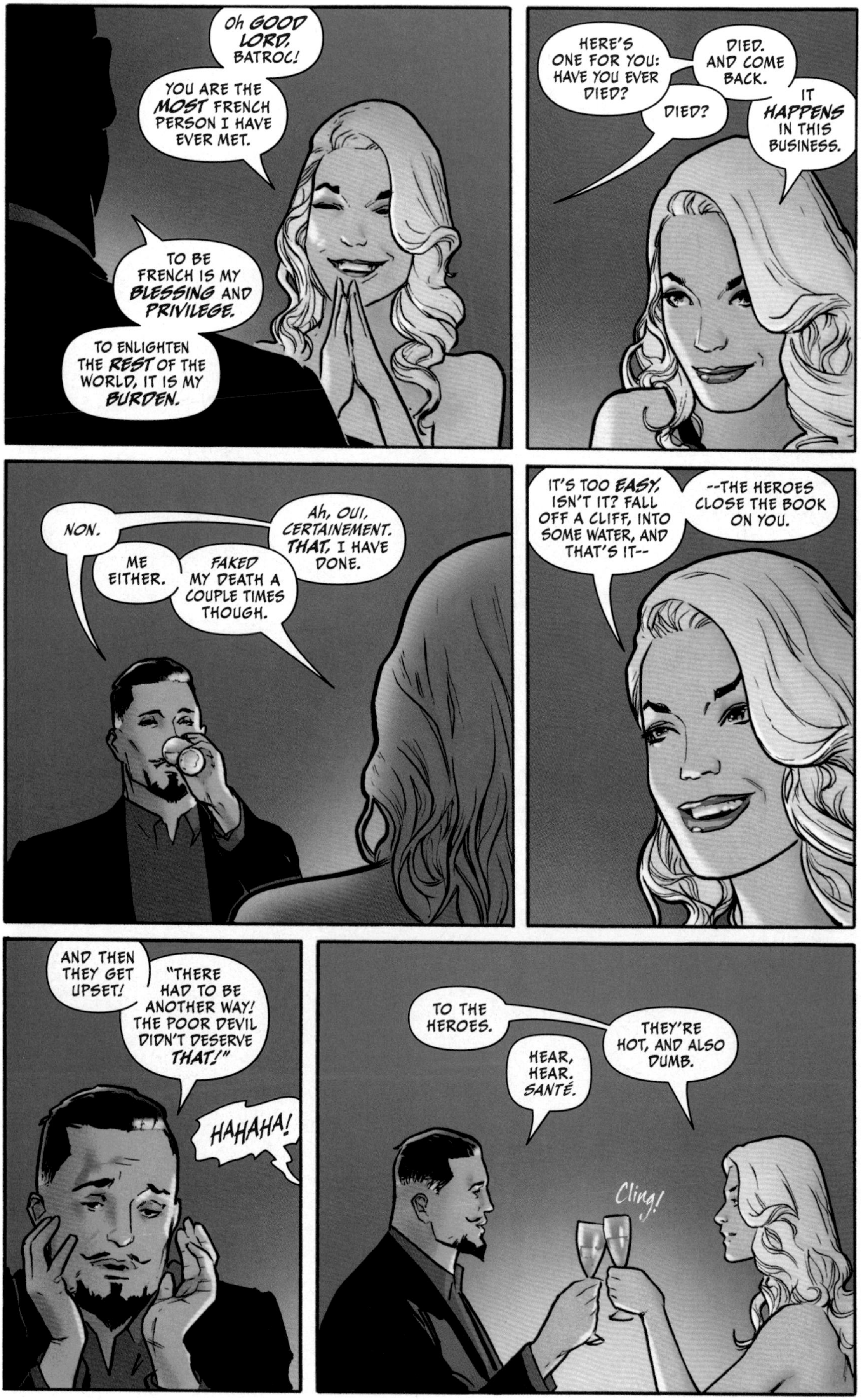

Oh GOOD LORD, BATROC!
YOU ARE THE MOST FRENCH PERSON I HAVE EVER MET.
TO BE FRENCH IS MY BLESSING AND PRIVILEGE.
TO ENLIGHTEN THE REST OF THE WORLD, IT IS MY BURDEN.
HERE'S ONE FOR YOU: HAVE YOU EVER DIED?
DIED?
DIED. AND COME BACK.
IT HAPPENS IN THIS BUSINESS.
NON.
Ah, OUI, CERTAINEMENT. THAT, I HAVE DONE.
ME EITHER.
FAKED MY DEATH A COUPLE TIMES THOUGH.
IT'S TOO EASY, ISN'T IT? FALL OFF A CLIFF, INTO SOME WATER, AND THAT'S IT--
--THE HEROES CLOSE THE BOOK ON YOU.
AND THEN THEY GET UPSET!
"THERE HAD TO BE ANOTHER WAY! THE POOR DEVIL DIDN'T DESERVE THAT!"
HAHAHA!
TO THE HEROES.
THEY'RE HOT, AND ALSO DUMB.
HEAR, HEAR. SANTÉ.
Cling!

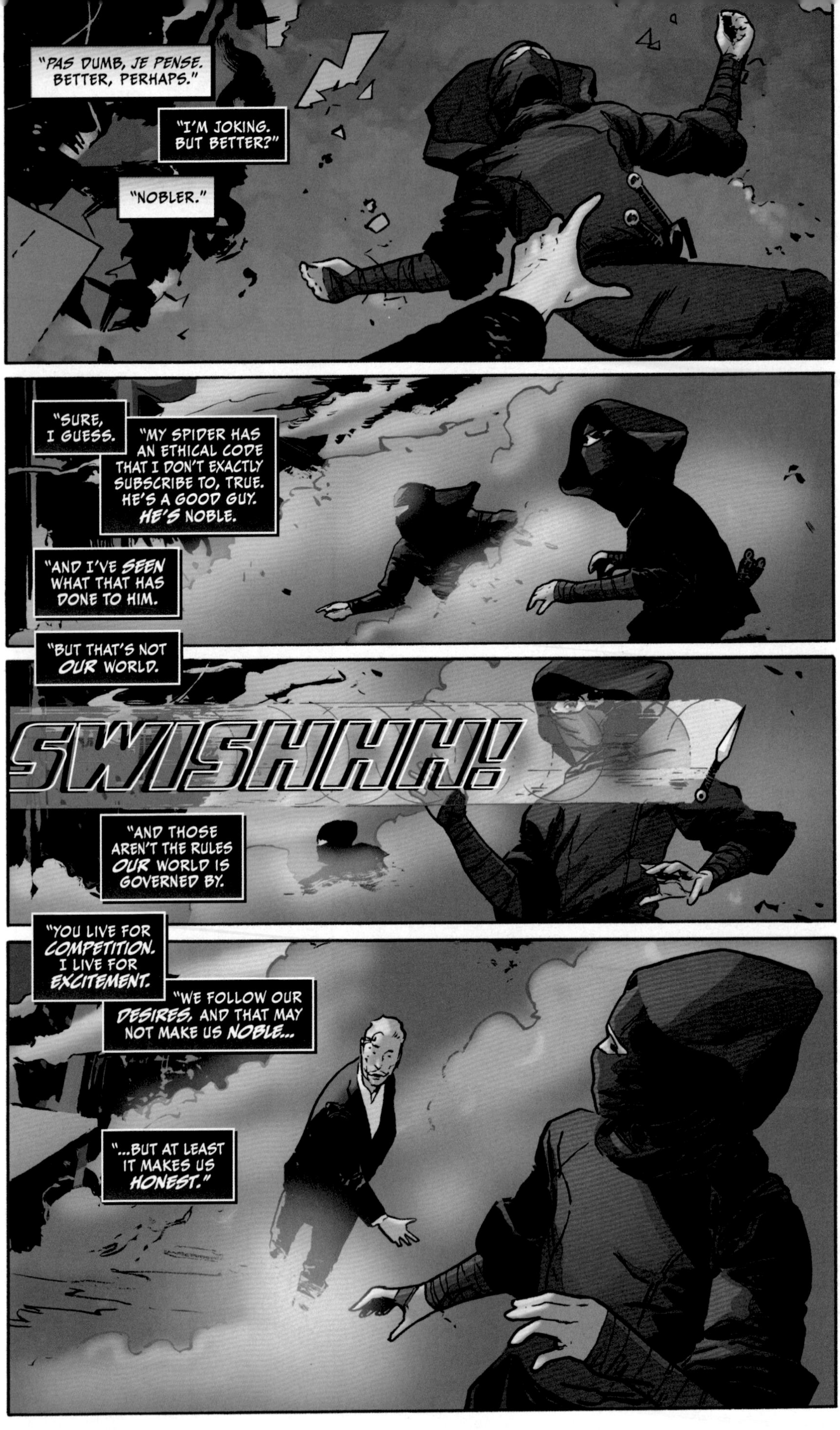
"PAS DUMB, JE PENSE. BETTER, PERHAPS."
"I'M JOKING. BUT BETTER?"
"NOBLER."
"SURE, I GUESS.
"MY SPIDER HAS AN ETHICAL CODE THAT I DON'T EXACTLY SUBSCRIBE TO, TRUE. HE'S A GOOD GUY. HE'S NOBLE.
"AND I'VE SEEN WHAT THAT HAS DONE TO HIM.
"BUT THAT'S NOT OUR WORLD.
SWISHHH!
"AND THOSE AREN'T THE RULES OUR WORLD IS GOVERNED BY.
"YOU LIVE FOR COMPETITION. I LIVE FOR EXCITEMENT.
"WE FOLLOW OUR DESIRES, AND THAT MAY NOT MAKE US NOBLE...
"...BUT AT LEAST IT MAKES US HONEST."

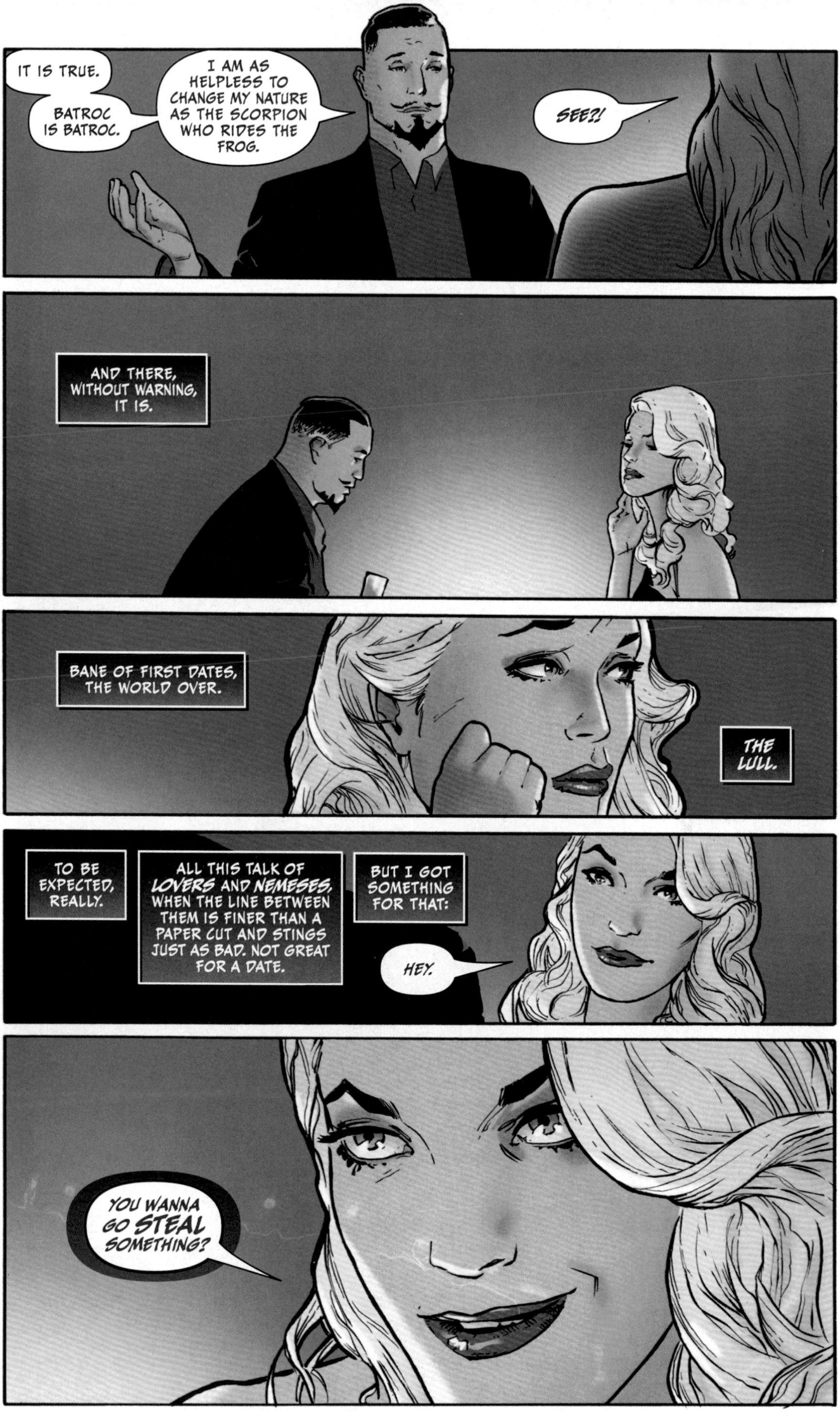
IT IS TRUE.
BATROC IS BATROC.
I AM AS HELPLESS TO CHANGE MY NATURE AS THE SCORPION WHO RIDES THE FROG.
SEE?!
AND THERE, WITHOUT WARNING, IT IS.
BANE OF FIRST DATES, THE WORLD OVER.
THE LULL.
TO BE EXPECTED, REALLY.
ALL THIS TALK OF LOVERS AND NEMESES, WHEN THE LINE BETWEEN THEM IS FINER THAN A PAPER CUT AND STINGS JUST AS BAD. NOT GREAT FOR A DATE.
BUT I GOT SOMETHING FOR THAT:
HEY.
YOU WANNA GO STEAL SOMETHING?

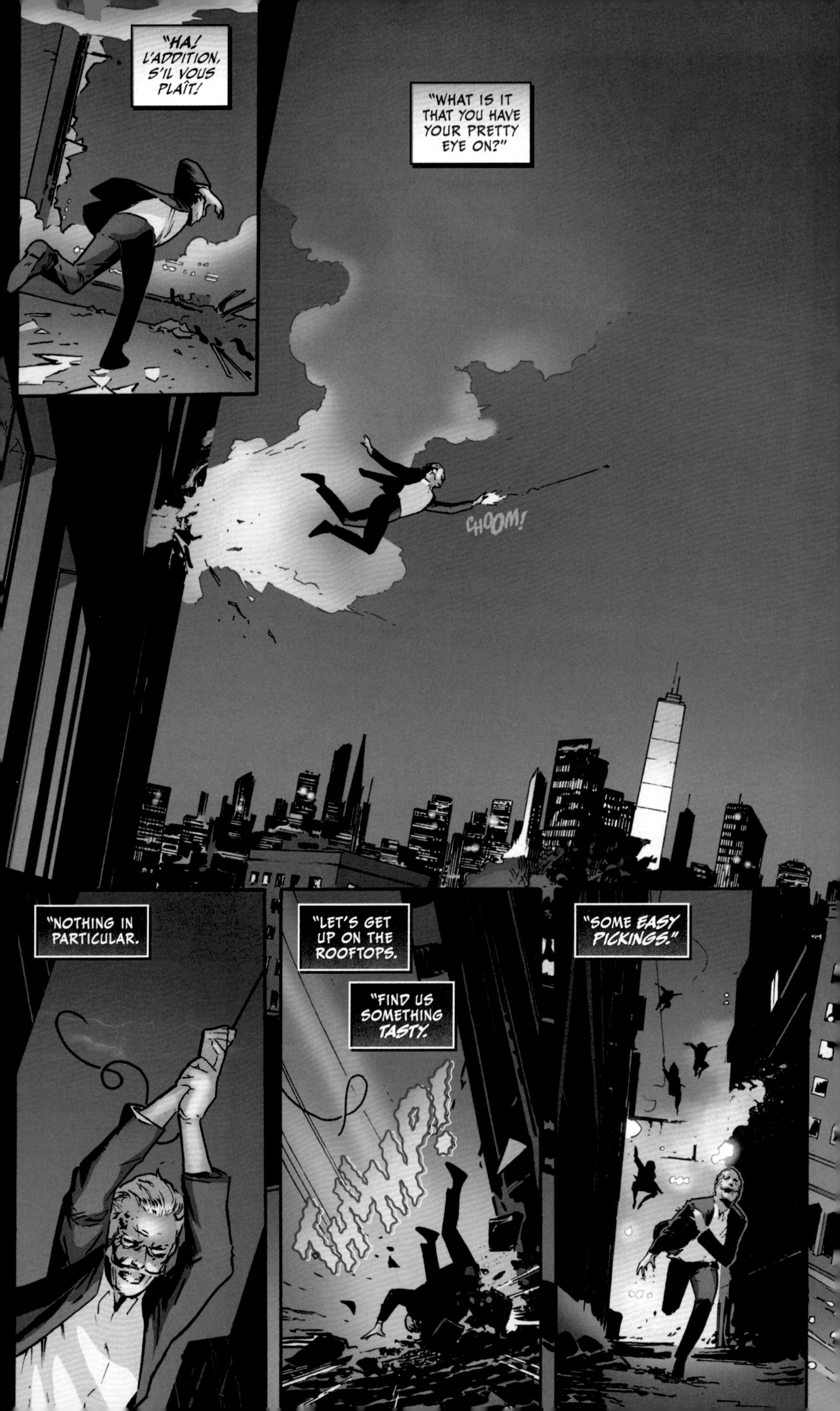
"HA! L'ADDITION, S'IL VOUS PLAÎT!
"WHAT IS IT THAT YOU HAVE YOUR PRETTY EYE ON?"
CHOOM!
"NOTHING IN PARTICULAR.
"LET'S GET UP ON THE ROOFTOPS.
"FIND US SOMETHING TASTY.
"SOME EASY PICKINGS."

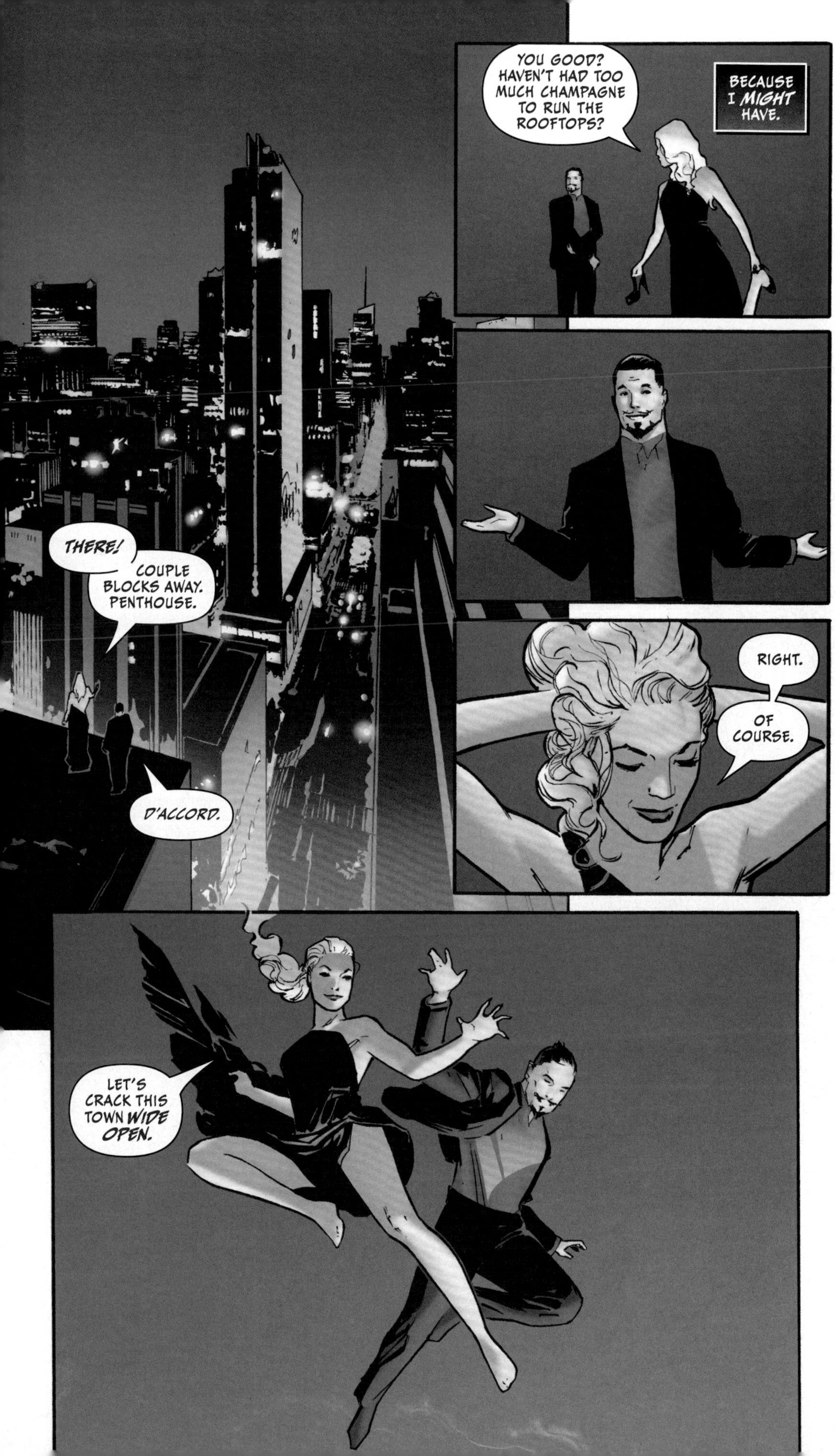
THERE!
COUPLE BLOCKS AWAY. PENTHOUSE.
D'ACCORD.
YOU GOOD? HAVEN'T HAD TOO MUCH CHAMPAGNE TO RUN THE ROOFTOPS?
BECAUSE I MIGHT HAVE.
RIGHT.
OF COURSE.
LET'S CRACK THIS TOWN WIDE OPEN.

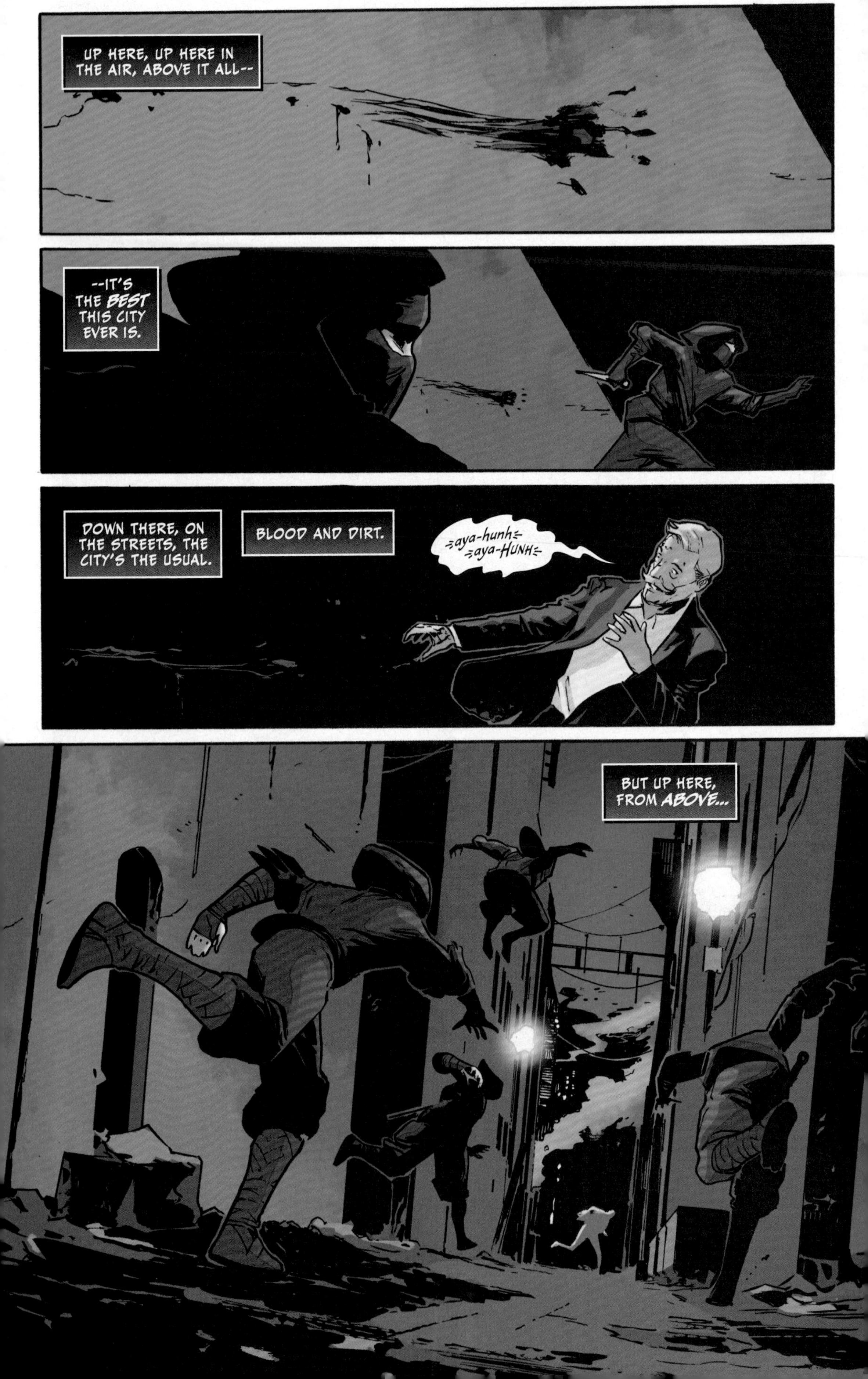
UP HERE, UP HERE IN THE AIR, ABOVE IT ALL--
--IT'S THE BEST THIS CITY EVER IS.
DOWN THERE, ON THE STREETS, THE CITY'S THE USUAL.
BLOOD AND DIRT.
aya-hunh aya-HUNH
BUT UP HERE, FROM ABOVE...

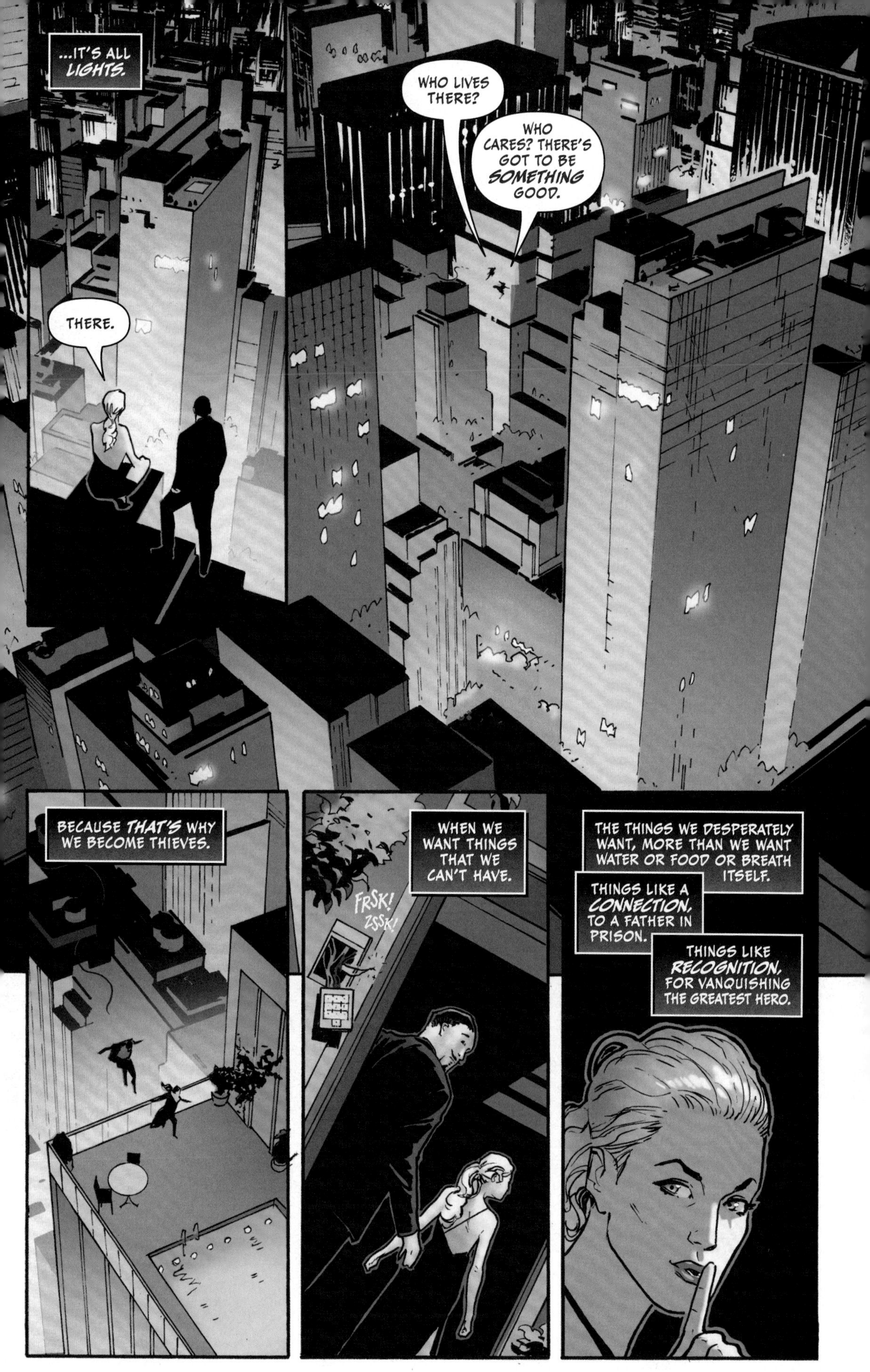
...IT'S ALL LIGHTS.
THERE.
WHO LIVES THERE?
WHO CARES? THERE'S GOT TO BE SOMETHING GOOD.
BECAUSE THAT'S WHY WE BECOME THIEVES.
WHEN WE WANT THINGS THAT WE CAN'T HAVE.
FRSK!
ZSSK!
THE THINGS WE DESPERATELY WANT, MORE THAN WE WANT WATER OR FOOD OR BREATH ITSELF.
THINGS LIKE A CONNECTION, TO A FATHER IN PRISON.
THINGS LIKE RECOGNITION, FOR VANQUISHING THE GREATEST HERO.

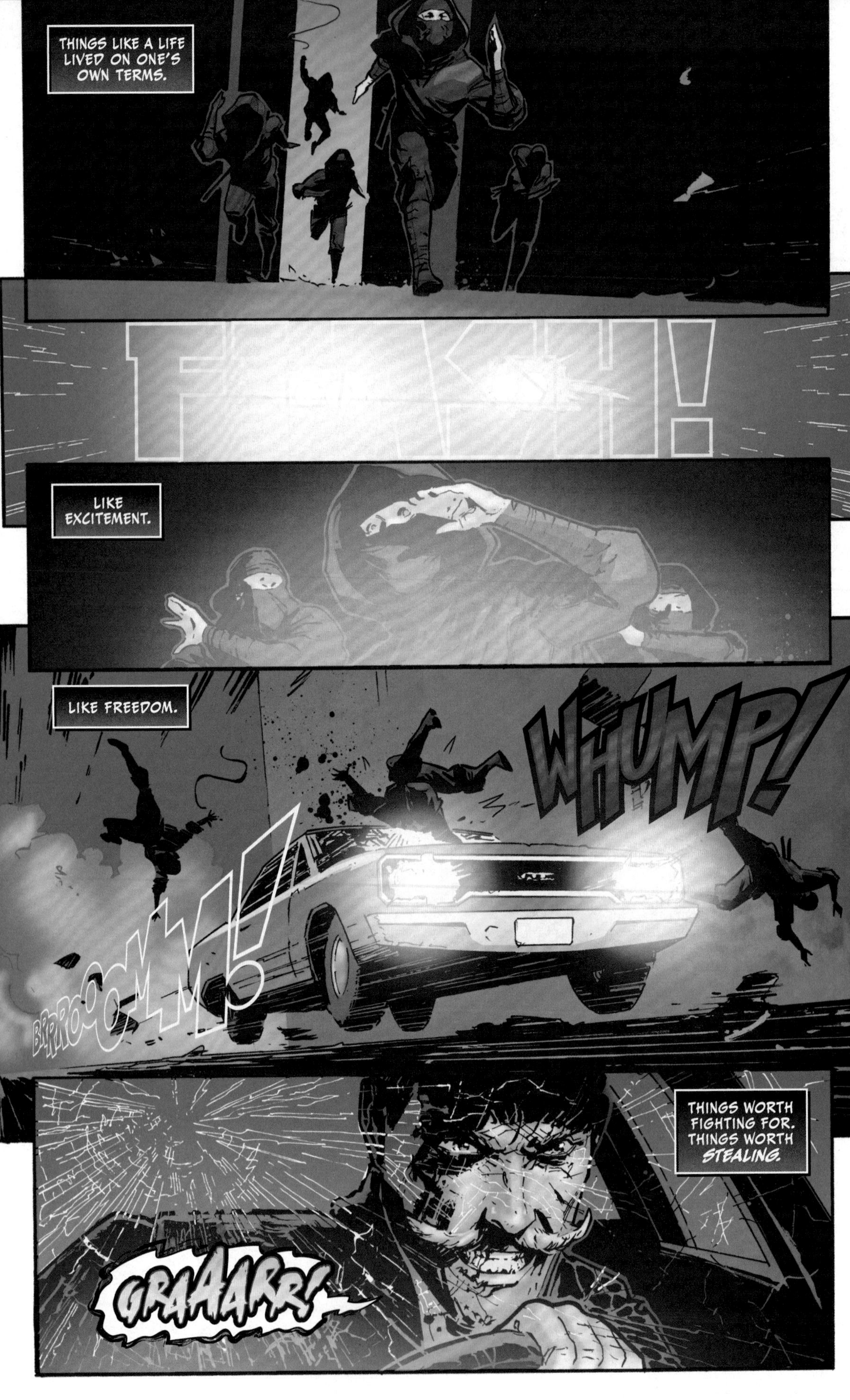
THINGS LIKE A LIFE LIVED ON ONE'S OWN TERMS.
LIKE EXCITEMENT.
LIKE FREEDOM.
WHUMP!
BRRROOOMM!
THINGS WORTH FIGHTING FOR. THINGS WORTH *STEALING.*
GRAAARR!

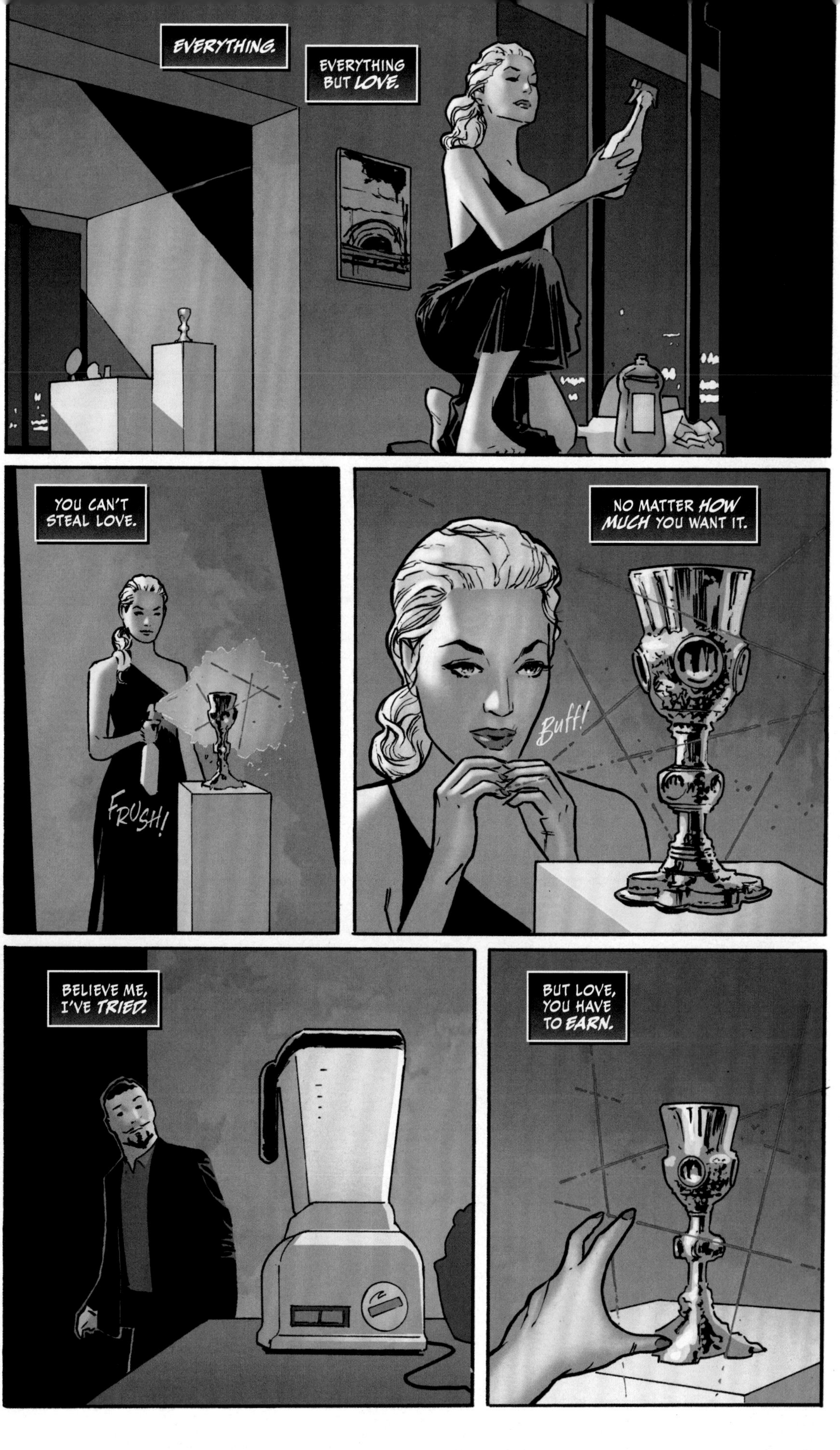
EVERYTHING.
EVERYTHING BUT LOVE.
YOU CAN'T STEAL LOVE.
FRUSH!
NO MATTER HOW MUCH YOU WANT IT.
Buff!
BELIEVE ME, I'VE TRIED.
BUT LOVE, YOU HAVE TO EARN.

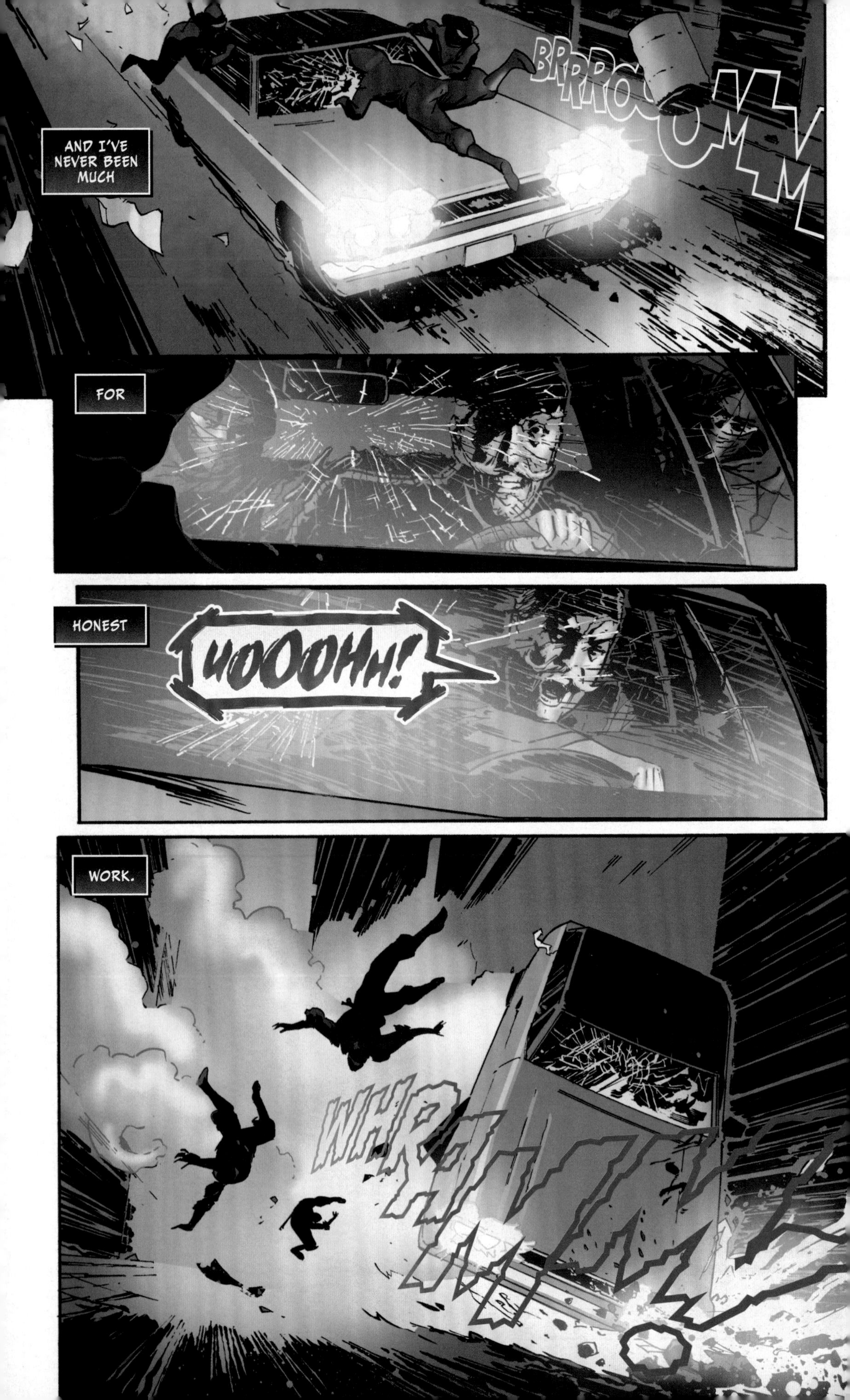

AND I'VE NEVER BEEN MUCH
BRRROOOMM
FOR
HONEST
UOOOHH!
WORK.
WHRAMM

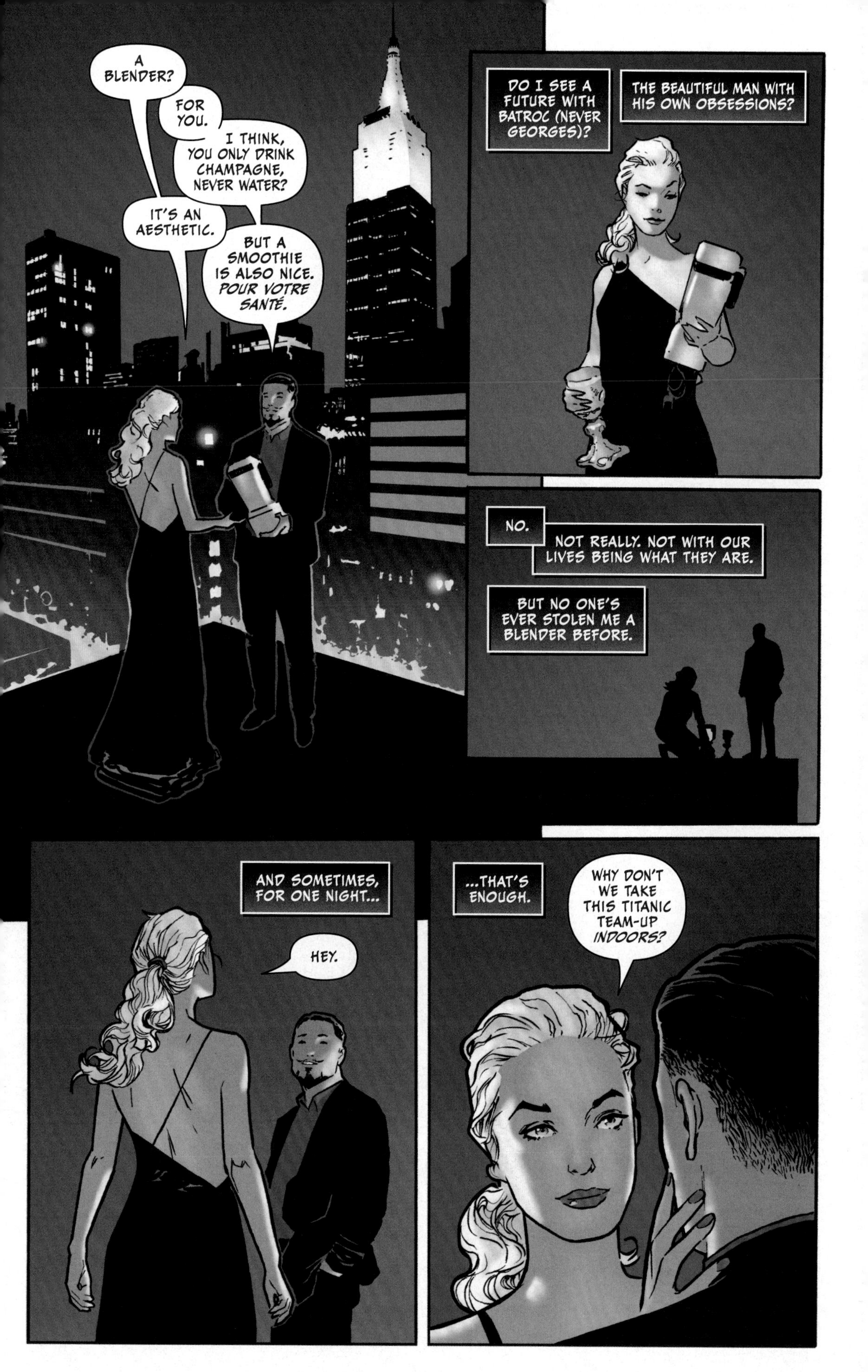
A BLENDER?
FOR YOU.
I THINK, YOU ONLY DRINK CHAMPAGNE, NEVER WATER?
IT'S AN AESTHETIC.
BUT A SMOOTHIE IS ALSO NICE. *POUR VOTRE SANTÉ.*
DO I SEE A FUTURE WITH BATROC (NEVER GEORGES)?
THE BEAUTIFUL MAN WITH HIS OWN OBSESSIONS?
NO.
NOT REALLY. NOT WITH OUR LIVES BEING WHAT THEY ARE.
BUT NO ONE'S EVER STOLEN ME A BLENDER BEFORE.
AND SOMETIMES, FOR ONE NIGHT...
HEY.
...THAT'S ENOUGH.
WHY DON'T WE TAKE THIS TITANIC TEAM-UP *INDOORS?*

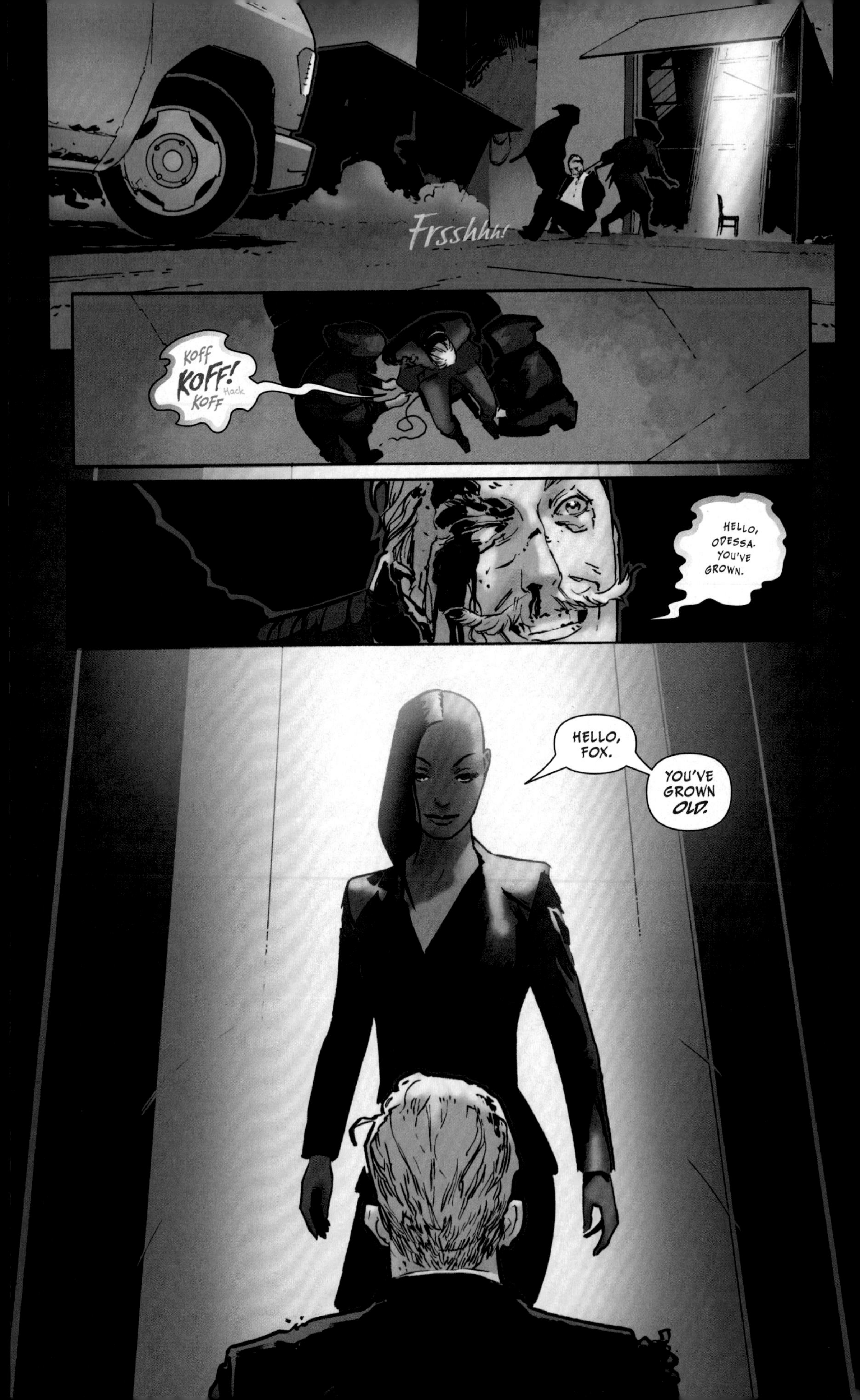
Frsshhh!
KOFF KOFF! KOFF Hack
HELLO, ODESSA. YOU'VE GROWN.
HELLO, FOX.
YOU'VE GROWN OLD.

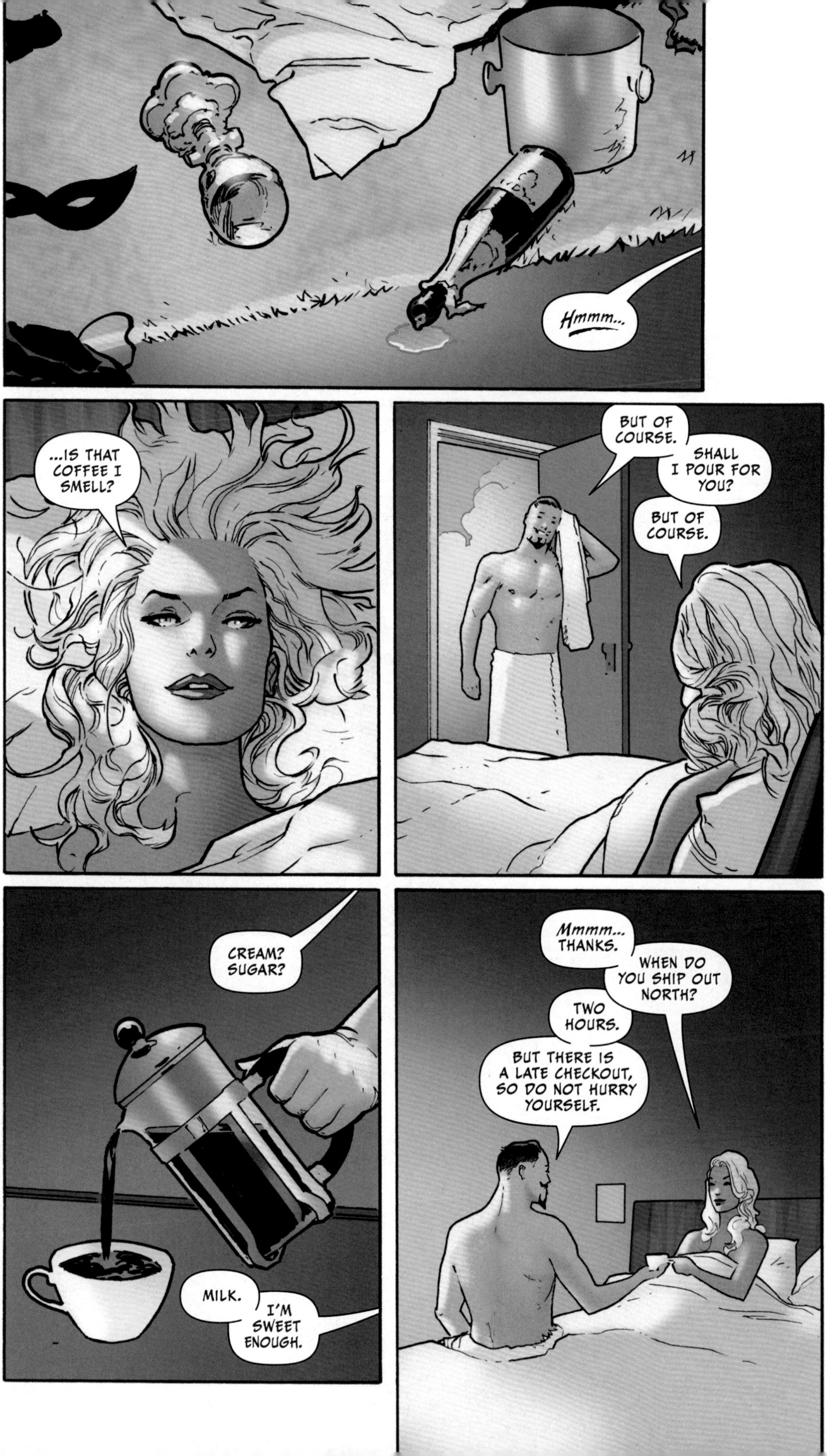
Hmmm...
...IS THAT COFFEE I SMELL?
BUT OF COURSE.
SHALL I POUR FOR YOU?
BUT OF COURSE.
CREAM? SUGAR?
MILK.
I'M SWEET ENOUGH.
Mmmm... THANKS.
WHEN DO YOU SHIP OUT NORTH?
TWO HOURS.
BUT THERE IS A LATE CHECKOUT, SO DO NOT HURRY YOURSELF.

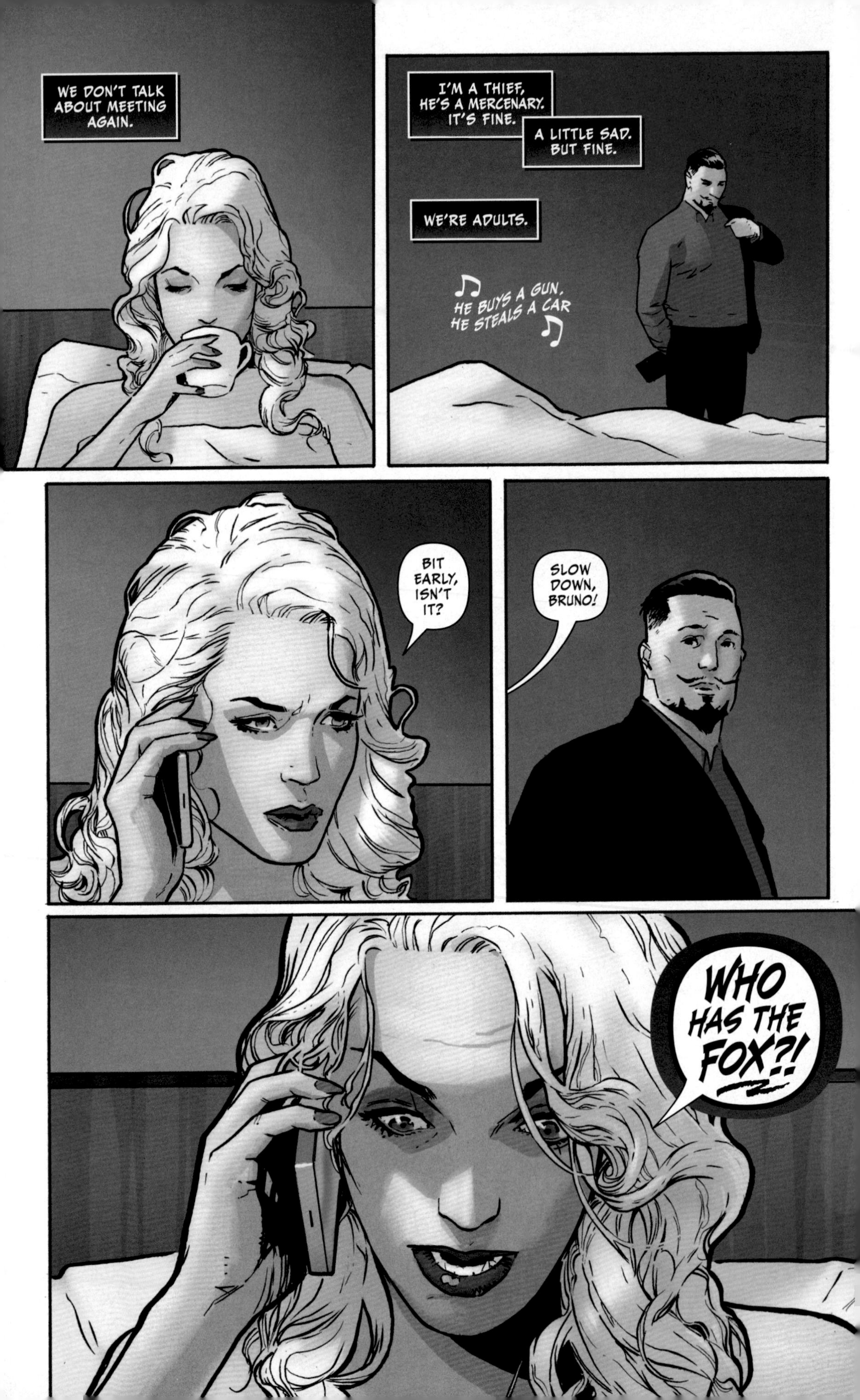
WE DON'T TALK ABOUT MEETING AGAIN.
I'M A THIEF, HE'S A MERCENARY. IT'S FINE.
A LITTLE SAD. BUT FINE.
WE'RE ADULTS.
♫ HE BUYS A GUN, HE STEALS A CAR ♫
BIT EARLY, ISN'T IT?
SLOW DOWN, BRUNO!
WHO HAS THE FOX?!

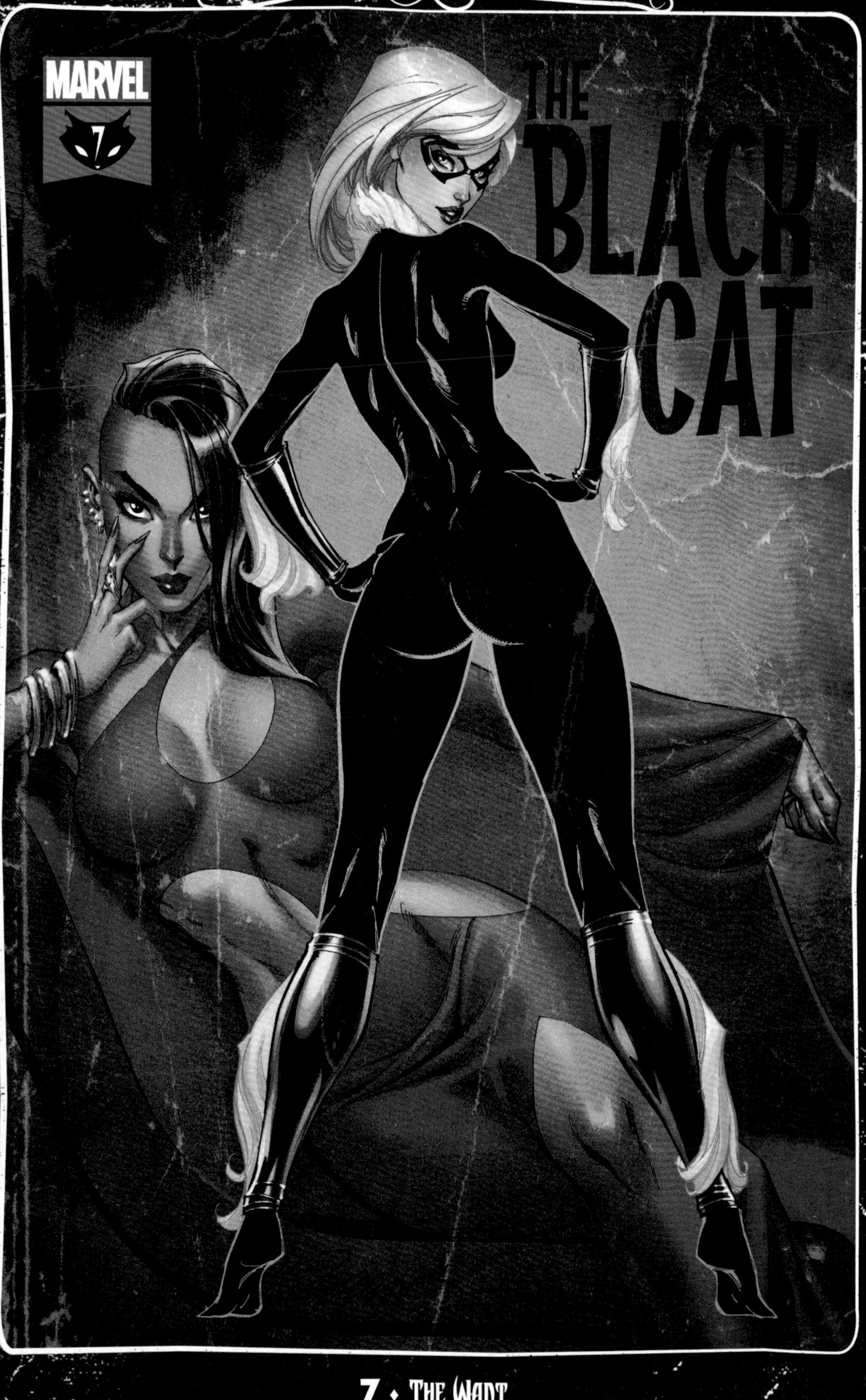
MARVEL
7
THE BLACK CAT

## 7 • The Want

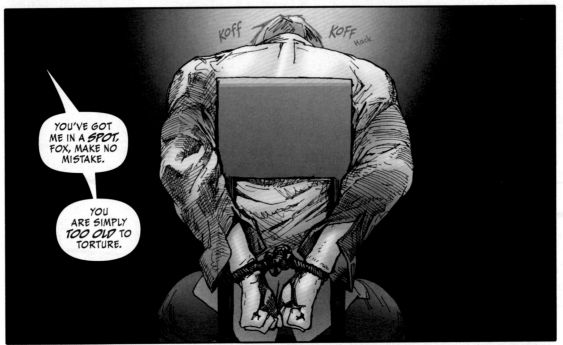

KOFF    KOFF
Hack

YOU'VE GOT ME IN A *SPOT*, FOX, MAKE NO MISTAKE.

YOU ARE SIMPLY *TOO OLD* TO TORTURE.

I WAS *HOPING* TO SPEND THIS TIME TOGETHER BEATING YOU WITHIN AN INCH OF YOUR LIFE...

...BUT YOU SIMPLY *DON'T HAVE* THAT INCH.

KOFF
KOFF!
Hack

YOUR EVIL OLD SOUL *WILL BE* SHUFFLING OFF THIS MORTAL COIL *SOON ENOUGH*, BUT I WON'T HAVE A *MOMENT* OF MY SATISFACTION STOLEN.

BECAUSE NO ONE STEALS FROM ME.

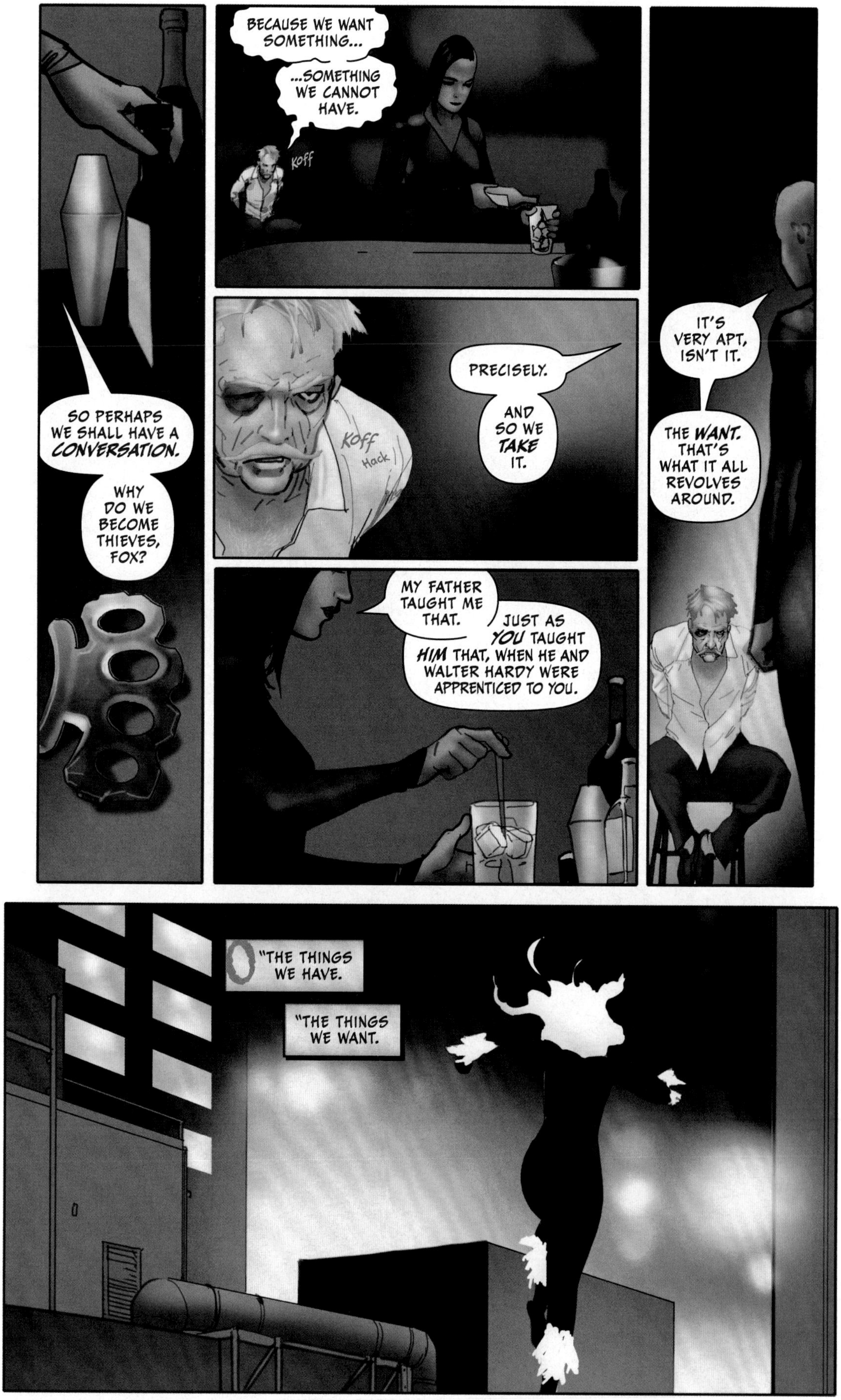

SO PERHAPS WE SHALL HAVE A CONVERSATION.
WHY DO WE BECOME THIEVES, FOX?
BECAUSE WE WANT SOMETHING...
...SOMETHING WE CANNOT HAVE.
KOFF
PRECISELY.
AND SO WE TAKE IT.
KOFF
HACK
MY FATHER TAUGHT ME THAT.
JUST AS YOU TAUGHT HIM THAT, WHEN HE AND WALTER HARDY WERE APPRENTICED TO YOU.
IT'S VERY APT, ISN'T IT.
THE WANT. THAT'S WHAT IT ALL REVOLVES AROUND.
"THE THINGS WE HAVE.
"THE THINGS WE WANT.

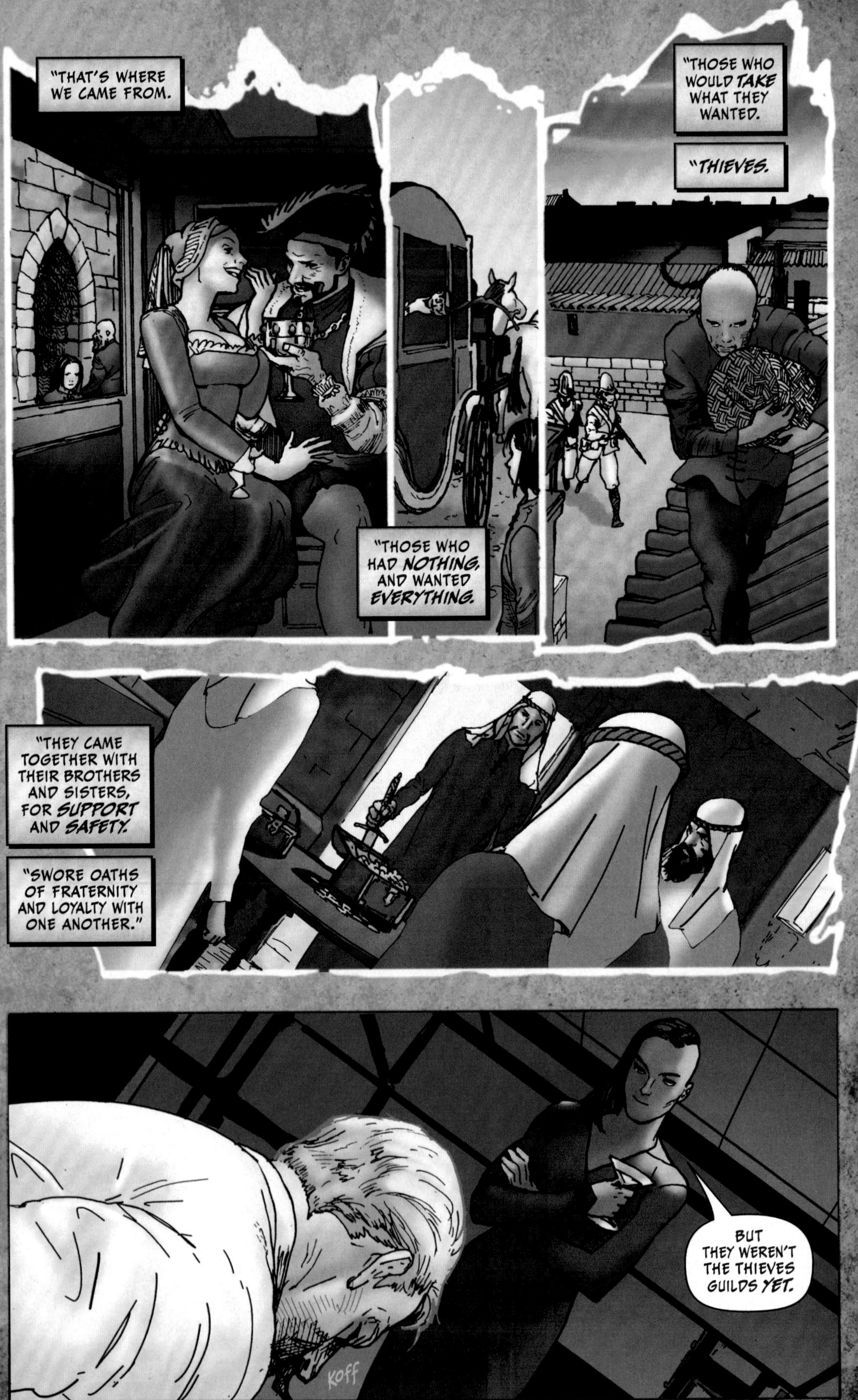
"THAT'S WHERE WE CAME FROM.
"THOSE WHO HAD NOTHING, AND WANTED EVERYTHING.
"THOSE WHO WOULD TAKE WHAT THEY WANTED.
"THIEVES.
"THEY CAME TOGETHER WITH THEIR BROTHERS AND SISTERS, FOR SUPPORT AND SAFETY.
"SWORE OATHS OF FRATERNITY AND LOYALTY WITH ONE ANOTHER."
BUT THEY WEREN'T THE THIEVES GUILDS YET.
KOFF

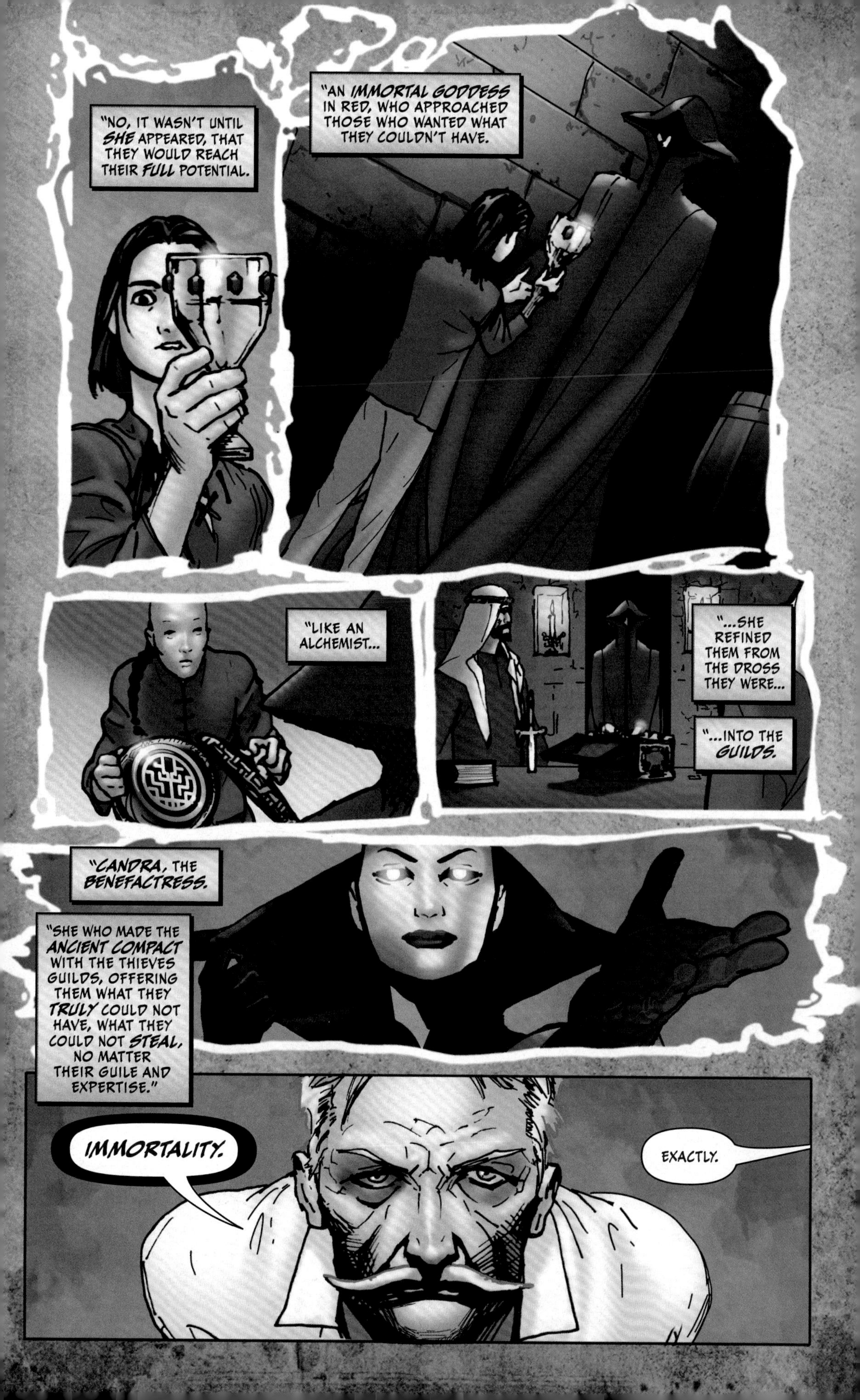
"NO, IT WASN'T UNTIL SHE APPEARED, THAT THEY WOULD REACH THEIR FULL POTENTIAL.
"AN IMMORTAL GODDESS IN RED, WHO APPROACHED THOSE WHO WANTED WHAT THEY COULDN'T HAVE.
"LIKE AN ALCHEMIST...
"...SHE REFINED THEM FROM THE DROSS THEY WERE...
"...INTO THE GUILDS.
"CANDRA, THE BENEFACTRESS.
"SHE WHO MADE THE ANCIENT COMPACT WITH THE THIEVES GUILDS, OFFERING THEM WHAT THEY TRULY COULD NOT HAVE, WHAT THEY COULD NOT STEAL, NO MATTER THEIR GUILE AND EXPERTISE."
IMMORTALITY.
EXACTLY.

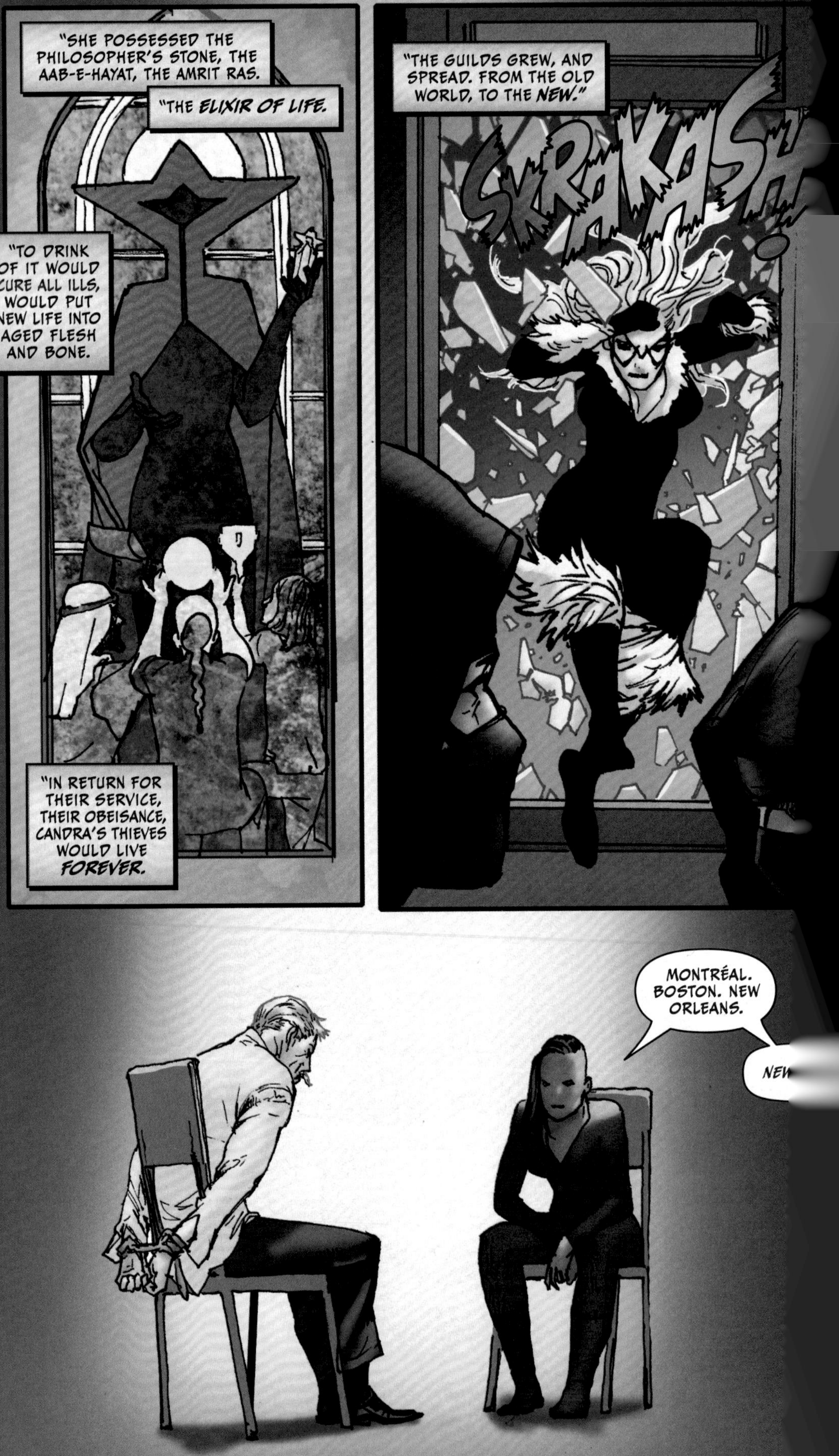
"SHE POSSESSED THE PHILOSOPHER'S STONE, THE AAB-E-HAYAT, THE AMRIT RAS.
"THE ELIXIR OF LIFE.
"TO DRINK OF IT WOULD CURE ALL ILLS, WOULD PUT NEW LIFE INTO AGED FLESH AND BONE.
"IN RETURN FOR THEIR SERVICE, THEIR OBEISANCE, CANDRA'S THIEVES WOULD LIVE FOREVER.
"THE GUILDS GREW, AND SPREAD. FROM THE OLD WORLD, TO THE NEW."
SKRAKASH!
MONTRÉAL. BOSTON. NEW ORLEANS.
NEW

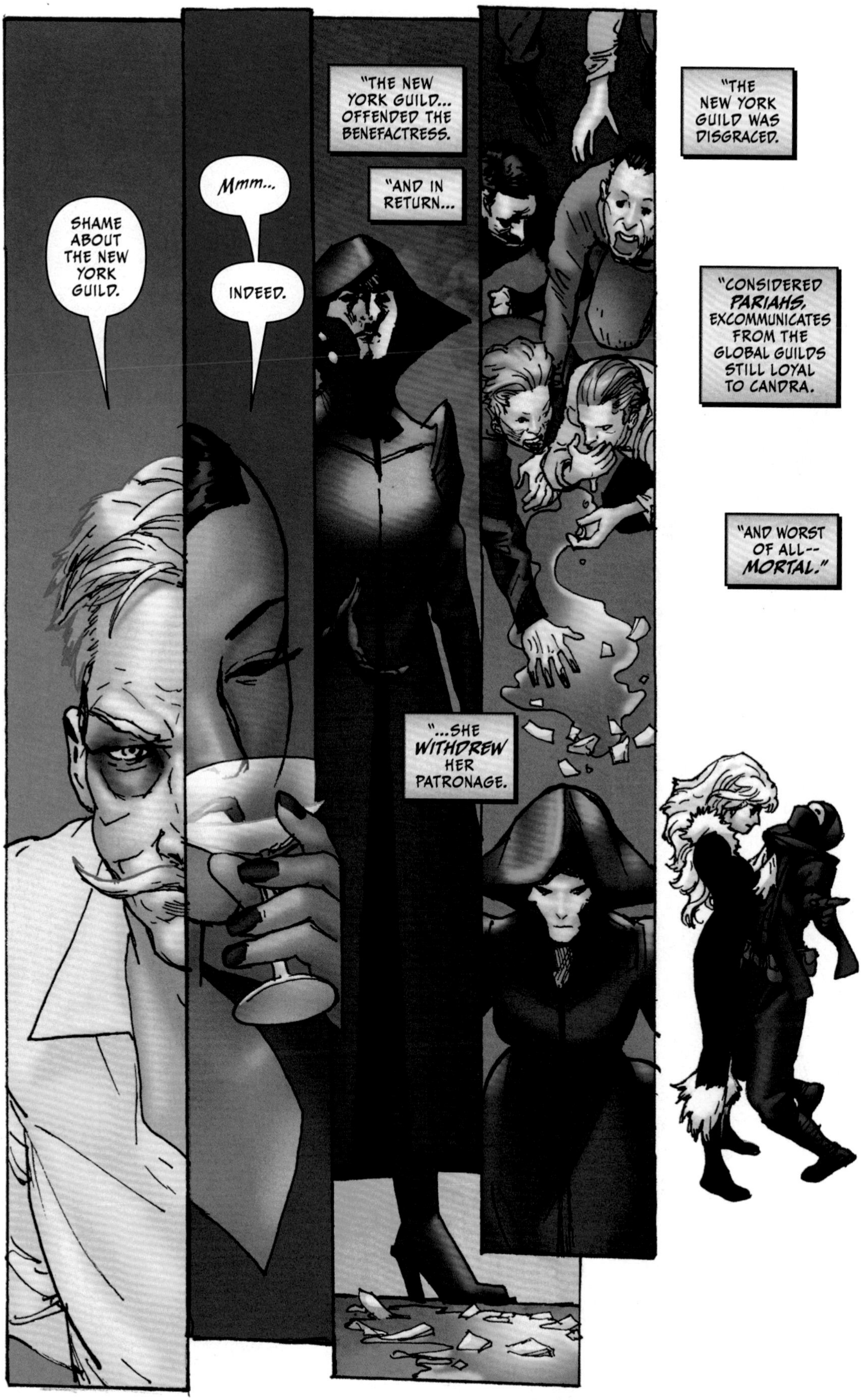

SHAME ABOUT THE NEW YORK GUILD.
Mmm...
INDEED.
"THE NEW YORK GUILD... OFFENDED THE BENEFACTRESS.
"AND IN RETURN...
"...SHE WITHDREW HER PATRONAGE.
"THE NEW YORK GUILD WAS DISGRACED.
"CONSIDERED PARIAHS, EXCOMMUNICATES FROM THE GLOBAL GUILDS STILL LOYAL TO CANDRA.
"AND WORST OF ALL-- MORTAL."

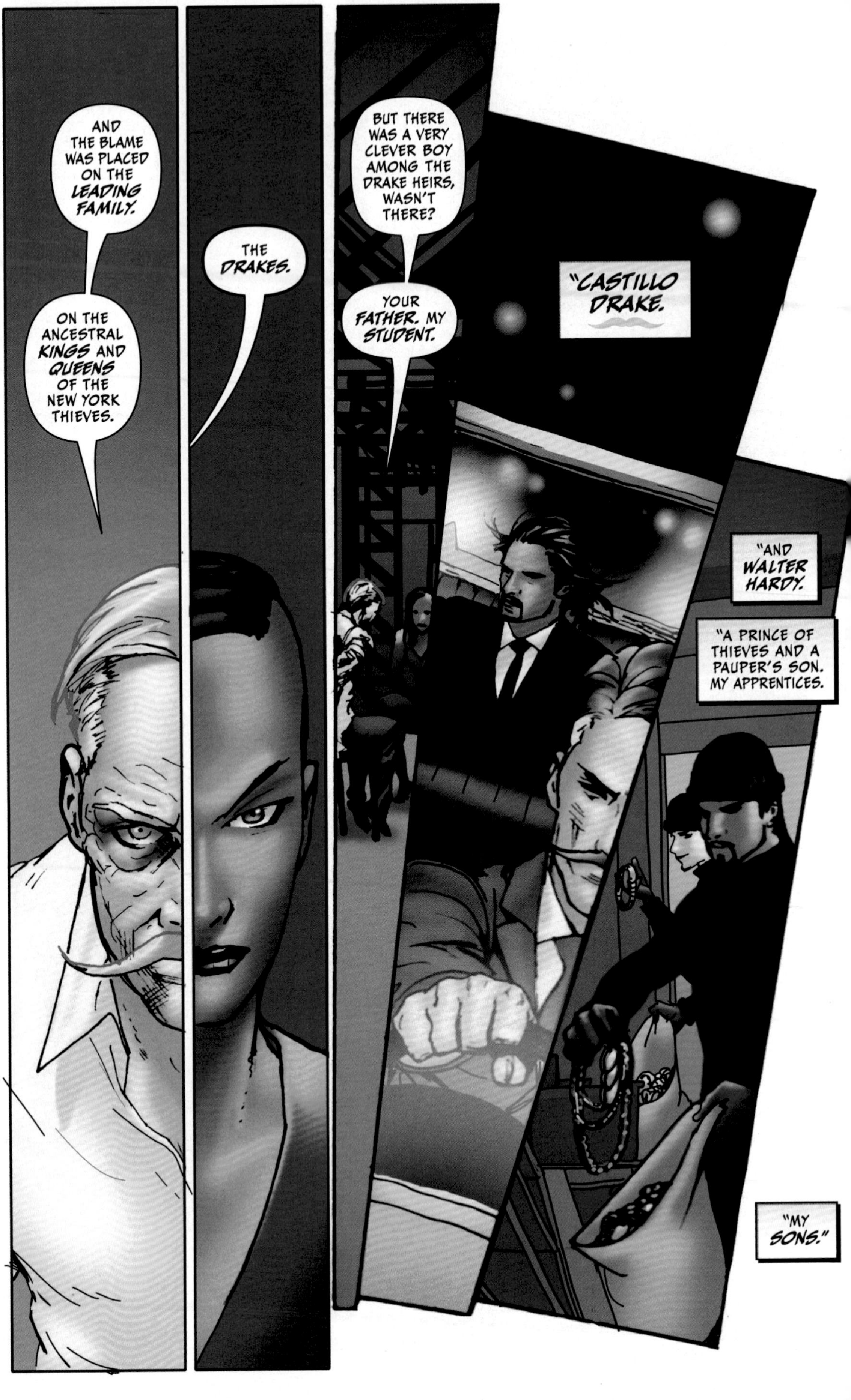
AND THE BLAME WAS PLACED ON THE LEADING FAMILY.
ON THE ANCESTRAL KINGS AND QUEENS OF THE NEW YORK THIEVES.
THE DRAKES.
BUT THERE WAS A VERY CLEVER BOY AMONG THE DRAKE HEIRS, WASN'T THERE?
YOUR FATHER. MY STUDENT.
"CASTILLO DRAKE.
"AND WALTER HARDY.
"A PRINCE OF THIEVES AND A PAUPER'S SON. MY APPRENTICES.
"MY SONS."

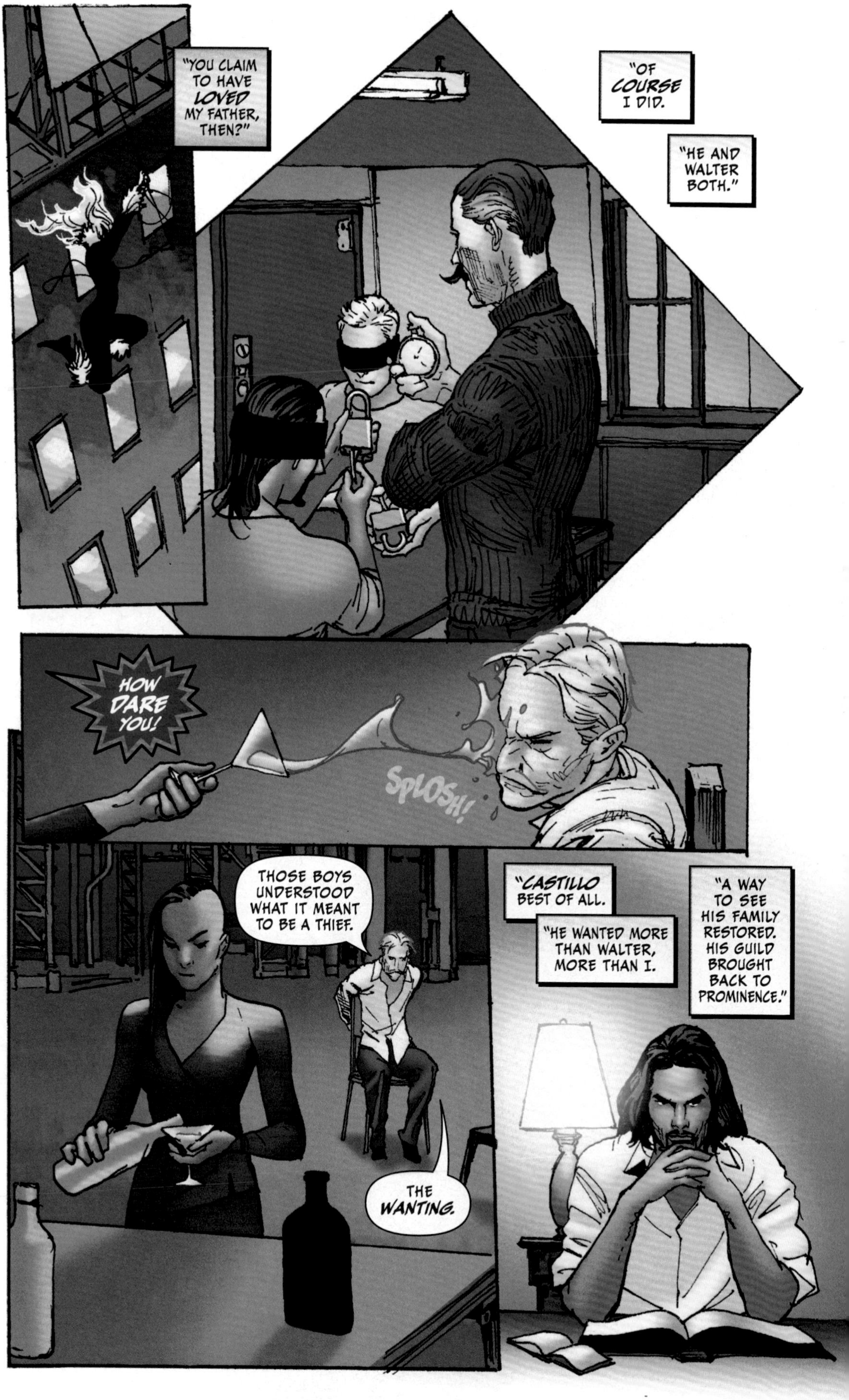
"YOU CLAIM TO HAVE LOVED MY FATHER, THEN?"
"OF COURSE I DID.
"HE AND WALTER BOTH."
HOW DARE YOU!
SPLOSH!
THOSE BOYS UNDERSTOOD WHAT IT MEANT TO BE A THIEF.
THE WANTING.
"CASTILLO BEST OF ALL.
"HE WANTED MORE THAN WALTER, MORE THAN I.
"A WAY TO SEE HIS FAMILY RESTORED. HIS GUILD BROUGHT BACK TO PROMINENCE."

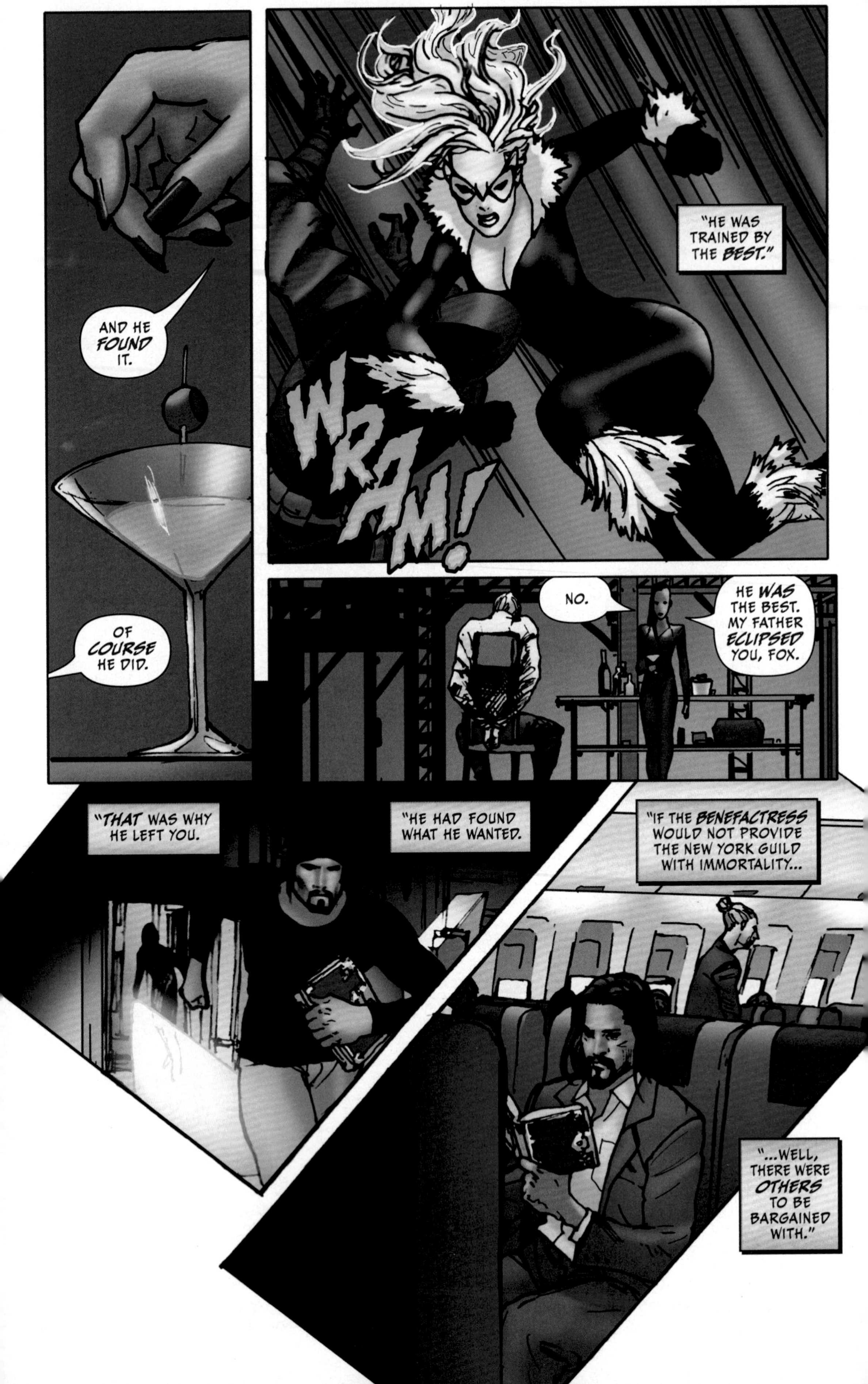
AND HE FOUND IT.
"HE WAS TRAINED BY THE BEST."
WRAM!
OF COURSE HE DID.
NO.
HE WAS THE BEST. MY FATHER ECLIPSED YOU, FOX.
"THAT WAS WHY HE LEFT YOU.
"HE HAD FOUND WHAT HE WANTED.
"IF THE BENEFACTRESS WOULD NOT PROVIDE THE NEW YORK GUILD WITH IMMORTALITY...
"...WELL, THERE WERE OTHERS TO BE BARGAINED WITH."

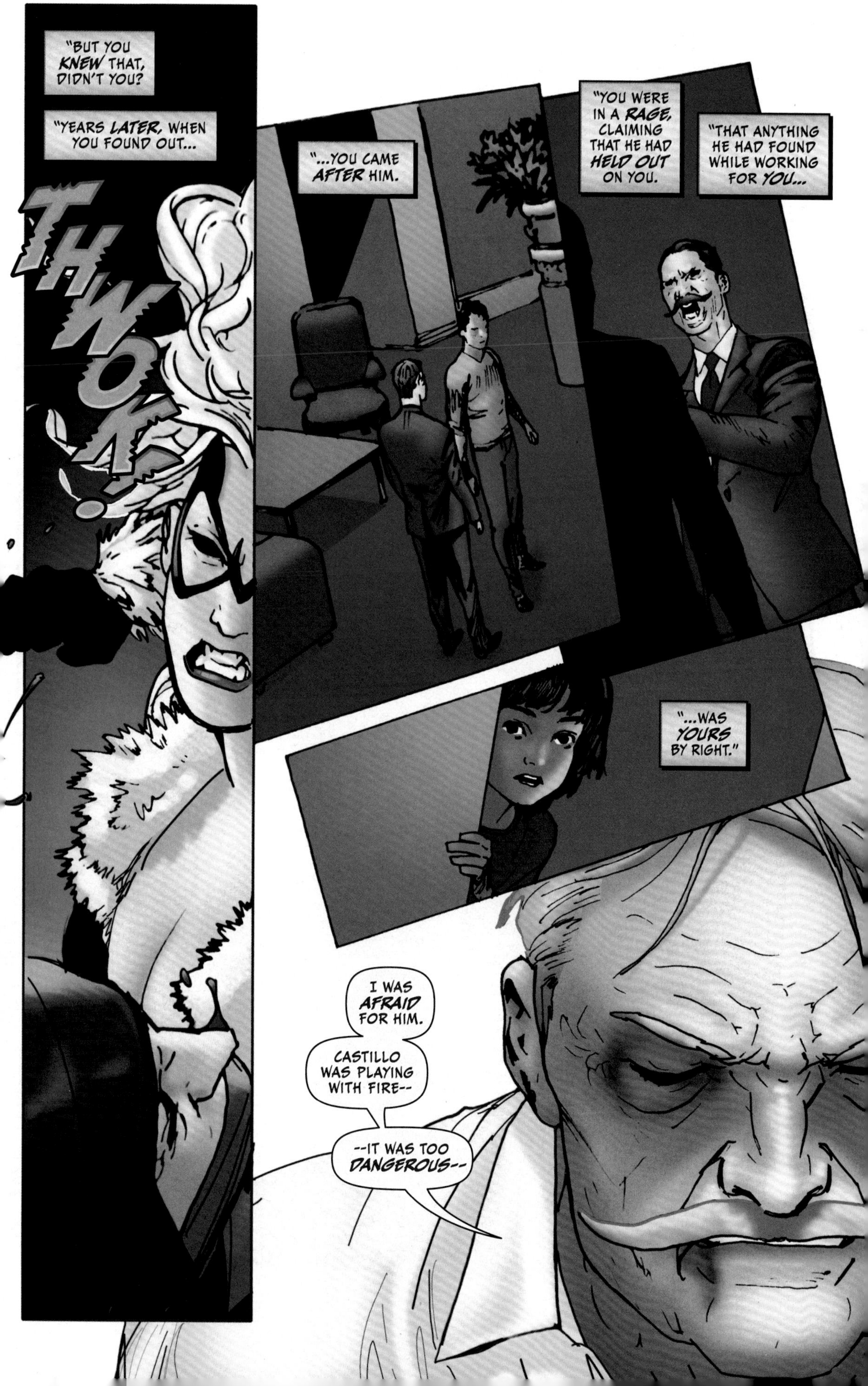
"BUT YOU KNEW THAT, DIDN'T YOU?
"YEARS LATER, WHEN YOU FOUND OUT...
THWOK!
"...YOU CAME AFTER HIM.
"YOU WERE IN A RAGE, CLAIMING THAT HE HAD HELD OUT ON YOU.
"THAT ANYTHING HE HAD FOUND WHILE WORKING FOR YOU...
"...WAS YOURS BY RIGHT."
I WAS AFRAID FOR HIM.
CASTILLO WAS PLAYING WITH FIRE--
--IT WAS TOO DANGEROUS--

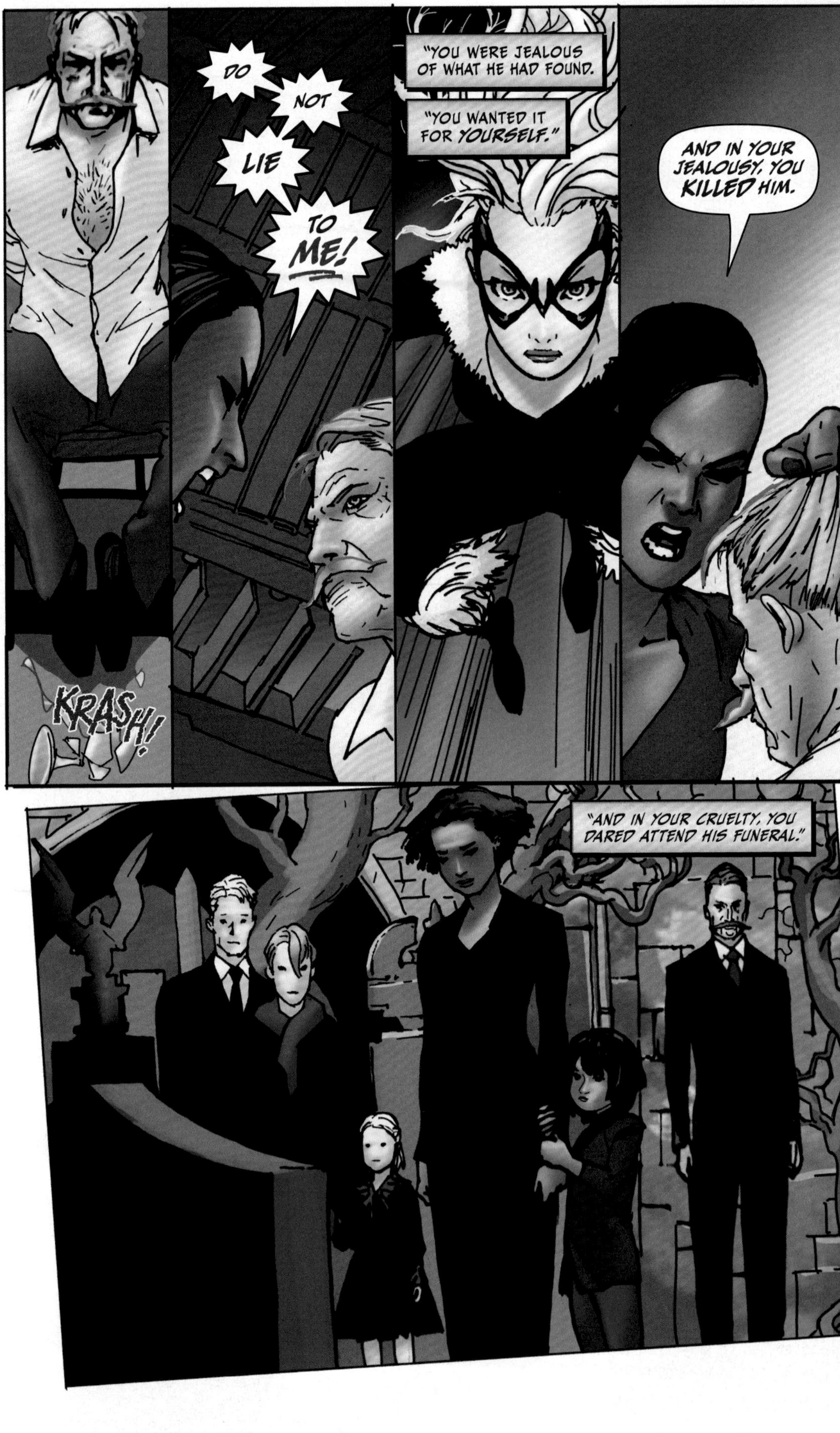
KRASH!
DO
NOT
LIE
TO
ME!
"YOU WERE JEALOUS OF WHAT HE HAD FOUND.
"YOU WANTED IT FOR YOURSELF."
AND IN YOUR JEALOUSY, YOU KILLED HIM.
"AND IN YOUR CRUELTY, YOU DARED ATTEND HIS FUNERAL."

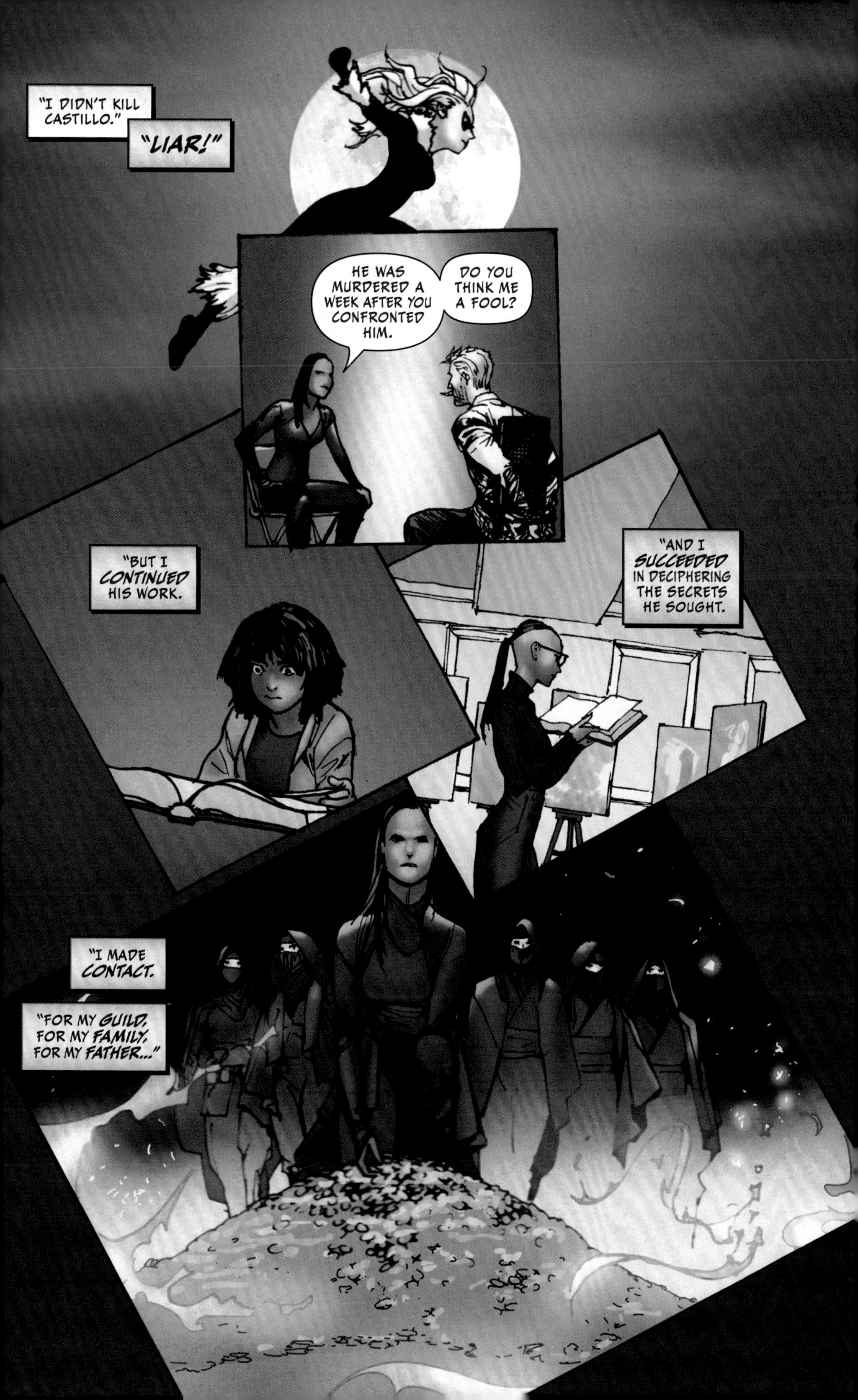
"I DIDN'T KILL CASTILLO."
"LIAR!"
HE WAS MURDERED A WEEK AFTER YOU CONFRONTED HIM.
DO YOU THINK ME A FOOL?
"BUT I CONTINUED HIS WORK.
"AND I SUCCEEDED IN DECIPHERING THE SECRETS HE SOUGHT.
"I MADE CONTACT.
"FOR MY GUILD, FOR MY FAMILY, FOR MY FATHER..."

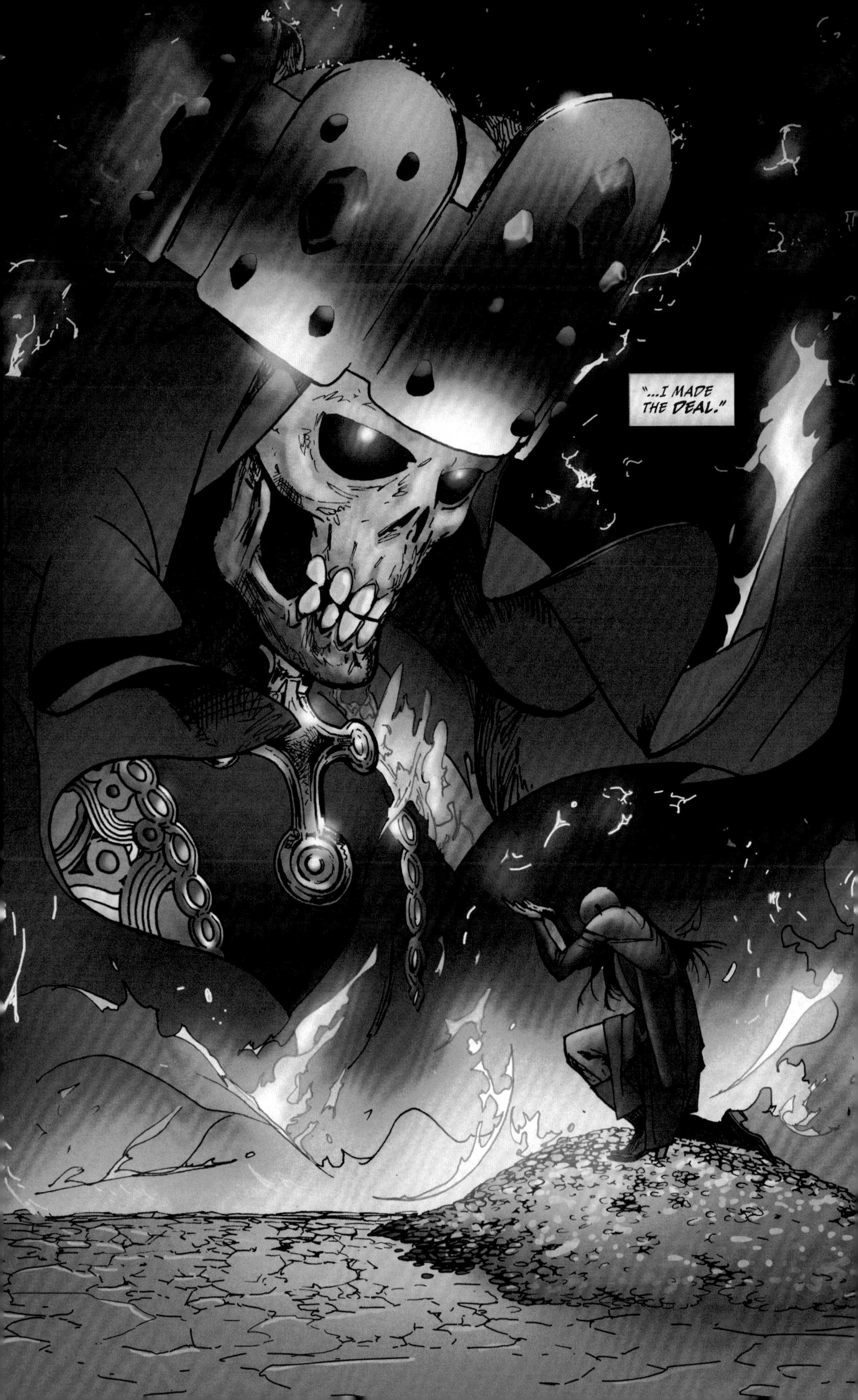
"...I MADE THE DEAL."

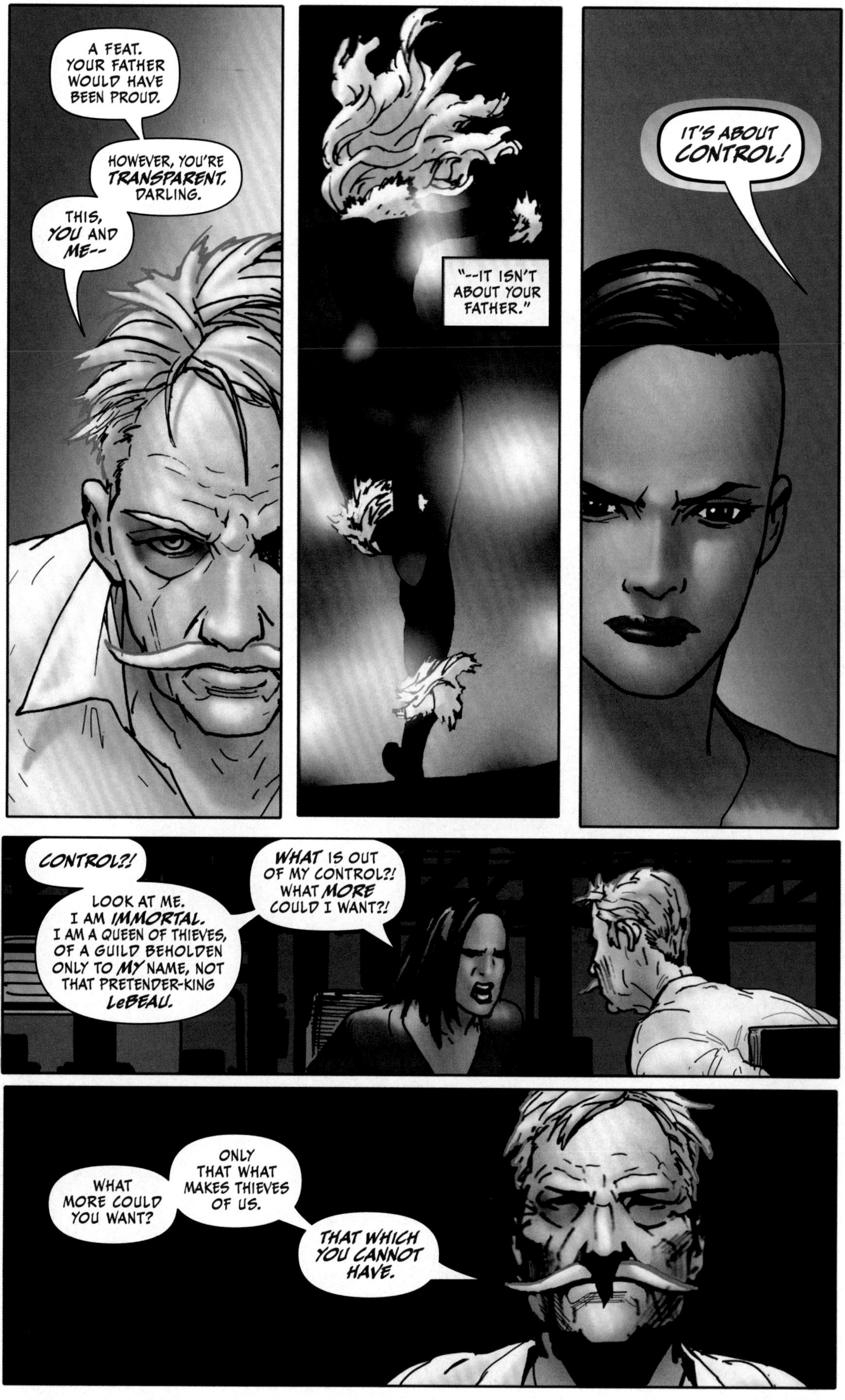
A FEAT. YOUR FATHER WOULD HAVE BEEN PROUD.
HOWEVER, YOU'RE TRANSPARENT, DARLING.
THIS, YOU AND ME--
"--IT ISN'T ABOUT YOUR FATHER."
IT'S ABOUT CONTROL!
CONTROL?!
LOOK AT ME. I AM IMMORTAL. I AM A QUEEN OF THIEVES, OF A GUILD BEHOLDEN ONLY TO MY NAME, NOT THAT PRETENDER-KING LeBEAU.
WHAT IS OUT OF MY CONTROL?! WHAT MORE COULD I WANT?!
WHAT MORE COULD YOU WANT?
ONLY THAT WHAT MAKES THIEVES OF US.
THAT WHICH YOU CANNOT HAVE.

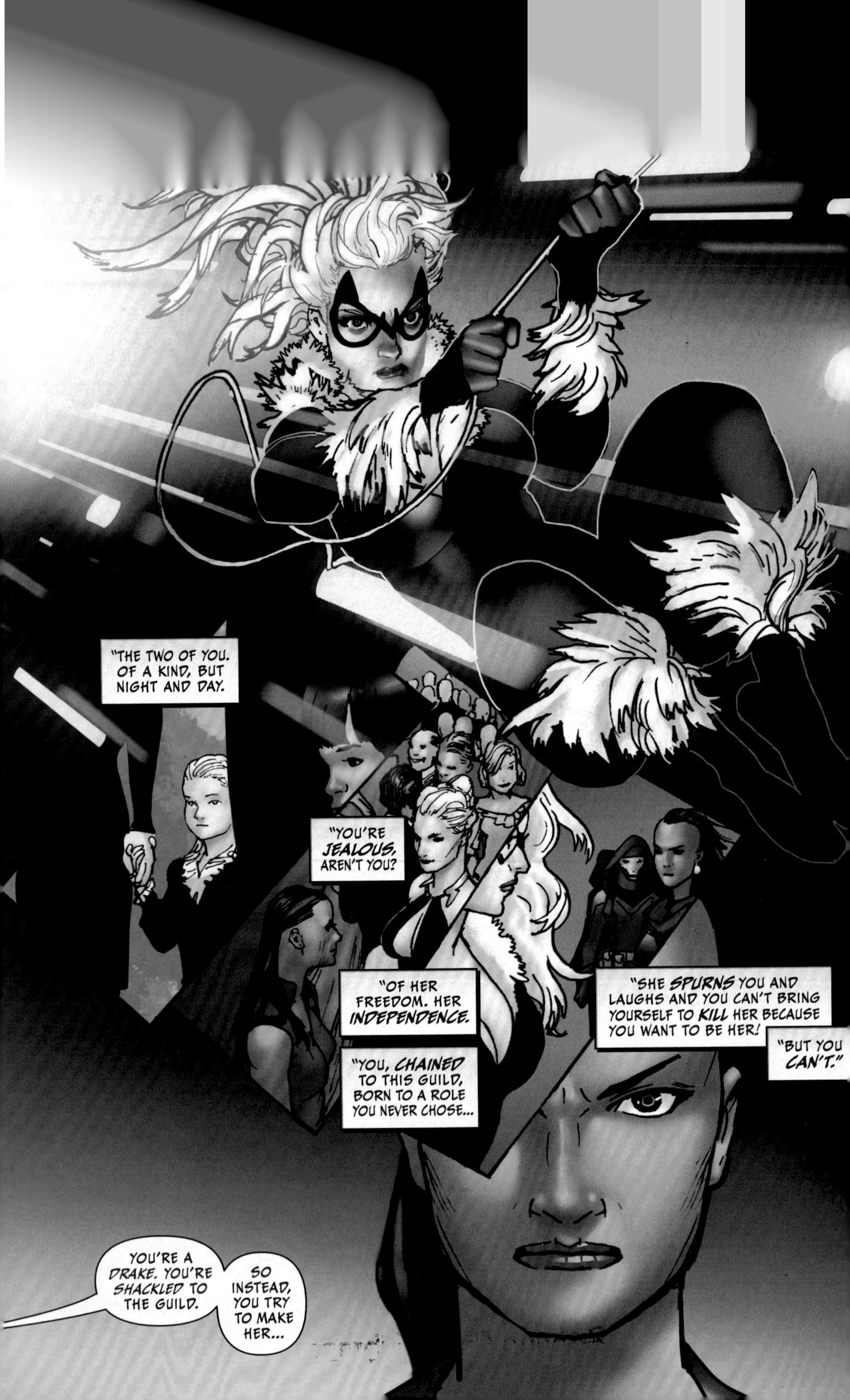
"THE TWO OF YOU. OF A KIND, BUT NIGHT AND DAY.
"YOU'RE JEALOUS, AREN'T YOU?
"OF HER FREEDOM. HER INDEPENDENCE.
"YOU, CHAINED TO THIS GUILD, BORN TO A ROLE YOU NEVER CHOSE...
"SHE SPURNS YOU AND LAUGHS AND YOU CAN'T BRING YOURSELF TO KILL HER BECAUSE YOU WANT TO BE HER!
"BUT YOU CAN'T."
YOU'RE A DRAKE. YOU'RE SHACKLED TO THE GUILD.
SO INSTEAD, YOU TRY TO MAKE HER...

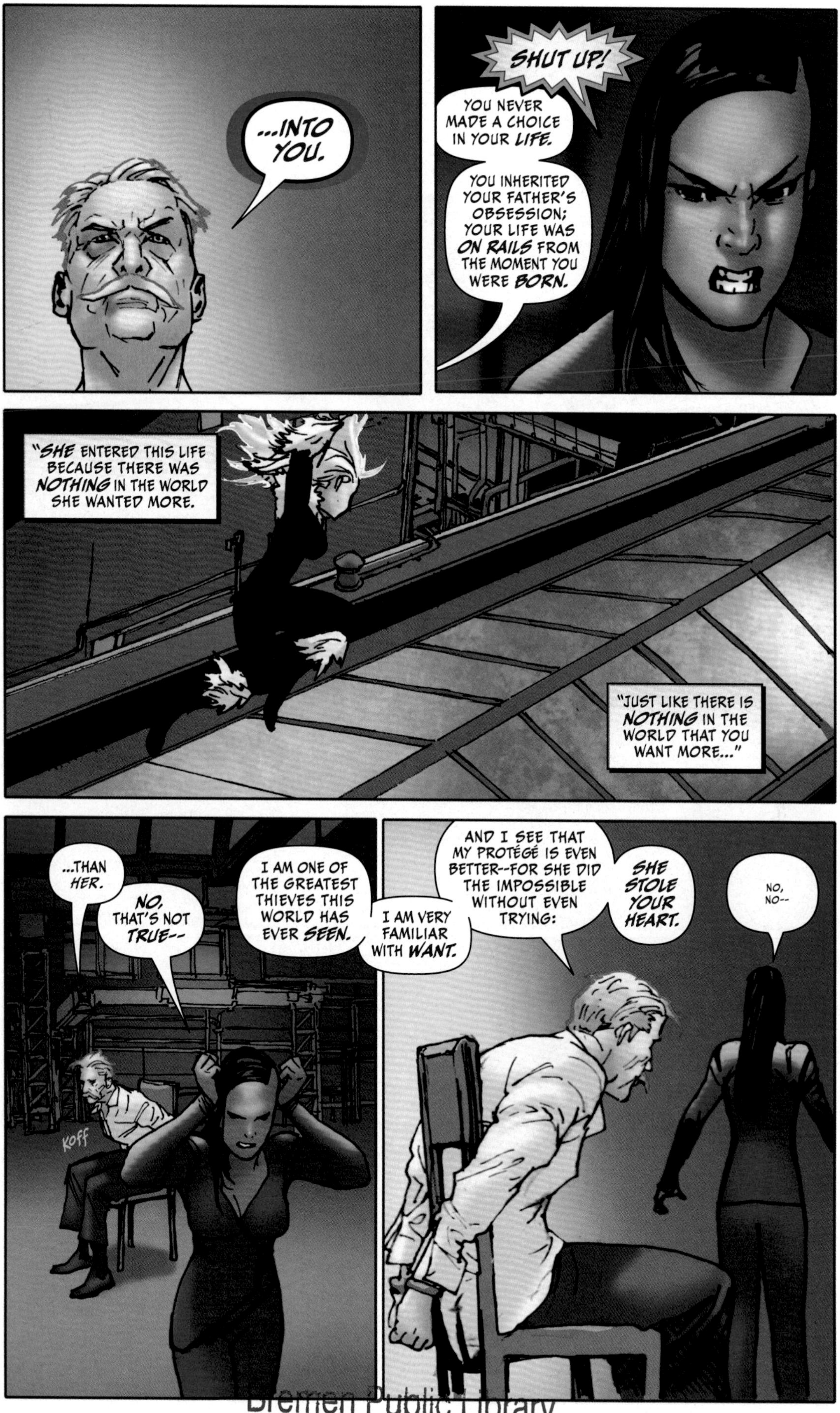
...INTO YOU.
SHUT UP!
YOU NEVER MADE A CHOICE IN YOUR LIFE.
YOU INHERITED YOUR FATHER'S OBSESSION; YOUR LIFE WAS ON RAILS FROM THE MOMENT YOU WERE BORN.
"SHE ENTERED THIS LIFE BECAUSE THERE WAS NOTHING IN THE WORLD SHE WANTED MORE.
"JUST LIKE THERE IS NOTHING IN THE WORLD THAT YOU WANT MORE..."
...THAN HER.
NO, THAT'S NOT TRUE--
I AM ONE OF THE GREATEST THIEVES THIS WORLD HAS EVER SEEN.
I AM VERY FAMILIAR WITH WANT.
KOFF
AND I SEE THAT MY PROTÉGÉ IS EVEN BETTER--FOR SHE DID THE IMPOSSIBLE WITHOUT EVEN TRYING:
SHE STOLE YOUR HEART.
NO, NO--

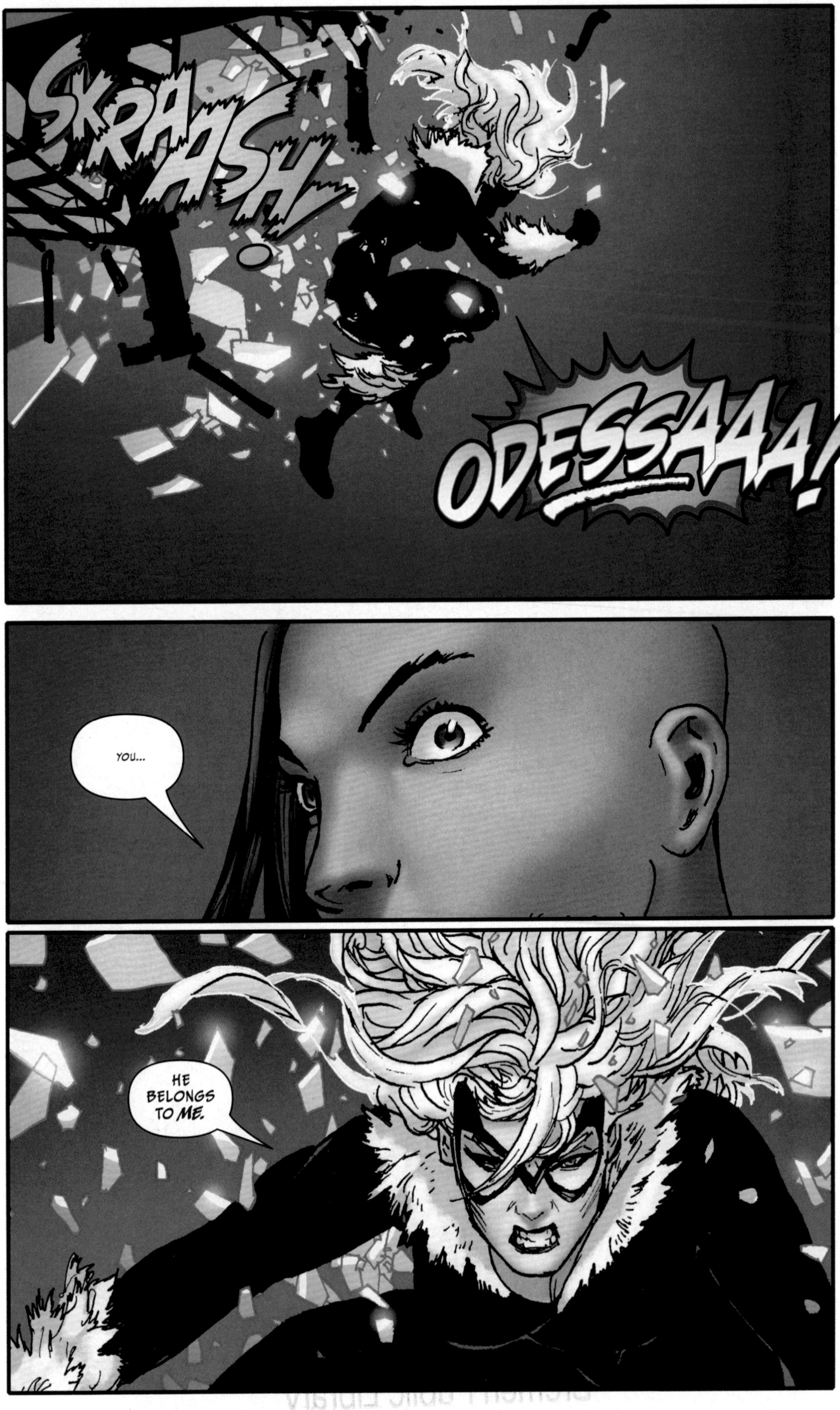
SKRASH
ODESSAAA!
YOU...
HE BELONGS TO ME.

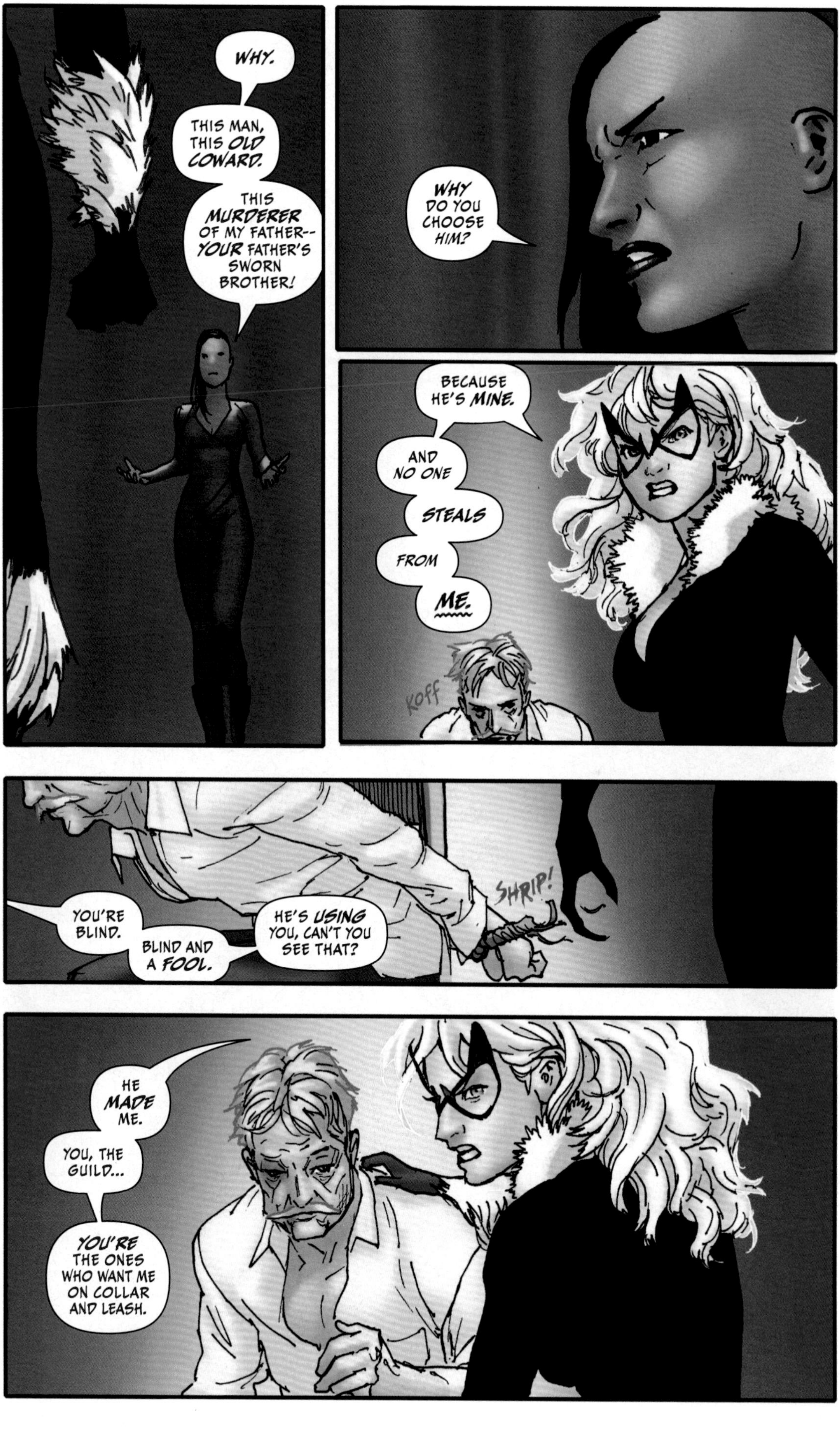
WHY.
THIS MAN, THIS OLD COWARD.
THIS MURDERER OF MY FATHER-- YOUR FATHER'S SWORN BROTHER!
WHY DO YOU CHOOSE HIM?
BECAUSE HE'S MINE.
AND NO ONE
STEALS
FROM
ME.
KOFF
YOU'RE BLIND.
BLIND AND A FOOL.
HE'S USING YOU, CAN'T YOU SEE THAT?
SHRIP!
HE MADE ME.
YOU, THE GUILD...
YOU'RE THE ONES WHO WANT ME ON COLLAR AND LEASH.

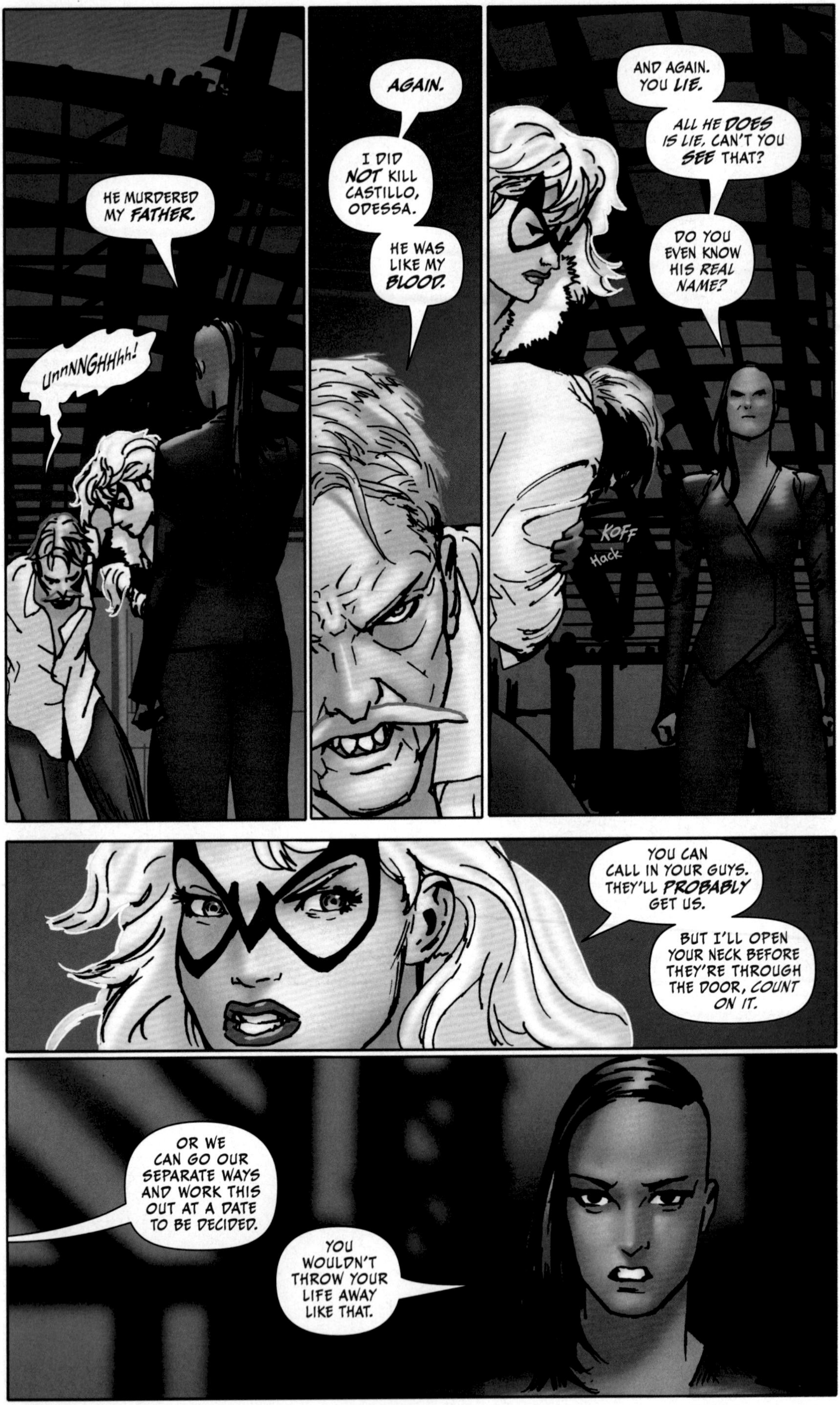
HE MURDERED MY FATHER.
UnnnNGHhhh!
AGAIN.
I DID NOT KILL CASTILLO, ODESSA.
HE WAS LIKE MY BLOOD.
AND AGAIN. YOU LIE.
ALL HE DOES IS LIE, CAN'T YOU SEE THAT?
DO YOU EVEN KNOW HIS REAL NAME?
KOFF
Hack
YOU CAN CALL IN YOUR GUYS. THEY'LL PROBABLY GET US.
BUT I'LL OPEN YOUR NECK BEFORE THEY'RE THROUGH THE DOOR, COUNT ON IT.
OR WE CAN GO OUR SEPARATE WAYS AND WORK THIS OUT AT A DATE TO BE DECIDED.
YOU WOULDN'T THROW YOUR LIFE AWAY LIKE THAT.

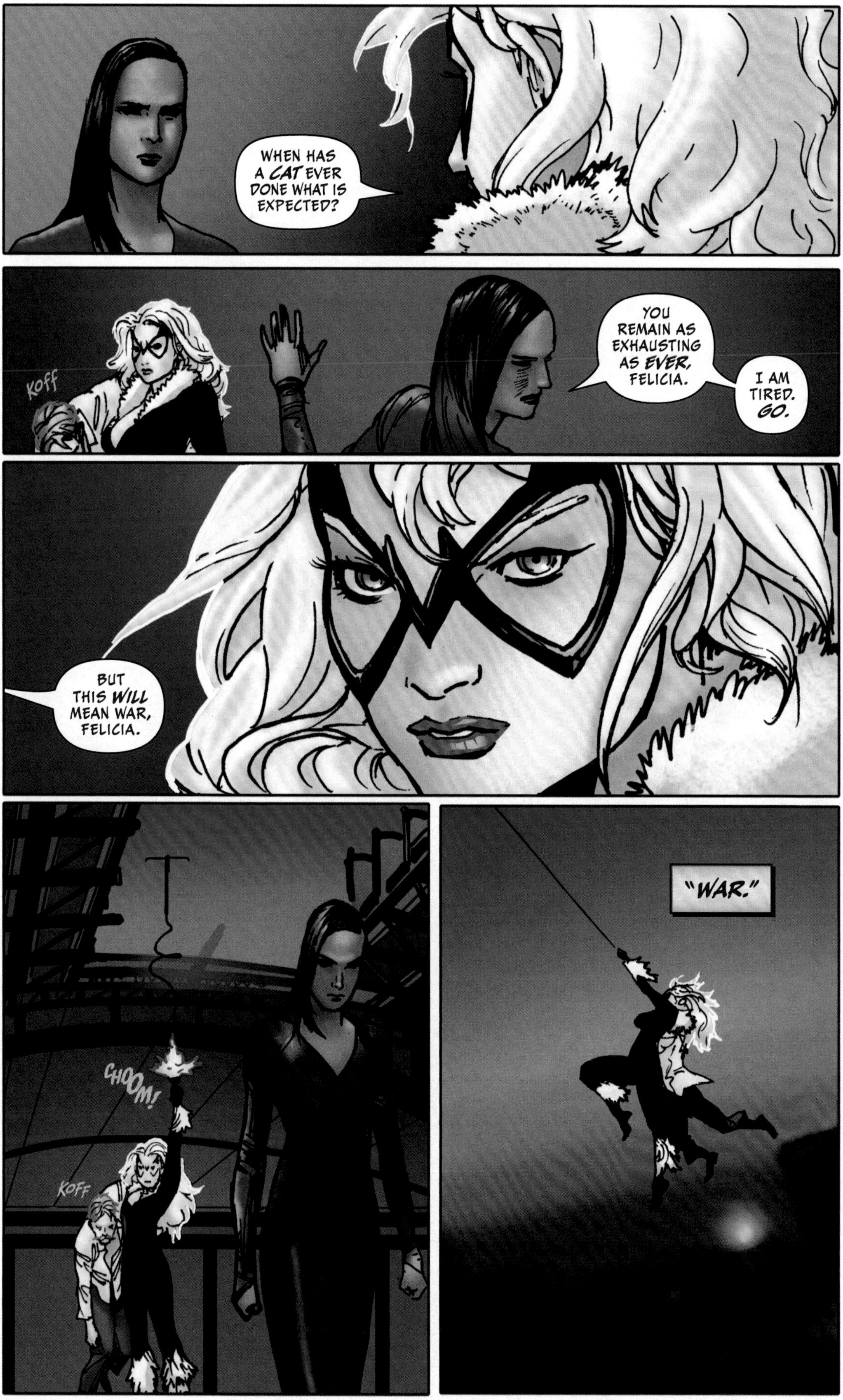

WHEN HAS A *CAT* EVER DONE WHAT IS EXPECTED?
KOFF
YOU REMAIN AS EXHAUSTING AS *EVER*, FELICIA.
I AM TIRED. *GO.*
BUT THIS *WILL* MEAN WAR, FELICIA.
CHOOM!
KOFF
"*WAR.*"

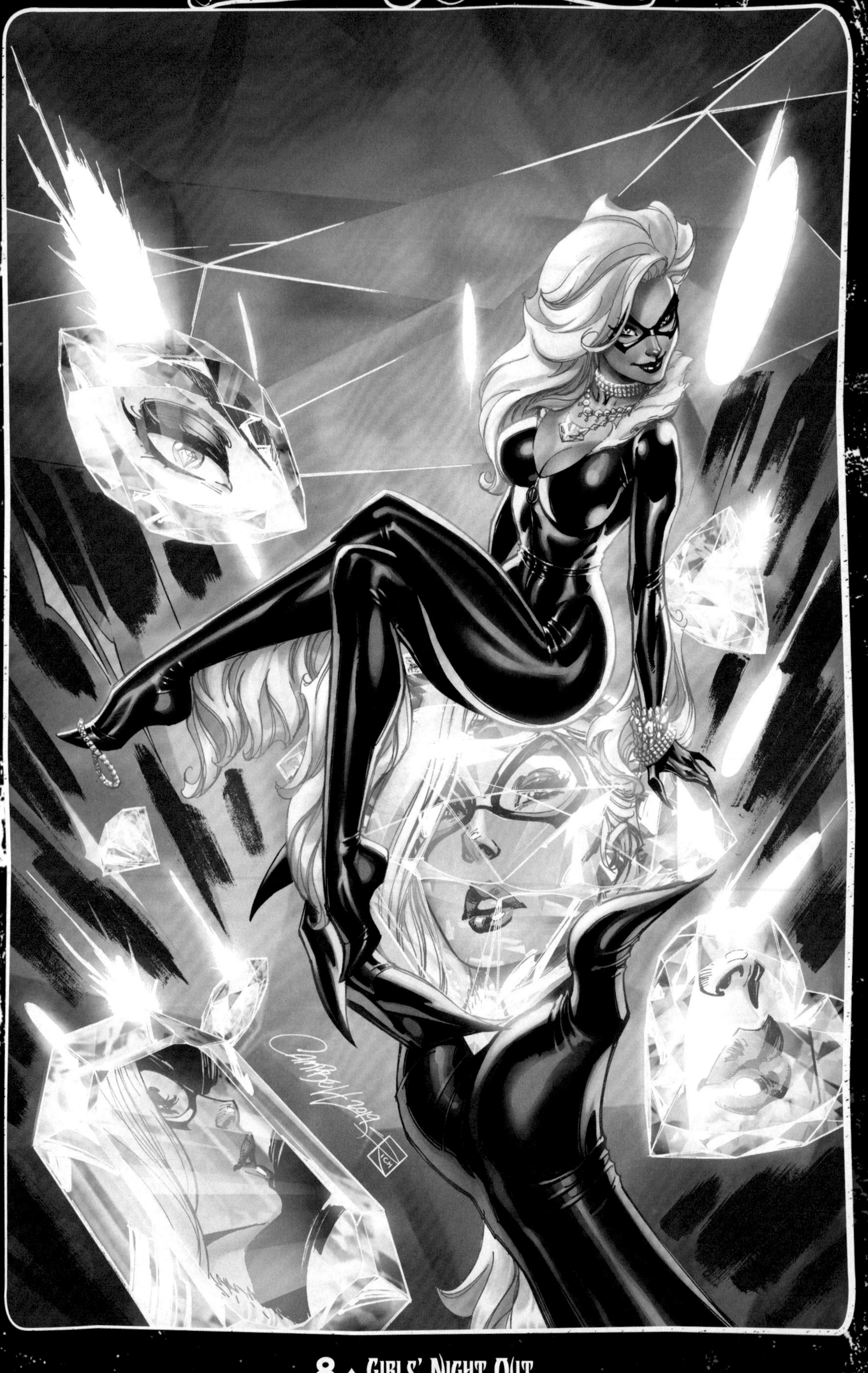

# 8 • Girls' Night Out

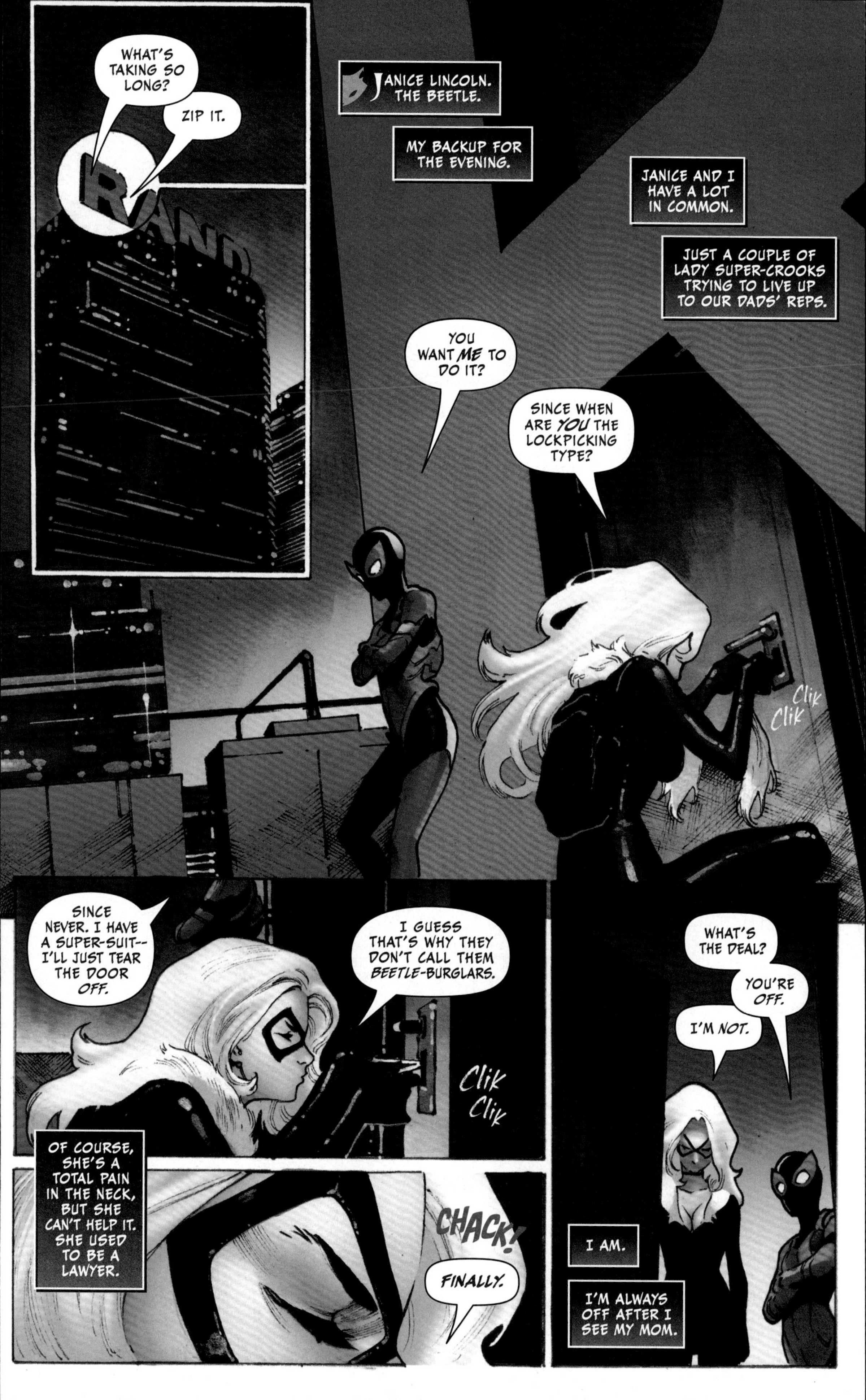
WHAT'S TAKING SO LONG?
ZIP IT.
RAND
JANICE LINCOLN. THE BEETLE.
MY BACKUP FOR THE EVENING.
JANICE AND I HAVE A LOT IN COMMON.
JUST A COUPLE OF LADY SUPER-CROOKS TRYING TO LIVE UP TO OUR DADS' REPS.
YOU WANT ME TO DO IT?
SINCE WHEN ARE YOU THE LOCKPICKING TYPE?
Clik Clik
SINCE NEVER. I HAVE A SUPER-SUIT-- I'LL JUST TEAR THE DOOR OFF.
I GUESS THAT'S WHY THEY DON'T CALL THEM BEETLE-BURGLARS.
Clik Clik
OF COURSE, SHE'S A TOTAL PAIN IN THE NECK, BUT SHE CAN'T HELP IT. SHE USED TO BE A LAWYER.
CHACK!
FINALLY.
WHAT'S THE DEAL?
YOU'RE OFF.
I'M NOT.
I AM.
I'M ALWAYS OFF AFTER I SEE MY MOM.

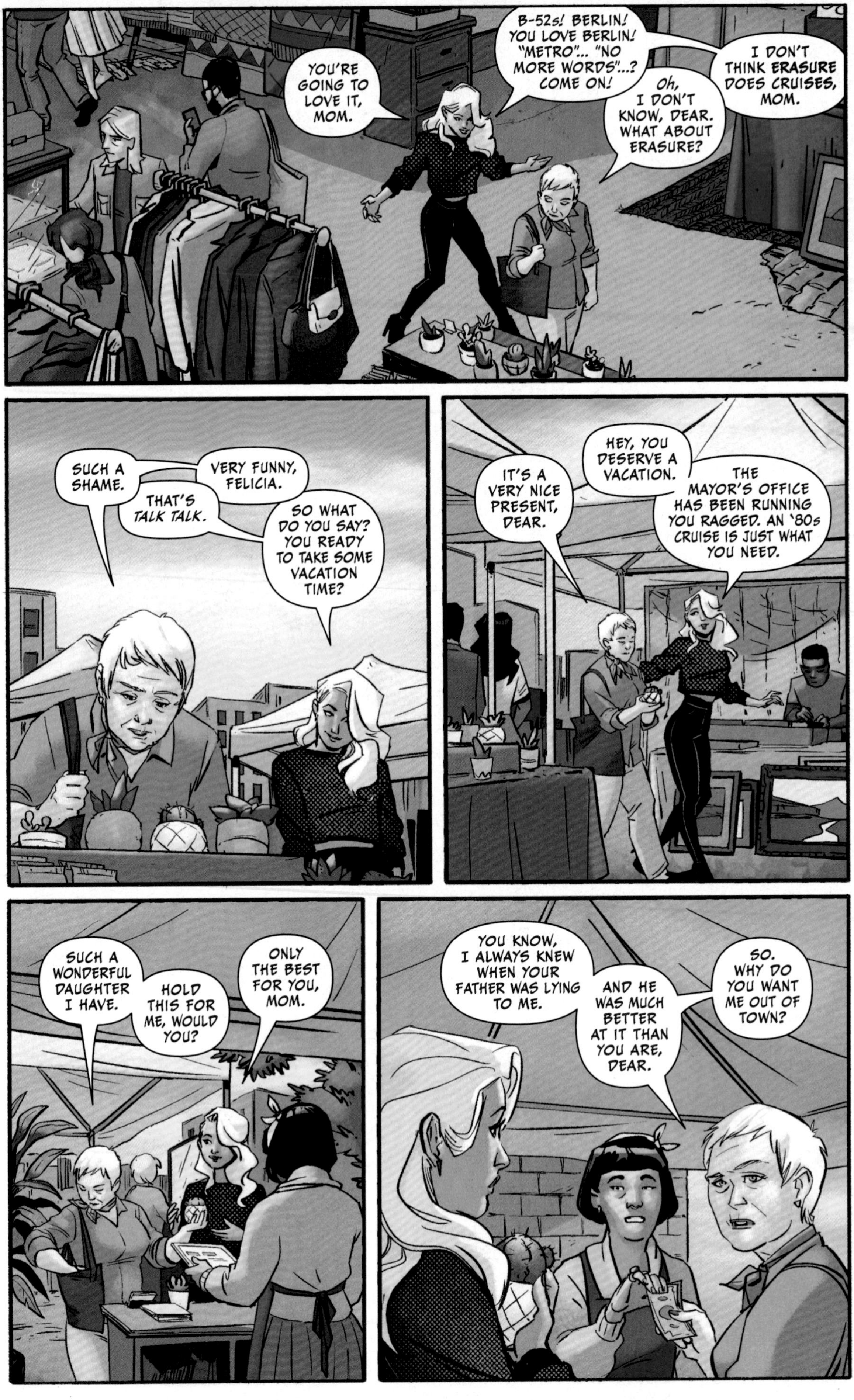
YOU'RE GOING TO LOVE IT, MOM.
B-52s! BERLIN! YOU LOVE BERLIN! "METRO"... "NO MORE WORDS"...? COME ON!
*Oh,* I DON'T KNOW, DEAR. WHAT ABOUT ERASURE?
I DON'T THINK **ERASURE** DOES CRUISES, MOM.
SUCH A SHAME.
VERY FUNNY, FELICIA.
THAT'S *TALK TALK.*
SO WHAT DO YOU SAY? YOU READY TO TAKE SOME VACATION TIME?
IT'S A VERY NICE PRESENT, DEAR.
HEY, YOU DESERVE A VACATION.
THE MAYOR'S OFFICE HAS BEEN RUNNING YOU RAGGED. AN '80s CRUISE IS JUST WHAT YOU NEED.
SUCH A WONDERFUL DAUGHTER I HAVE.
HOLD THIS FOR ME, WOULD YOU?
ONLY THE BEST FOR YOU, MOM.
YOU KNOW, I ALWAYS KNEW WHEN YOUR FATHER WAS LYING TO ME.
AND HE WAS MUCH BETTER AT IT THAN YOU ARE, DEAR.
SO. WHY DO YOU WANT ME OUT OF TOWN?

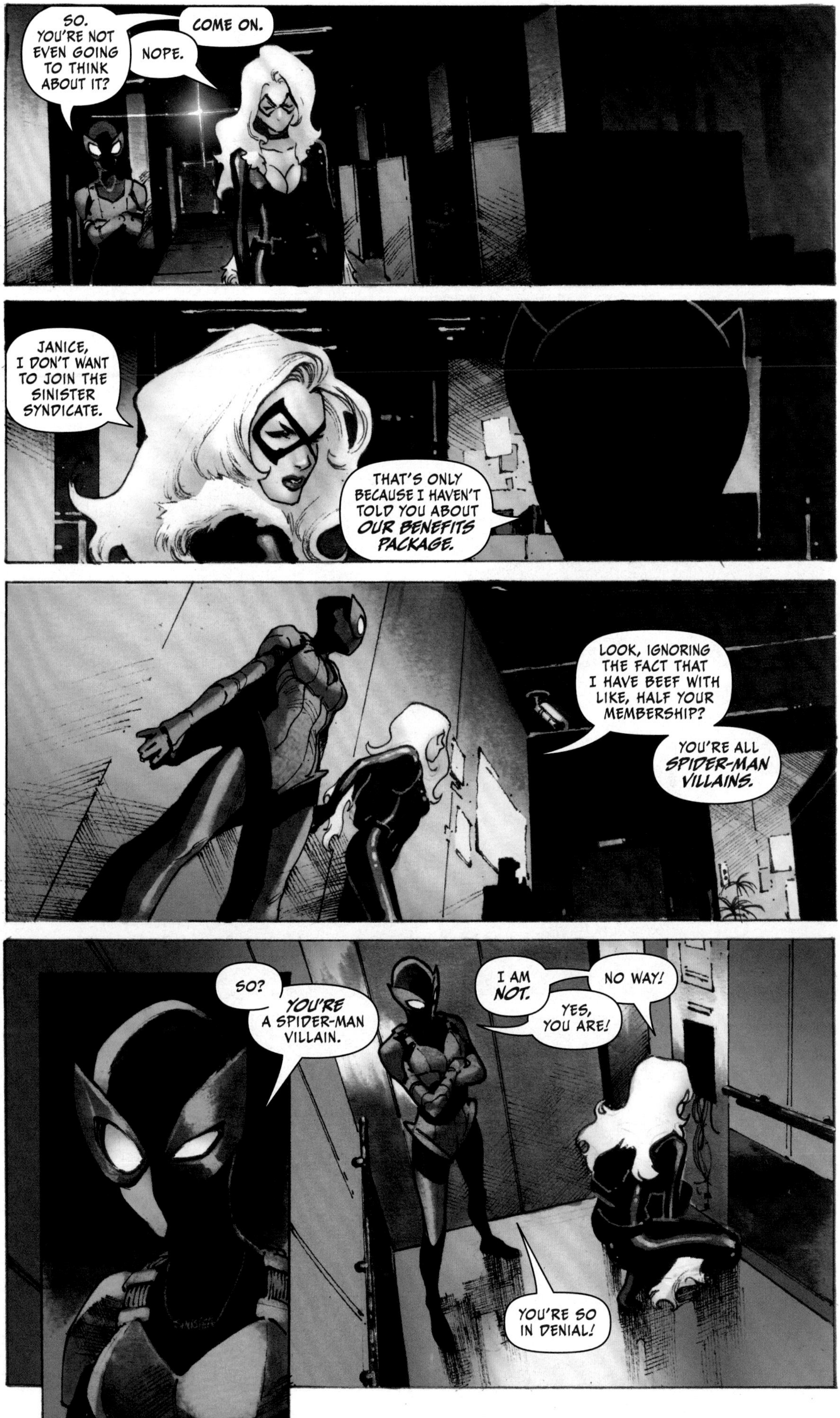
SO. YOU'RE NOT EVEN GOING TO THINK ABOUT IT?
NOPE.
COME ON.
JANICE, I DON'T WANT TO JOIN THE SINISTER SYNDICATE.
THAT'S ONLY BECAUSE I HAVEN'T TOLD YOU ABOUT OUR BENEFITS PACKAGE.
LOOK, IGNORING THE FACT THAT I HAVE BEEF WITH LIKE, HALF YOUR MEMBERSHIP?
YOU'RE ALL SPIDER-MAN VILLAINS.
SO? YOU'RE A SPIDER-MAN VILLAIN.
I AM NOT.
YES, YOU ARE!
NO WAY!
YOU'RE SO IN DENIAL!

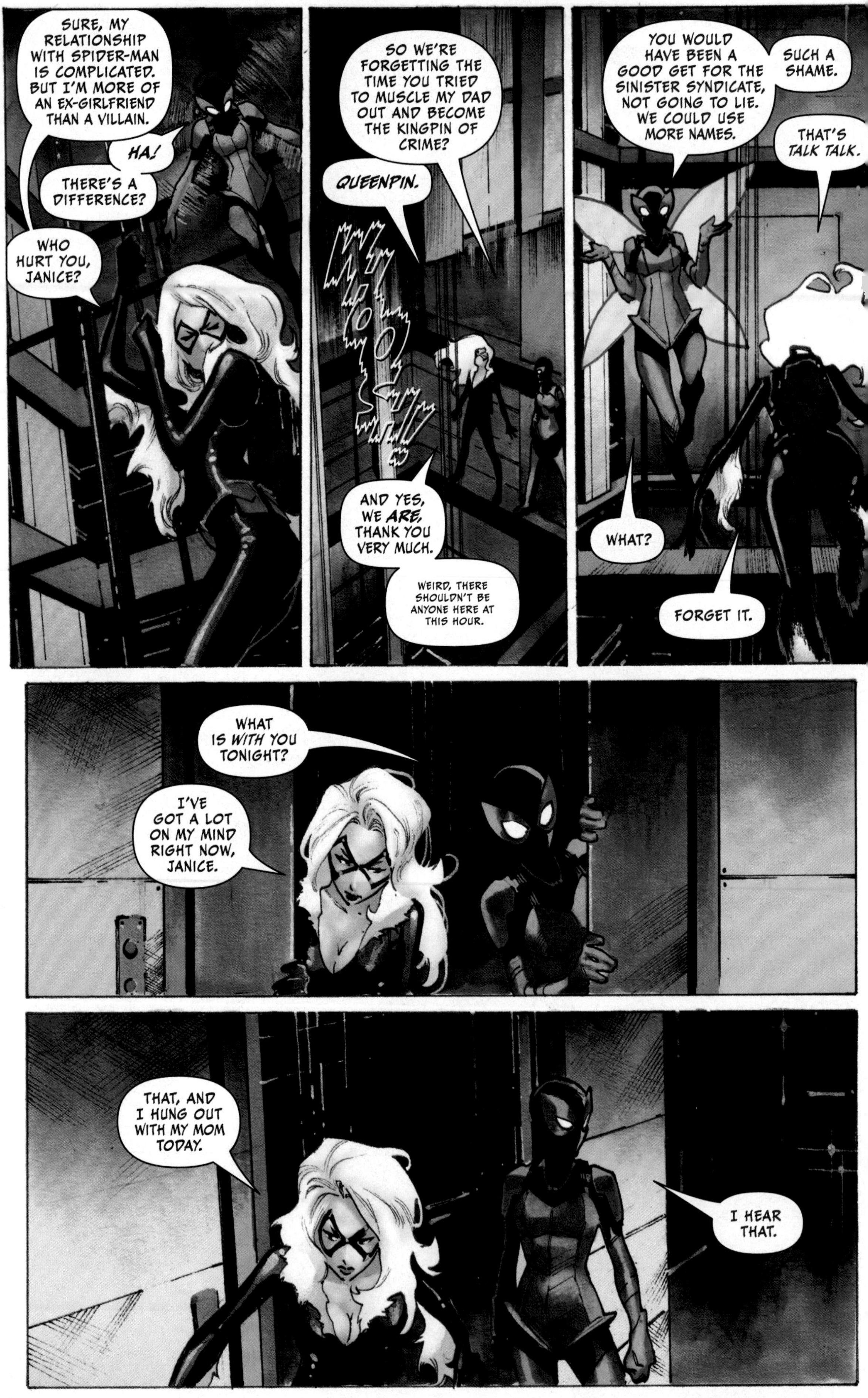
SURE, MY RELATIONSHIP WITH SPIDER-MAN IS COMPLICATED. BUT I'M MORE OF AN EX-GIRLFRIEND THAN A VILLAIN.
HA!
THERE'S A DIFFERENCE?
WHO HURT YOU, JANICE?
SO WE'RE FORGETTING THE TIME YOU TRIED TO MUSCLE MY DAD OUT AND BECOME THE KINGPIN OF CRIME?
QUEENPIN.
AND YES, WE ARE, THANK YOU VERY MUCH.
WEIRD, THERE SHOULDN'T BE ANYONE HERE AT THIS HOUR.
YOU WOULD HAVE BEEN A GOOD GET FOR THE SINISTER SYNDICATE, NOT GOING TO LIE. WE COULD USE MORE NAMES.
SUCH A SHAME.
THAT'S TALK TALK.
WHAT?
FORGET IT.
WHAT IS WITH YOU TONIGHT?
I'VE GOT A LOT ON MY MIND RIGHT NOW, JANICE.
THAT, AND I HUNG OUT WITH MY MOM TODAY.
I HEAR THAT.

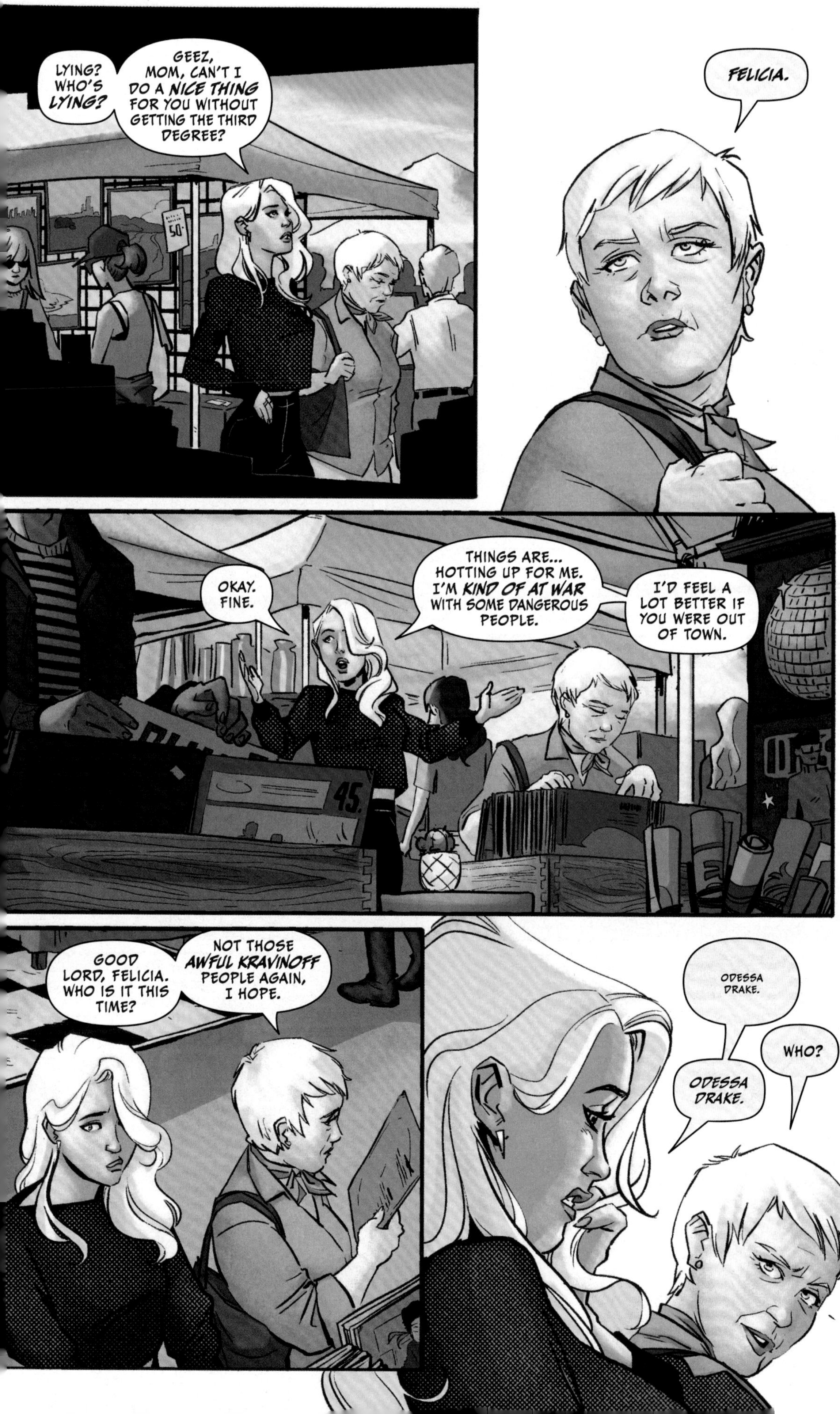
LYING? WHO'S LYING?
GEEZ, MOM, CAN'T I DO A NICE THING FOR YOU WITHOUT GETTING THE THIRD DEGREE?
50
FELICIA.
OKAY. FINE.
THINGS ARE... HOTTING UP FOR ME. I'M KIND OF AT WAR WITH SOME DANGEROUS PEOPLE.
I'D FEEL A LOT BETTER IF YOU WERE OUT OF TOWN.
45.
GOOD LORD, FELICIA. WHO IS IT THIS TIME?
NOT THOSE AWFUL KRAVINOFF PEOPLE AGAIN, I HOPE.
ODESSA DRAKE.
WHO?
ODESSA DRAKE.

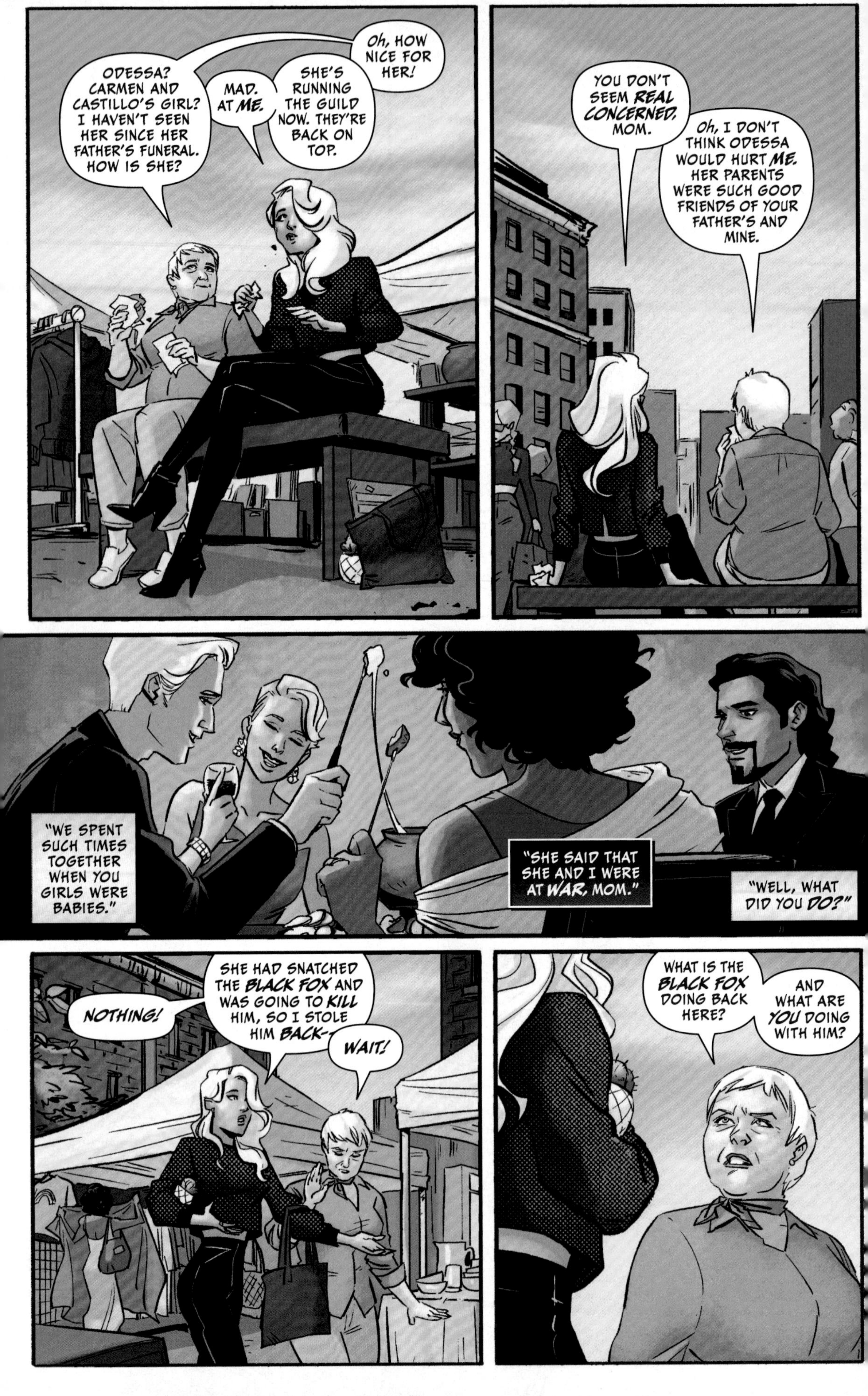
ODESSA? CARMEN AND CASTILLO'S GIRL? I HAVEN'T SEEN HER SINCE HER FATHER'S FUNERAL. HOW IS SHE?
MAD. AT ME.
SHE'S RUNNING THE GUILD NOW. THEY'RE BACK ON TOP.
Oh, HOW NICE FOR HER!
YOU DON'T SEEM REAL CONCERNED, MOM.
Oh, I DON'T THINK ODESSA WOULD HURT ME. HER PARENTS WERE SUCH GOOD FRIENDS OF YOUR FATHER'S AND MINE.
"WE SPENT SUCH TIMES TOGETHER WHEN YOU GIRLS WERE BABIES."
"SHE SAID THAT SHE AND I WERE AT WAR, MOM."
"WELL, WHAT DID YOU DO?"
NOTHING!
SHE HAD SNATCHED THE BLACK FOX AND WAS GOING TO KILL HIM, SO I STOLE HIM BACK-
WAIT!
WHAT IS THE BLACK FOX DOING BACK HERE?
AND WHAT ARE YOU DOING WITH HIM?

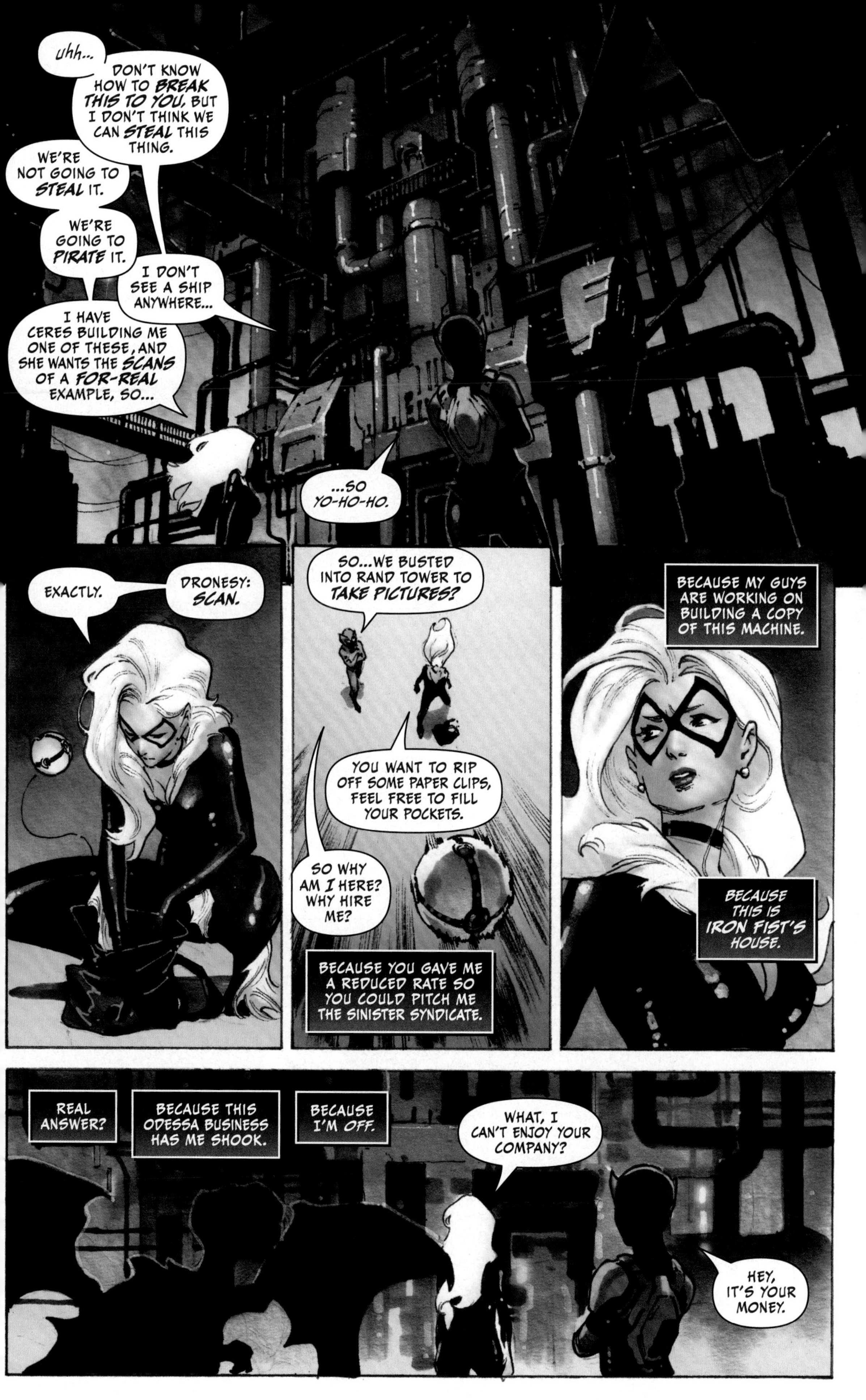
uhh...
DON'T KNOW HOW TO BREAK THIS TO YOU, BUT I DON'T THINK WE CAN STEAL THIS THING.
WE'RE NOT GOING TO STEAL IT.
WE'RE GOING TO PIRATE IT.
I DON'T SEE A SHIP ANYWHERE...
I HAVE CERES BUILDING ME ONE OF THESE, AND SHE WANTS THE SCANS OF A FOR-REAL EXAMPLE, SO...
...SO YO-HO-HO.
EXACTLY.
DRONESY: SCAN.
SO...WE BUSTED INTO RAND TOWER TO TAKE PICTURES?
YOU WANT TO RIP OFF SOME PAPER CLIPS, FEEL FREE TO FILL YOUR POCKETS.
SO WHY AM I HERE? WHY HIRE ME?
BECAUSE YOU GAVE ME A REDUCED RATE SO YOU COULD PITCH ME THE SINISTER SYNDICATE.
BECAUSE MY GUYS ARE WORKING ON BUILDING A COPY OF THIS MACHINE.
BECAUSE THIS IS IRON FIST'S HOUSE.
REAL ANSWER?
BECAUSE THIS ODESSA BUSINESS HAS ME SHOOK.
BECAUSE I'M OFF.
WHAT, I CAN'T ENJOY YOUR COMPANY?
HEY, IT'S YOUR MONEY.

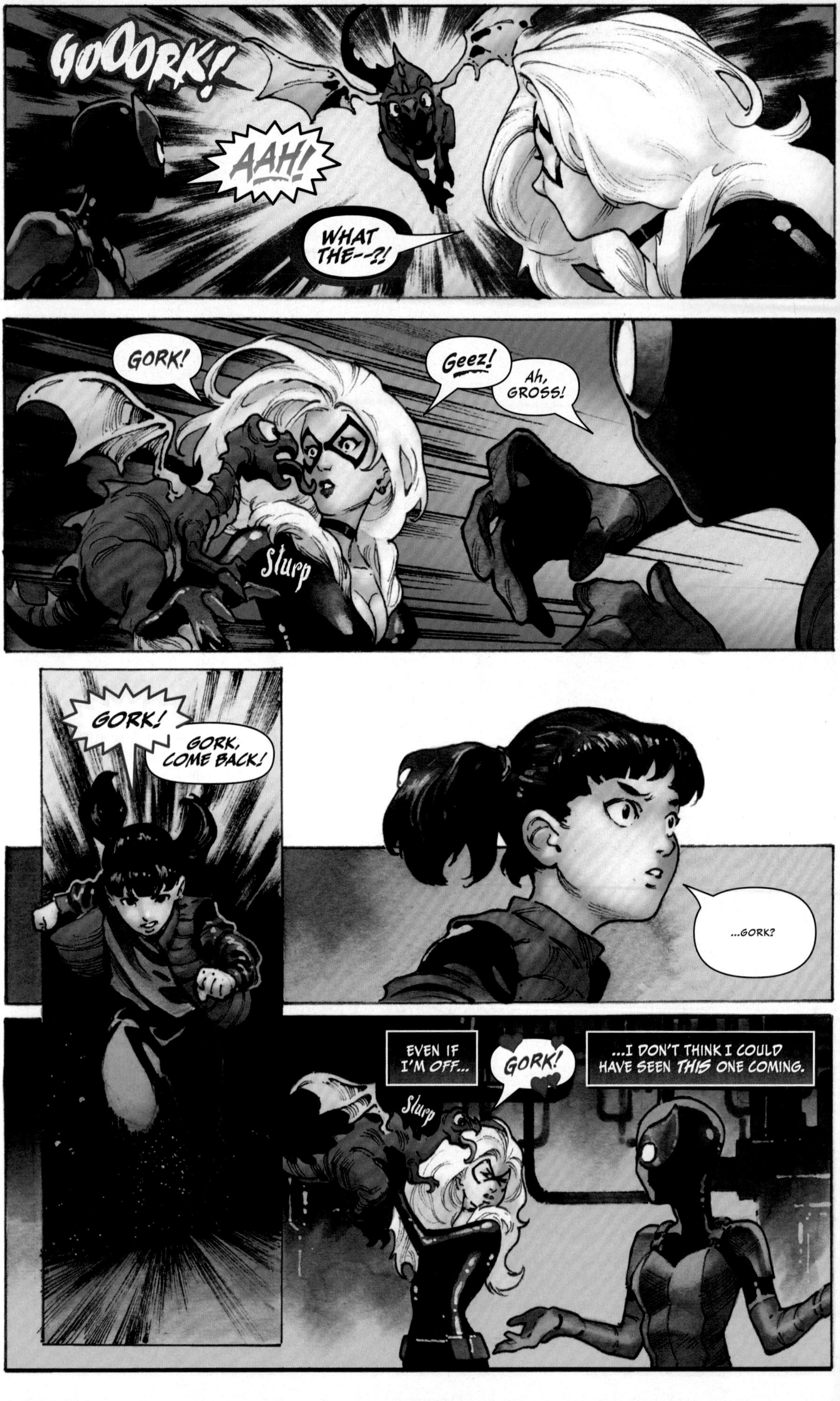
GOOOORK!
AAH!
WHAT THE--?!
GORK!
Geez!
Ah, GROSS!
Slurp
GORK!
GORK, COME BACK!
...GORK?
EVEN IF I'M OFF...
GORK!
...I DON'T THINK I COULD HAVE SEEN THIS ONE COMING.
Slurp

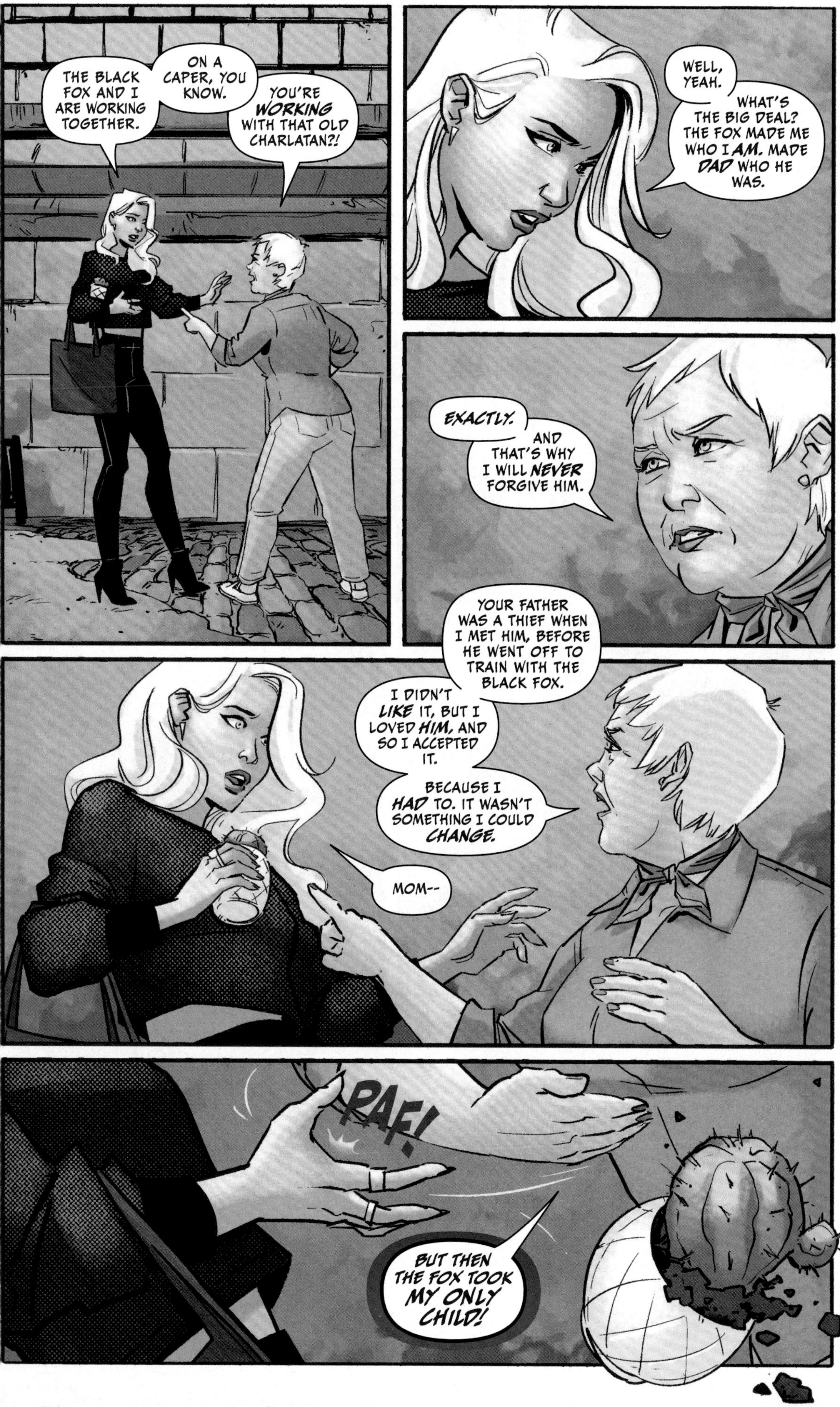
THE BLACK FOX AND I ARE WORKING TOGETHER.
ON A CAPER, YOU KNOW.
YOU'RE WORKING WITH THAT OLD CHARLATAN?!
WELL, YEAH.
WHAT'S THE BIG DEAL? THE FOX MADE ME WHO I AM. MADE DAD WHO HE WAS.
EXACTLY.
AND THAT'S WHY I WILL NEVER FORGIVE HIM.
YOUR FATHER WAS A THIEF WHEN I MET HIM, BEFORE HE WENT OFF TO TRAIN WITH THE BLACK FOX.
I DIDN'T LIKE IT, BUT I LOVED HIM, AND SO I ACCEPTED IT.
BECAUSE I HAD TO. IT WASN'T SOMETHING I COULD CHANGE.
MOM--
PAF!
BUT THEN THE FOX TOOK MY ONLY CHILD!

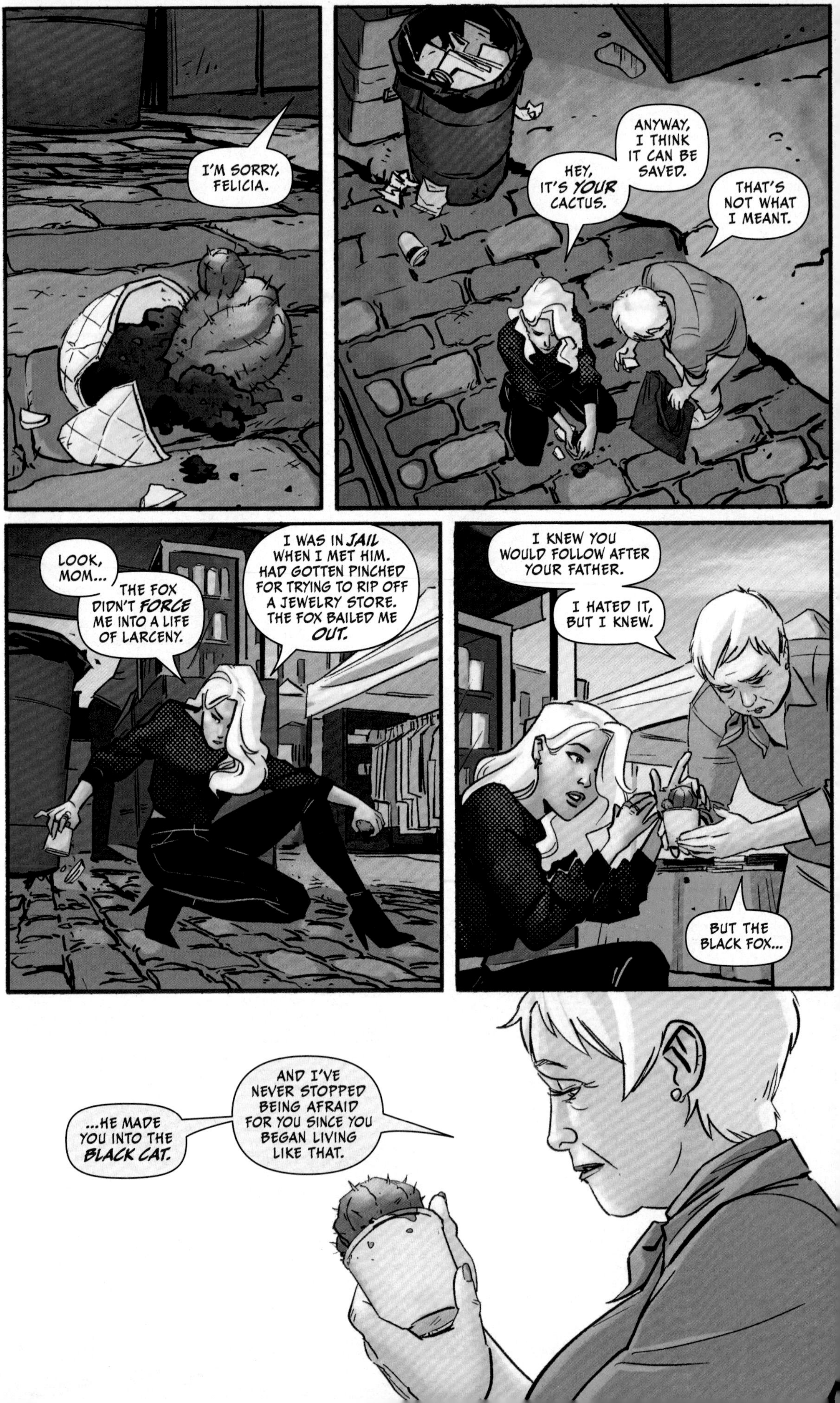
I'M SORRY, FELICIA.
HEY, IT'S YOUR CACTUS.
ANYWAY, I THINK IT CAN BE SAVED.
THAT'S NOT WHAT I MEANT.
LOOK, MOM...
THE FOX DIDN'T FORCE ME INTO A LIFE OF LARCENY.
I WAS IN JAIL WHEN I MET HIM. HAD GOTTEN PINCHED FOR TRYING TO RIP OFF A JEWELRY STORE. THE FOX BAILED ME OUT.
I KNEW YOU WOULD FOLLOW AFTER YOUR FATHER.
I HATED IT, BUT I KNEW.
BUT THE BLACK FOX...
...HE MADE YOU INTO THE BLACK CAT.
AND I'VE NEVER STOPPED BEING AFRAID FOR YOU SINCE YOU BEGAN LIVING LIKE THAT.

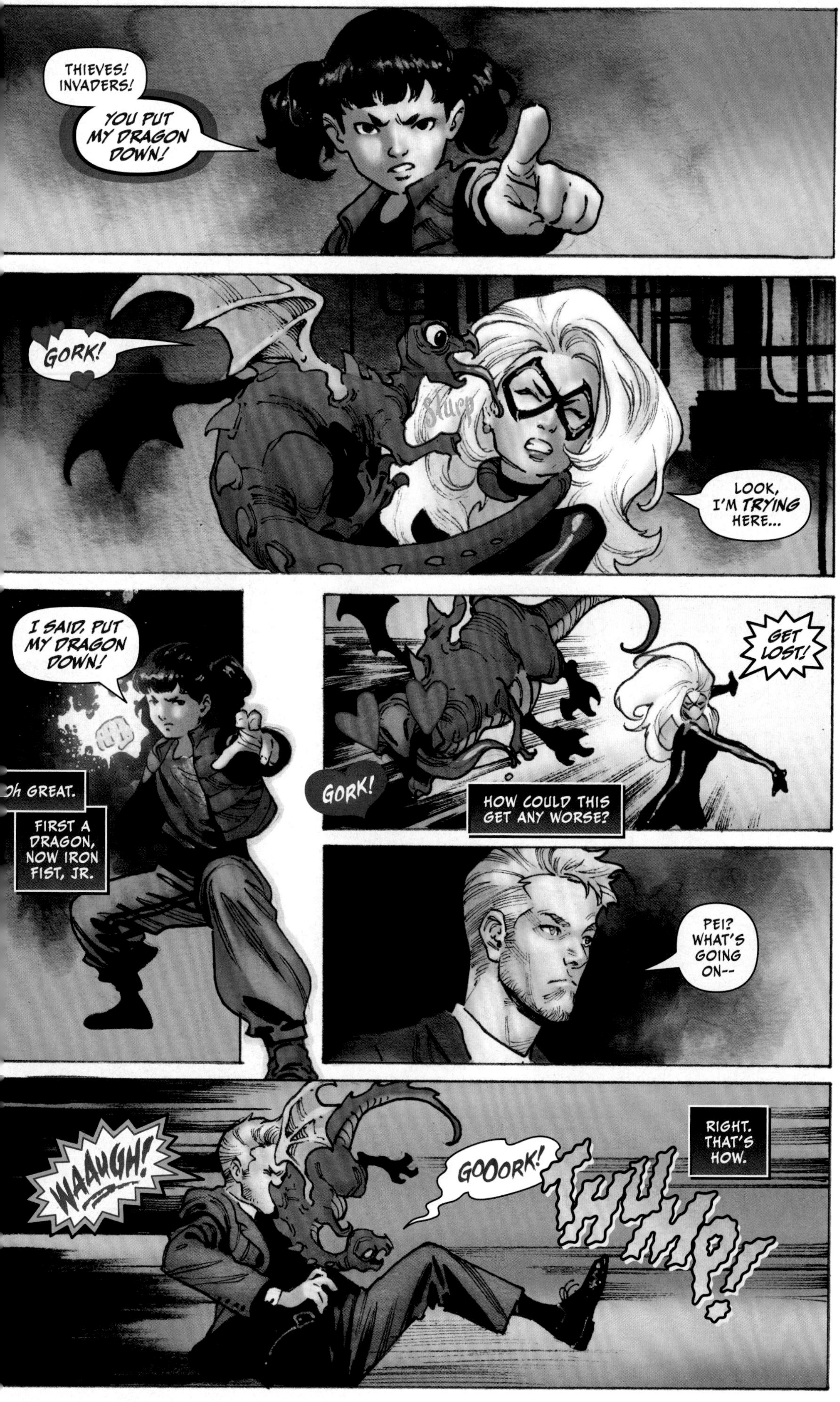

THIEVES! INVADERS!
YOU PUT MY DRAGON DOWN!
GORK!
Slurp
LOOK, I'M TRYING HERE...
I SAID, PUT MY DRAGON DOWN!
Oh GREAT.
FIRST A DRAGON, NOW IRON FIST, JR.
GET LOST!
GORK!
HOW COULD THIS GET ANY WORSE?
PEI? WHAT'S GOING ON--
WAAUGH!
GOOORK!
THUMP!!
RIGHT. THAT'S HOW.

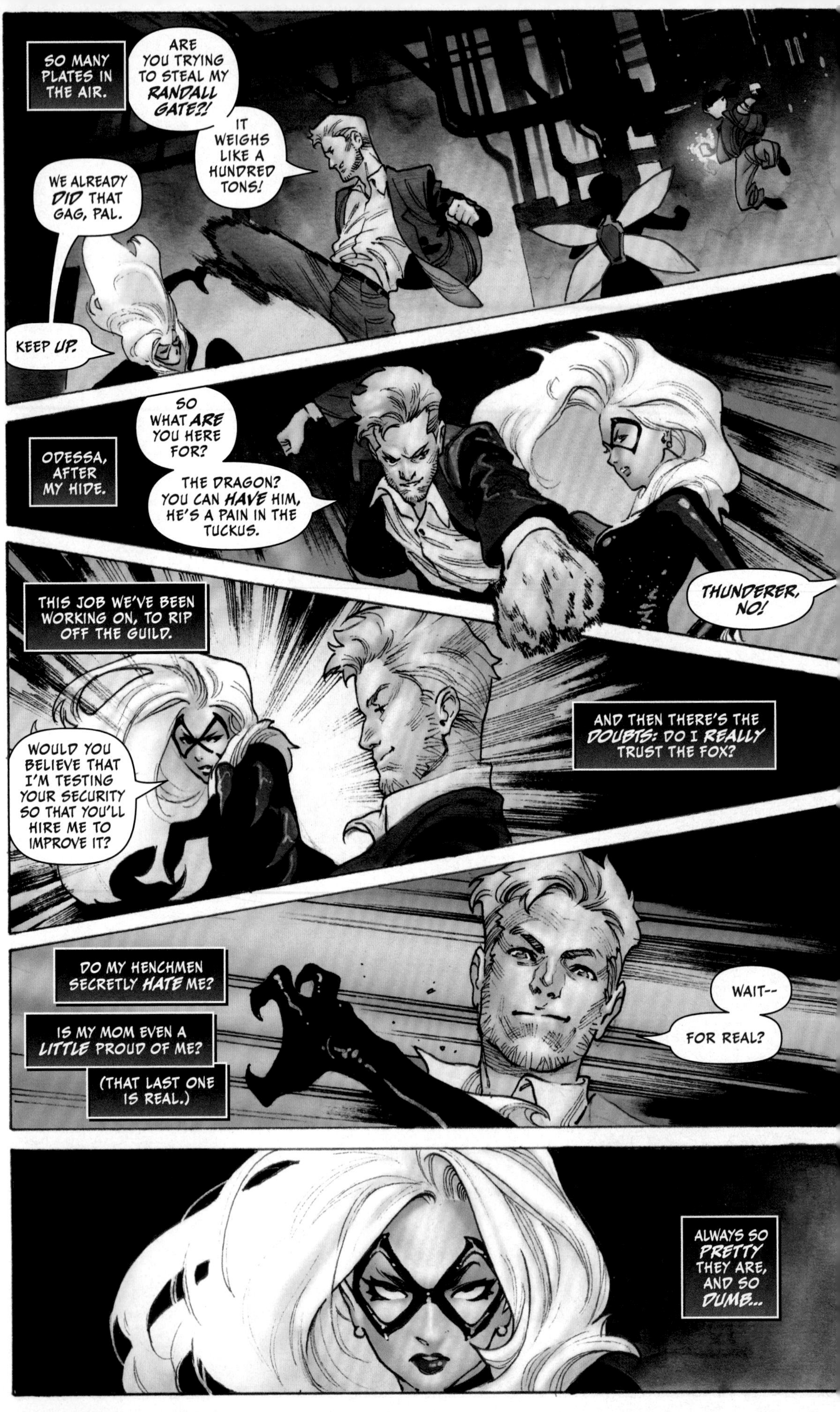

SO MANY PLATES IN THE AIR.
ARE YOU TRYING TO STEAL MY RANDALL GATE?!
IT WEIGHS LIKE A HUNDRED TONS!
WE ALREADY DID THAT GAG, PAL.
KEEP UP.
ODESSA, AFTER MY HIDE.
SO WHAT ARE YOU HERE FOR?
THE DRAGON? YOU CAN HAVE HIM, HE'S A PAIN IN THE TUCKUS.
THUNDERER, NO!
THIS JOB WE'VE BEEN WORKING ON, TO RIP OFF THE GUILD.
WOULD YOU BELIEVE THAT I'M TESTING YOUR SECURITY SO THAT YOU'LL HIRE ME TO IMPROVE IT?
AND THEN THERE'S THE DOUBTS: DO I REALLY TRUST THE FOX?
DO MY HENCHMEN SECRETLY HATE ME?
IS MY MOM EVEN A LITTLE PROUD OF ME?
(THAT LAST ONE IS REAL.)
WAIT--
FOR REAL?
ALWAYS SO PRETTY THEY ARE, AND SO DUMB...

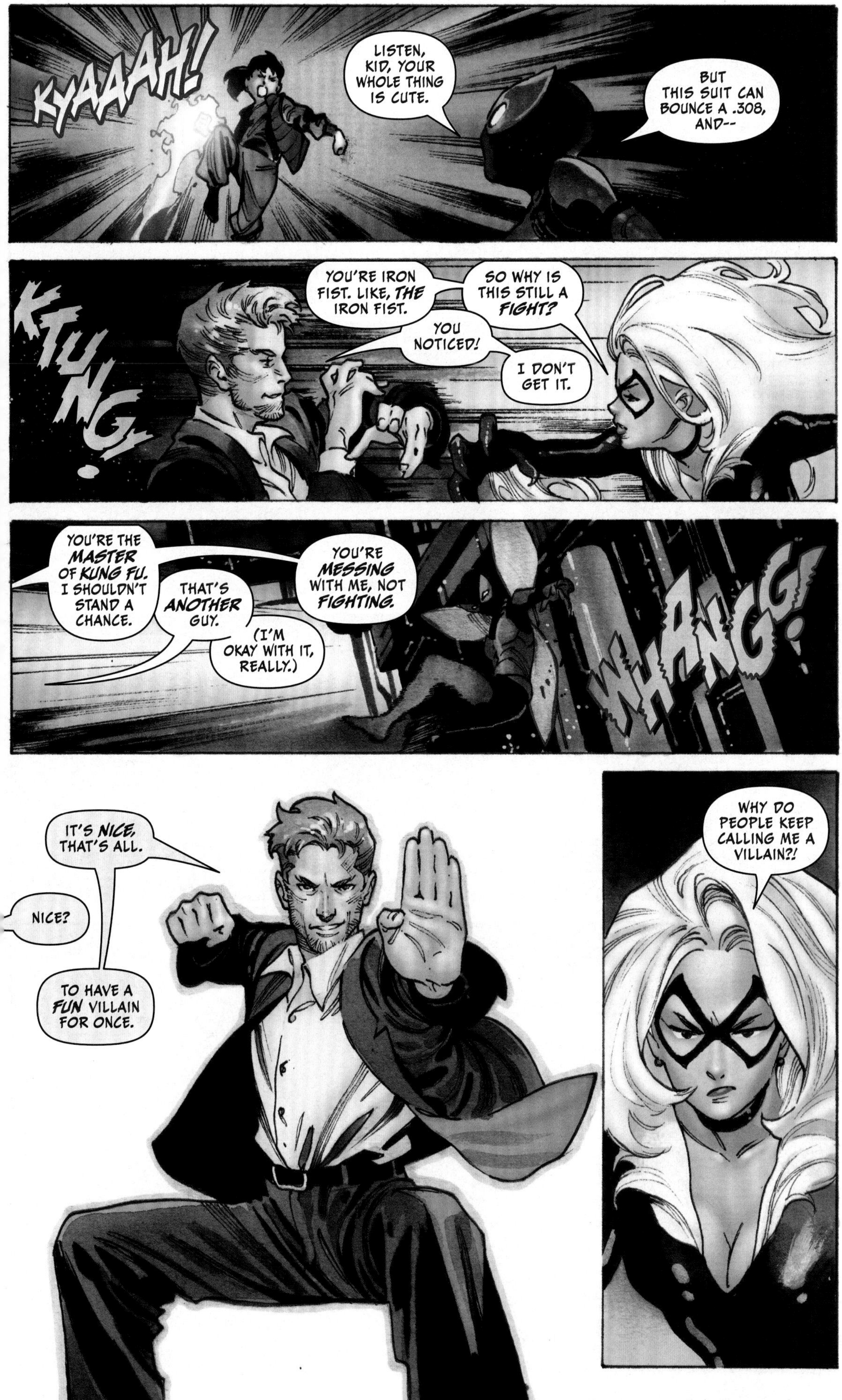
KYAAAH!
LISTEN, KID, YOUR WHOLE THING IS CUTE.
BUT THIS SUIT CAN BOUNCE A .308, AND--
KTUNG!
YOU'RE IRON FIST. LIKE, THE IRON FIST.
SO WHY IS THIS STILL A FIGHT?
YOU NOTICED!
I DON'T GET IT.
YOU'RE THE MASTER OF KUNG FU. I SHOULDN'T STAND A CHANCE.
YOU'RE MESSING WITH ME, NOT FIGHTING.
THAT'S ANOTHER GUY.
(I'M OKAY WITH IT, REALLY.)
WHANGG!
IT'S NICE, THAT'S ALL.
NICE?
TO HAVE A FUN VILLAIN FOR ONCE.
WHY DO PEOPLE KEEP CALLING ME A VILLAIN?!

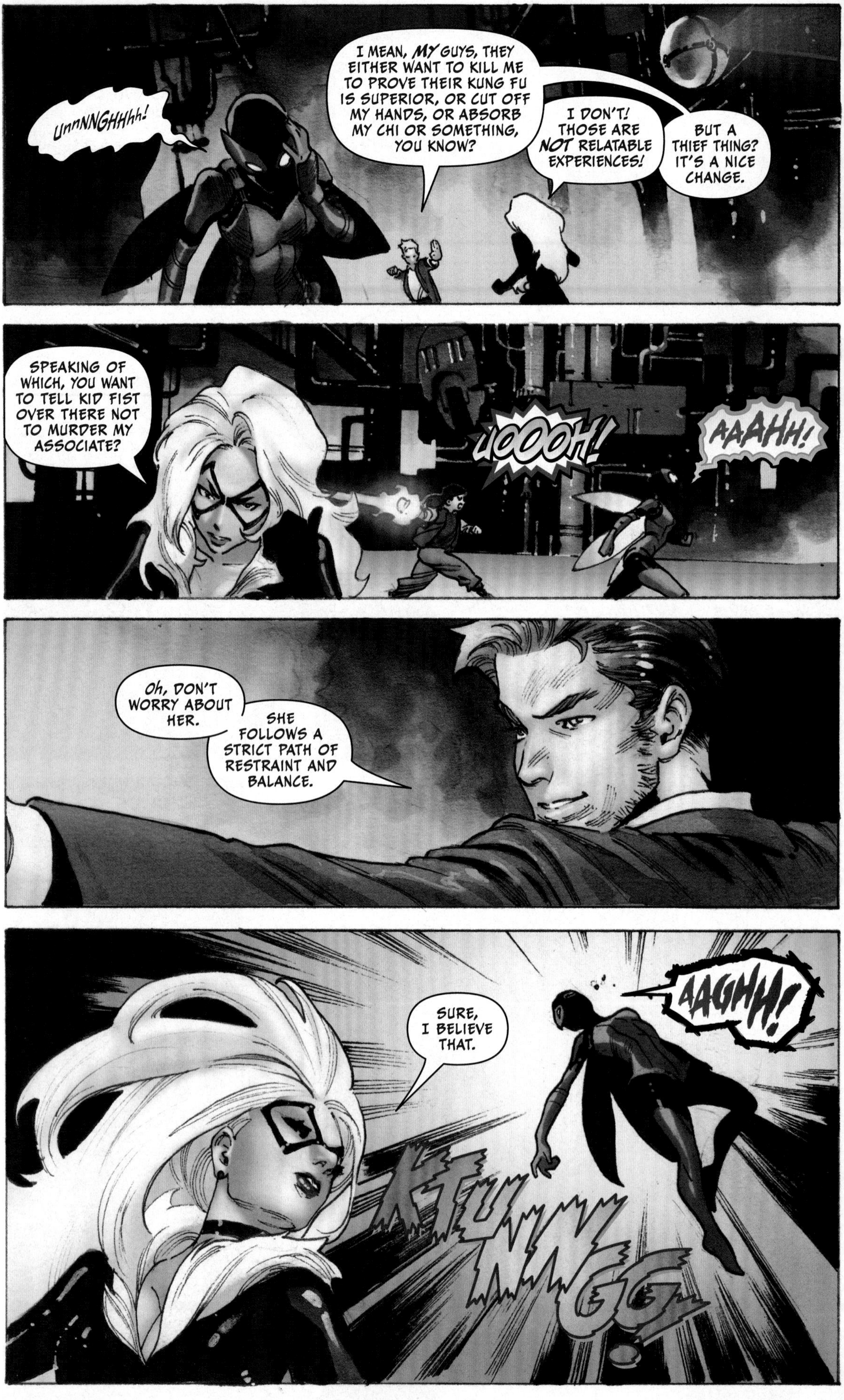
UnnNNGHHhh!
I MEAN, MY GUYS, THEY EITHER WANT TO KILL ME TO PROVE THEIR KUNG FU IS SUPERIOR, OR CUT OFF MY HANDS, OR ABSORB MY CHI OR SOMETHING, YOU KNOW?
I DON'T! THOSE ARE NOT RELATABLE EXPERIENCES!
BUT A THIEF THING? IT'S A NICE CHANGE.
SPEAKING OF WHICH, YOU WANT TO TELL KID FIST OVER THERE NOT TO MURDER MY ASSOCIATE?
UOOOH!
AAAHH!
Oh, DON'T WORRY ABOUT HER.
SHE FOLLOWS A STRICT PATH OF RESTRAINT AND BALANCE.
SURE, I BELIEVE THAT.
AAGHH!
KTUNNGG

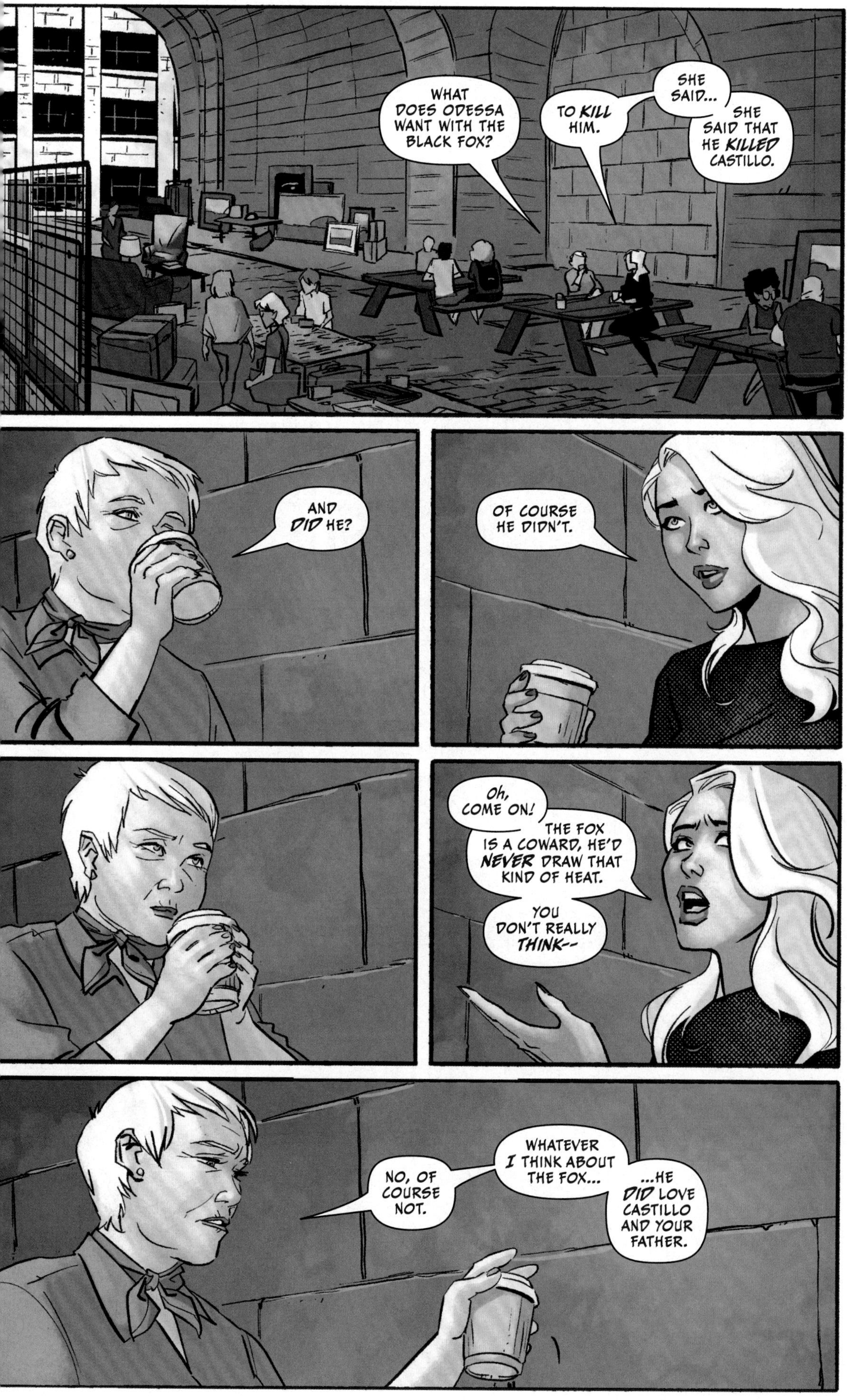
WHAT DOES ODESSA WANT WITH THE BLACK FOX?
SHE SAID...
SHE SAID THAT HE KILLED CASTILLO.
TO KILL HIM.
AND DID HE?
OF COURSE HE DIDN'T.
Oh, COME ON!
THE FOX IS A COWARD, HE'D NEVER DRAW THAT KIND OF HEAT.
YOU DON'T REALLY THINK--
NO, OF COURSE NOT.
WHATEVER I THINK ABOUT THE FOX...
...HE DID LOVE CASTILLO AND YOUR FATHER.

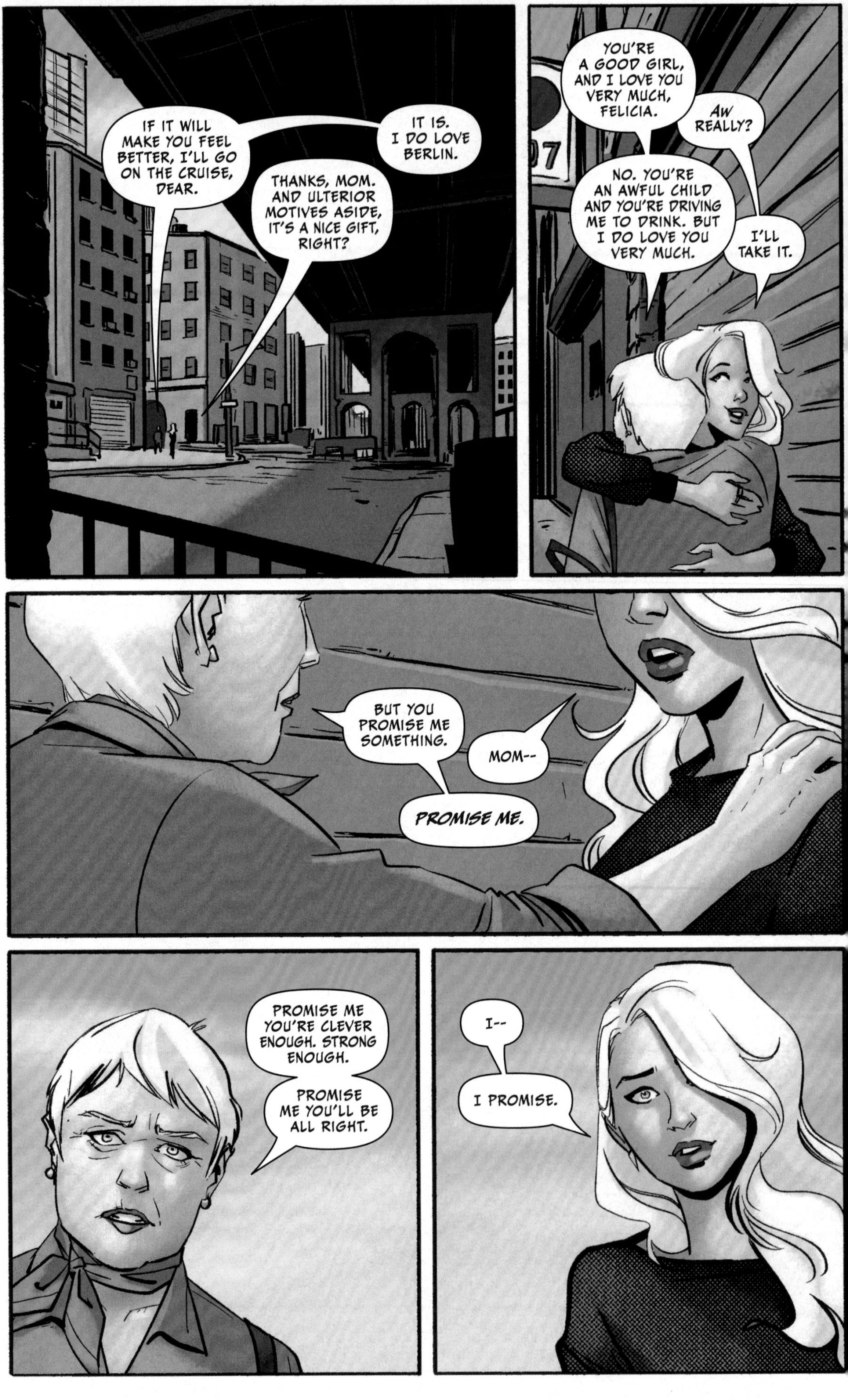
IF IT WILL MAKE YOU FEEL BETTER, I'LL GO ON THE CRUISE, DEAR.
IT IS. I DO LOVE BERLIN.
THANKS, MOM. AND ULTERIOR MOTIVES ASIDE, IT'S A NICE GIFT, RIGHT?
YOU'RE A GOOD GIRL, AND I LOVE YOU VERY MUCH, FELICIA.
AW REALLY?
NO. YOU'RE AN AWFUL CHILD AND YOU'RE DRIVING ME TO DRINK. BUT I DO LOVE YOU VERY MUCH.
I'LL TAKE IT.
BUT YOU PROMISE ME SOMETHING.
MOM--
PROMISE ME.
PROMISE ME YOU'RE CLEVER ENOUGH. STRONG ENOUGH.
PROMISE ME YOU'LL BE ALL RIGHT.
I--
I PROMISE.

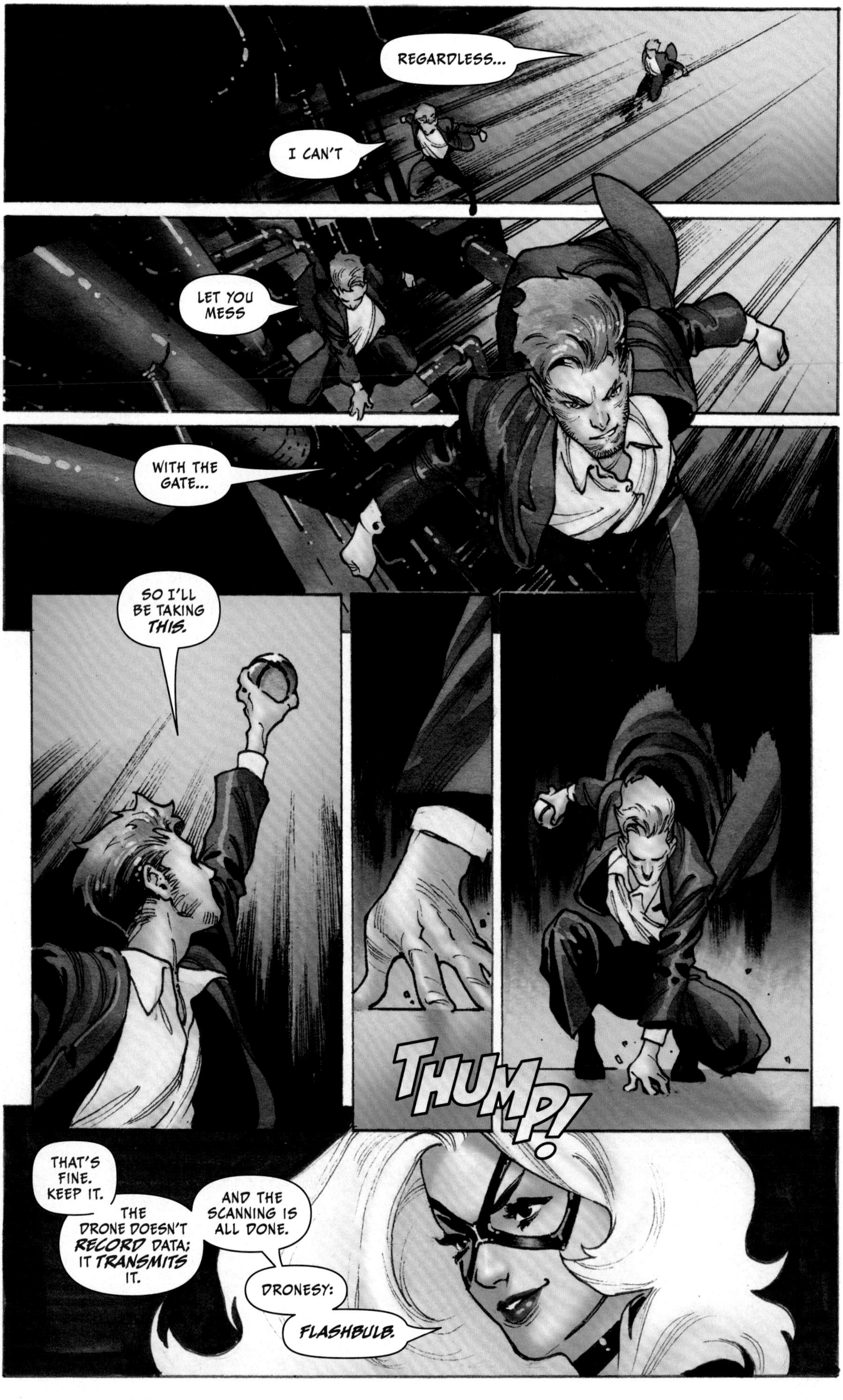
REGARDLESS...
I CAN'T
LET YOU MESS
WITH THE GATE...
SO I'LL BE TAKING *THIS.*
THUMP!
THAT'S FINE. KEEP IT.
THE DRONE DOESN'T *RECORD* DATA; IT *TRANSMITS* IT.
AND THE SCANNING IS ALL DONE.
DRONESY:
*FLASHBULB.*

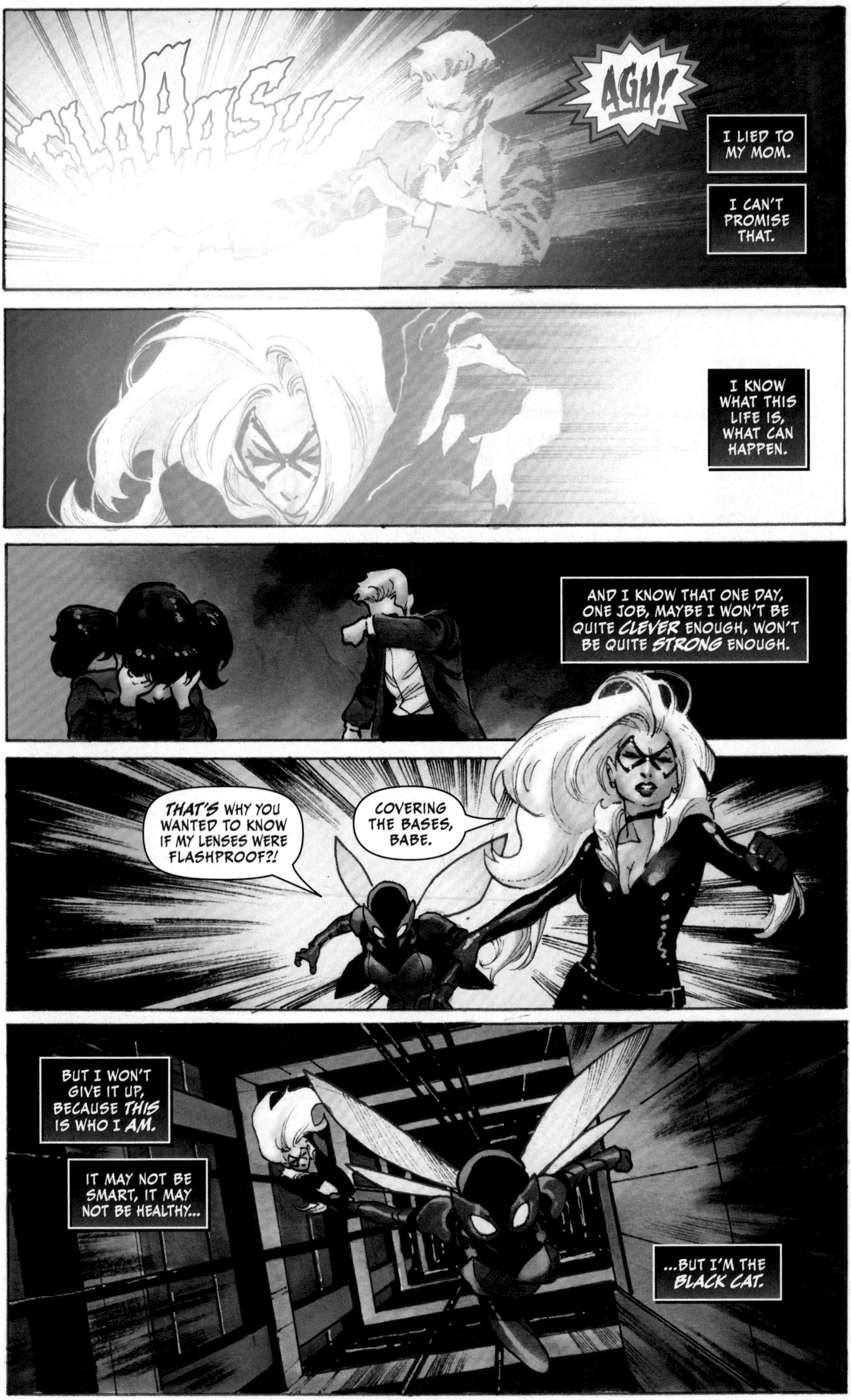
SHLAASH!!
AGH!
I LIED TO MY MOM.
I CAN'T PROMISE THAT.
I KNOW WHAT THIS LIFE IS, WHAT CAN HAPPEN.
AND I KNOW THAT ONE DAY, ONE JOB, MAYBE I WON'T BE QUITE CLEVER ENOUGH, WON'T BE QUITE STRONG ENOUGH.
THAT'S WHY YOU WANTED TO KNOW IF MY LENSES WERE FLASHPROOF?!
COVERING THE BASES, BABE.
BUT I WON'T GIVE IT UP, BECAUSE THIS IS WHO I AM.
IT MAY NOT BE SMART, IT MAY NOT BE HEALTHY...
...BUT I'M THE BLACK CAT.

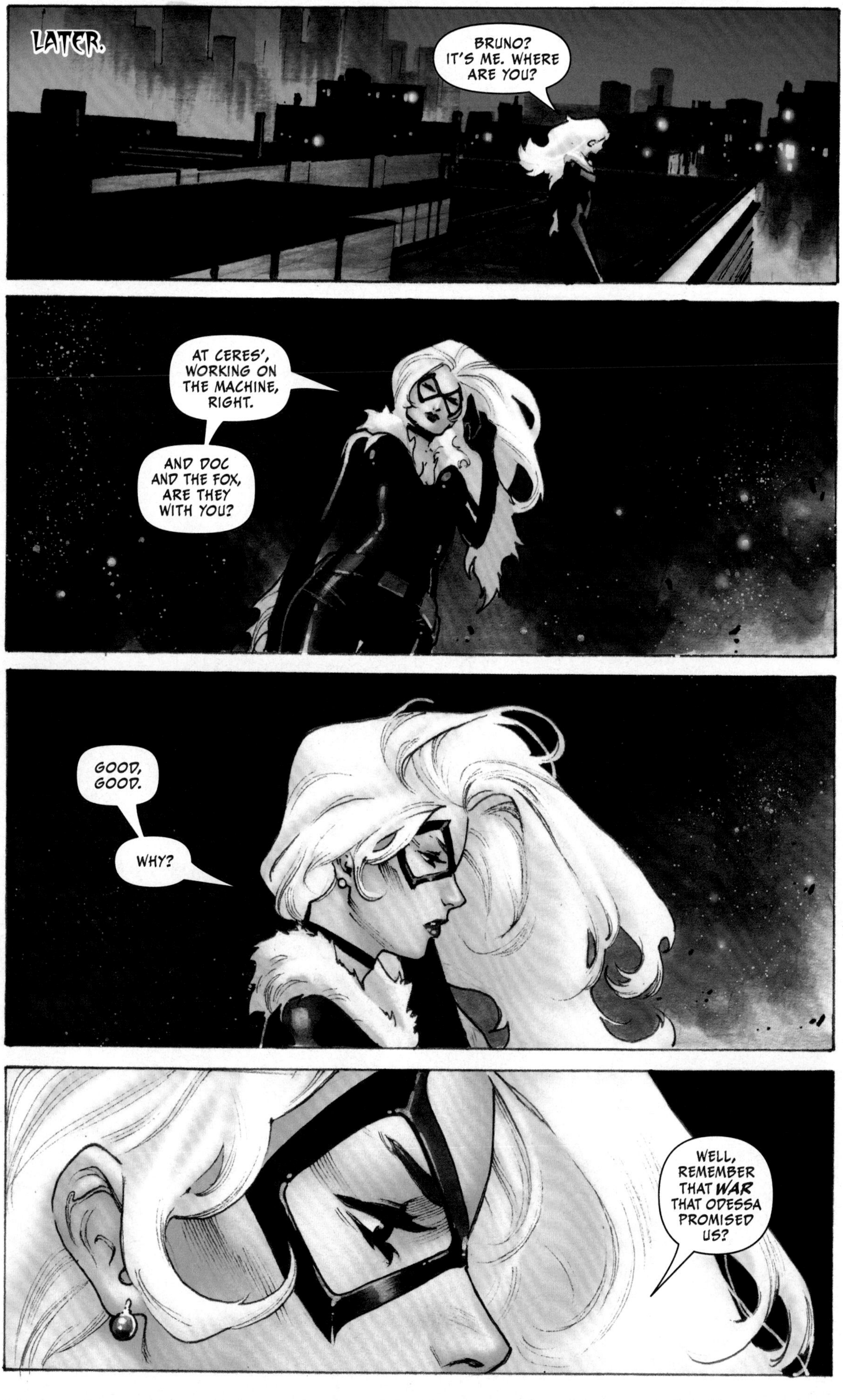
LATER.
BRUNO? IT'S ME. WHERE ARE YOU?
AT CERES', WORKING ON THE MACHINE, RIGHT.
AND DOC AND THE FOX, ARE THEY WITH YOU?
GOOD, GOOD.
WHY?
WELL, REMEMBER THAT WAR THAT ODESSA PROMISED US?

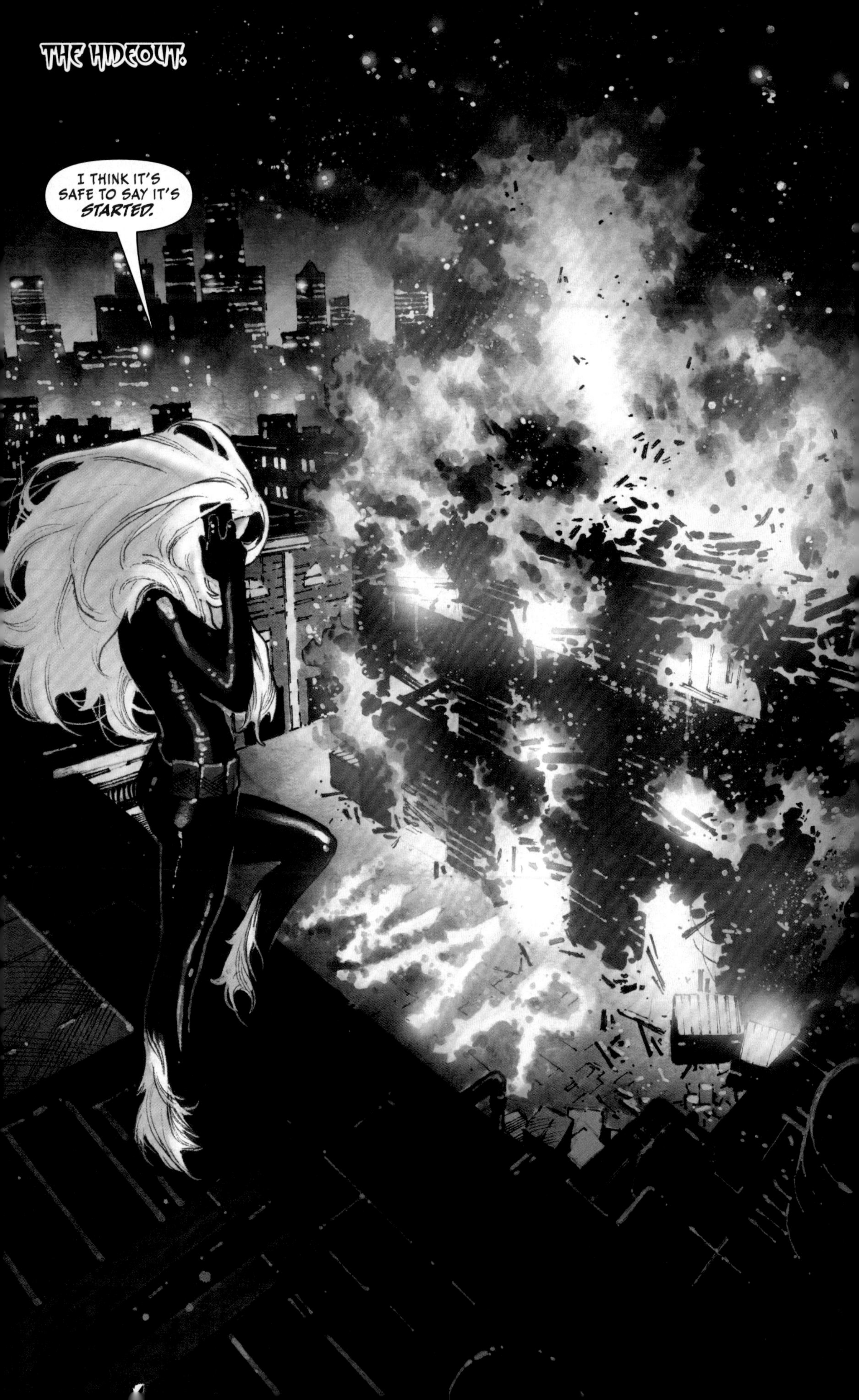
THE HIDEOUT.
I THINK IT'S SAFE TO SAY IT'S STARTED.

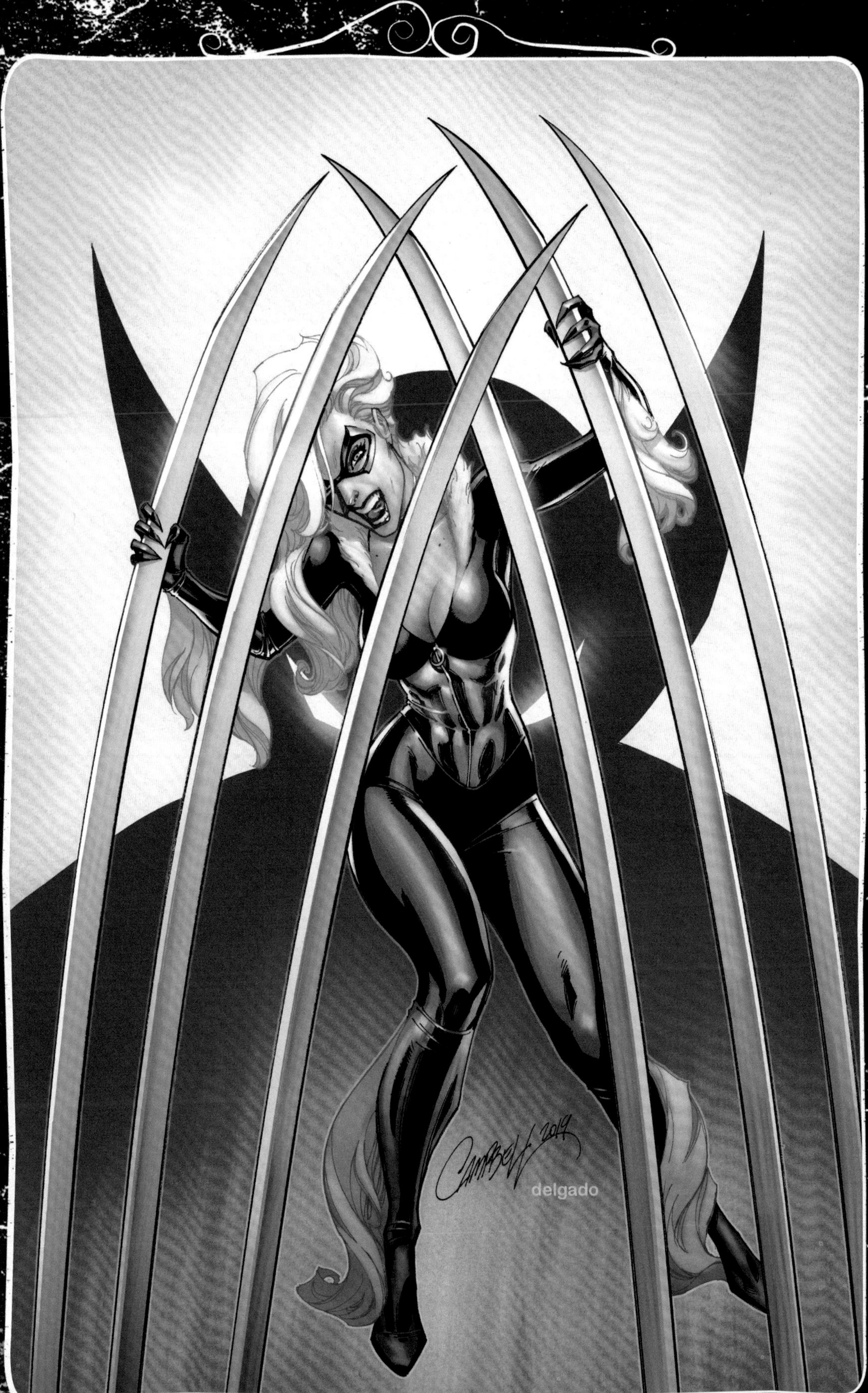
delgado

# 9 • Sleight of Hand PART 1

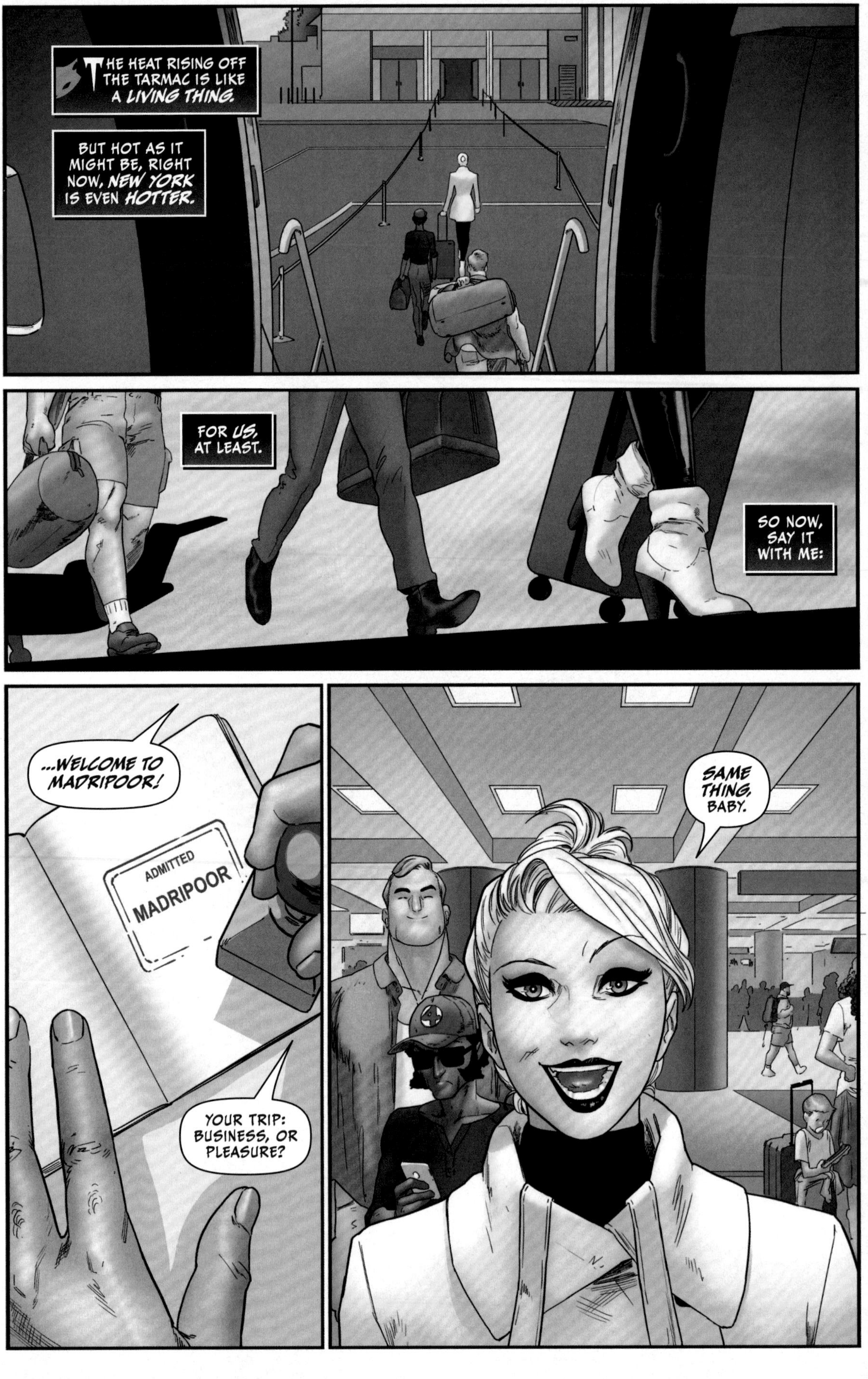
THE HEAT RISING OFF THE TARMAC IS LIKE A LIVING THING.
BUT HOT AS IT MIGHT BE, RIGHT NOW, NEW YORK IS EVEN HOTTER.
FOR US, AT LEAST.
SO NOW, SAY IT WITH ME:
...WELCOME TO MADRIPOOR!
ADMITTED
MADRIPOOR
YOUR TRIP: BUSINESS, OR PLEASURE?
SAME THING, BABY.

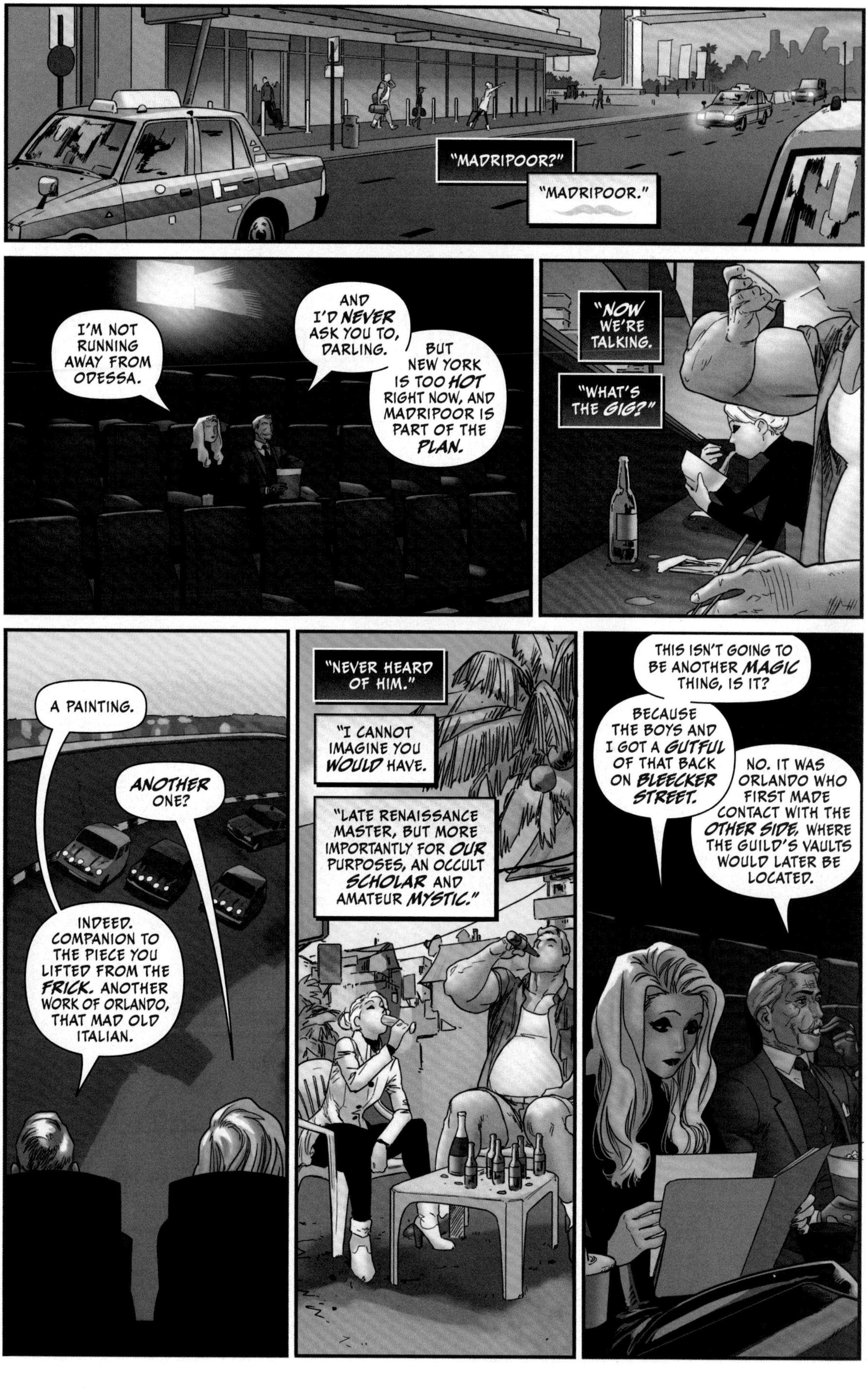
"MADRIPOOR?"
"MADRIPOOR."
I'M NOT RUNNING AWAY FROM ODESSA.
AND I'D NEVER ASK YOU TO, DARLING.
BUT NEW YORK IS TOO HOT RIGHT NOW, AND MADRIPOOR IS PART OF THE PLAN.
"NOW WE'RE TALKING.
"WHAT'S THE GIG?"
A PAINTING.
ANOTHER ONE?
INDEED. COMPANION TO THE PIECE YOU LIFTED FROM THE FRICK. ANOTHER WORK OF ORLANDO, THAT MAD OLD ITALIAN.
"NEVER HEARD OF HIM."
"I CANNOT IMAGINE YOU WOULD HAVE.
"LATE RENAISSANCE MASTER, BUT MORE IMPORTANTLY FOR OUR PURPOSES, AN OCCULT SCHOLAR AND AMATEUR MYSTIC."
THIS ISN'T GOING TO BE ANOTHER MAGIC THING, IS IT?
BECAUSE THE BOYS AND I GOT A GUTFUL OF THAT BACK ON BLEECKER STREET.
NO. IT WAS ORLANDO WHO FIRST MADE CONTACT WITH THE OTHER SIDE, WHERE THE GUILD'S VAULTS WOULD LATER BE LOCATED.

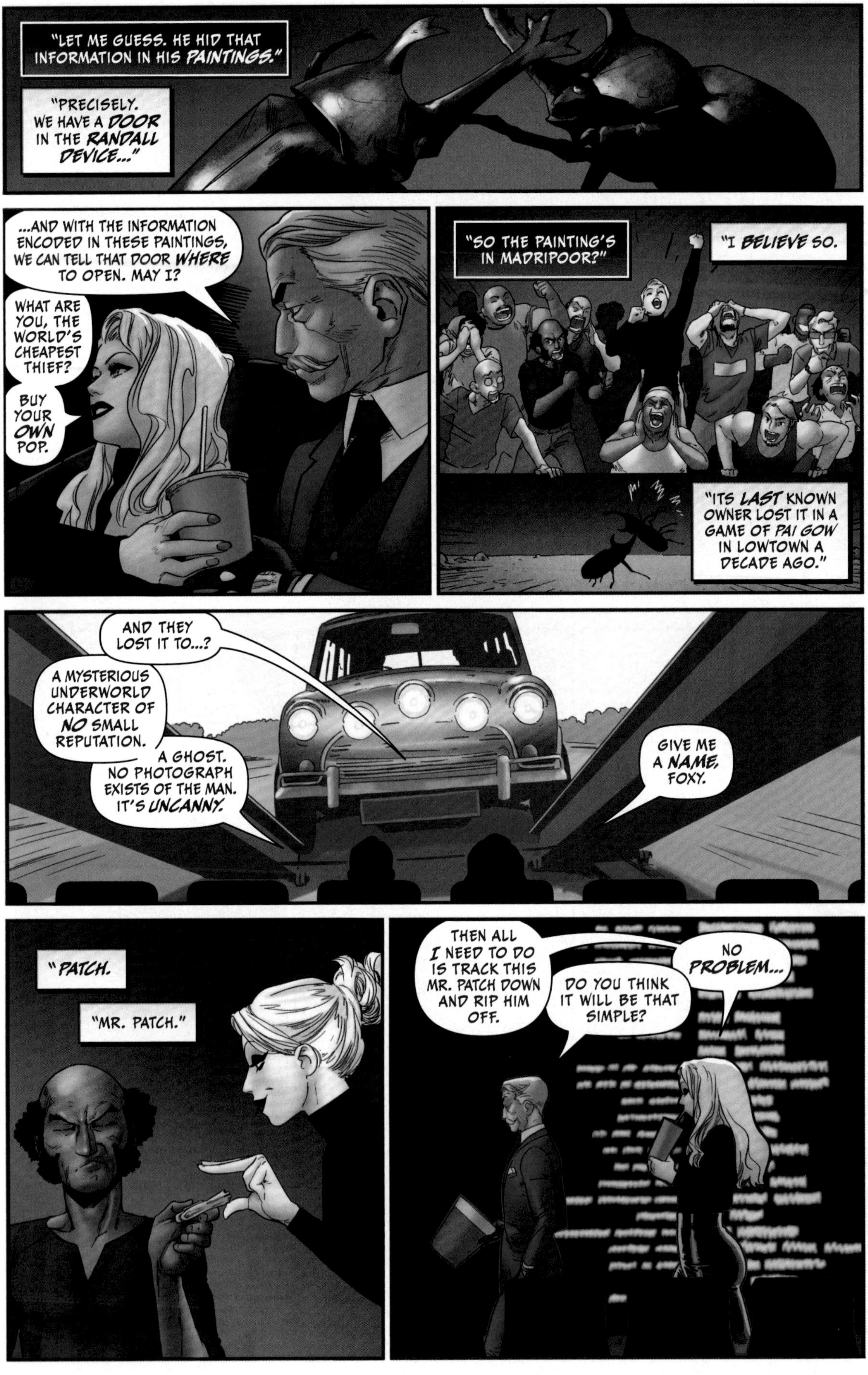
"LET ME GUESS. HE HID THAT INFORMATION IN HIS PAINTINGS."
"PRECISELY. WE HAVE A DOOR IN THE RANDALL DEVICE..."
...AND WITH THE INFORMATION ENCODED IN THESE PAINTINGS, WE CAN TELL THAT DOOR WHERE TO OPEN. MAY I?
WHAT ARE YOU, THE WORLD'S CHEAPEST THIEF?
BUY YOUR OWN POP.
"SO THE PAINTING'S IN MADRIPOOR?"
"I BELIEVE SO.
"ITS LAST KNOWN OWNER LOST IT IN A GAME OF PAI GOW IN LOWTOWN A DECADE AGO."
AND THEY LOST IT TO...?
A MYSTERIOUS UNDERWORLD CHARACTER OF NO SMALL REPUTATION.
A GHOST. NO PHOTOGRAPH EXISTS OF THE MAN. IT'S UNCANNY.
GIVE ME A NAME, FOXY.
"PATCH.
"MR. PATCH."
THEN ALL I NEED TO DO IS TRACK THIS MR. PATCH DOWN AND RIP HIM OFF.
DO YOU THINK IT WILL BE THAT SIMPLE?
NO PROBLEM...

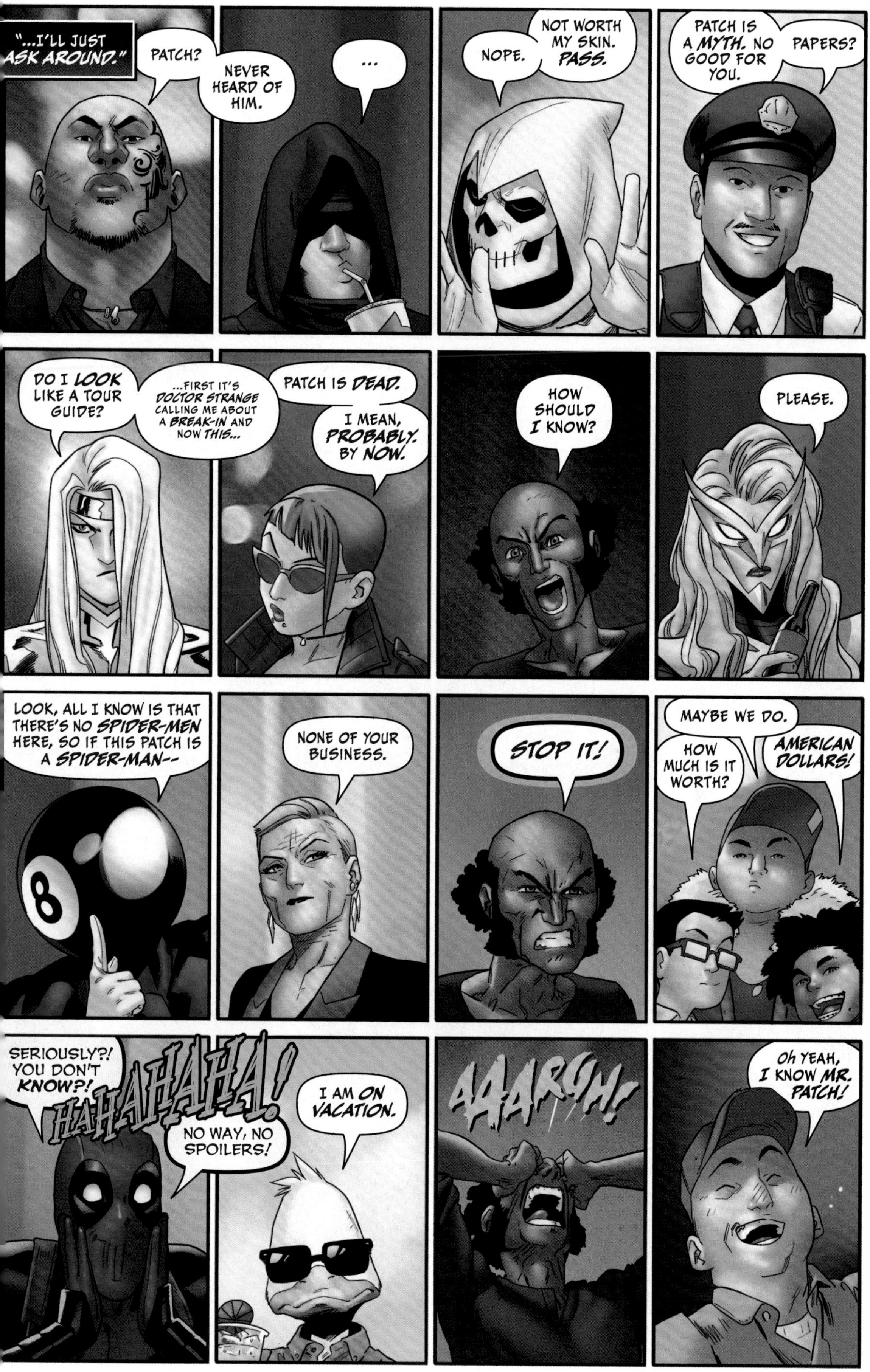
"...I'LL JUST ASK AROUND."
PATCH?
NEVER HEARD OF HIM.
...
NOPE.
NOT WORTH MY SKIN. PASS.
PATCH IS A MYTH. NO GOOD FOR YOU.
PAPERS?
DO I LOOK LIKE A TOUR GUIDE?
...FIRST IT'S DOCTOR STRANGE CALLING ME ABOUT A BREAK-IN AND NOW THIS...
PATCH IS DEAD.
I MEAN, PROBABLY. BY NOW.
HOW SHOULD I KNOW?
PLEASE.
LOOK, ALL I KNOW IS THAT THERE'S NO SPIDER-MEN HERE, SO IF THIS PATCH IS A SPIDER-MAN--
NONE OF YOUR BUSINESS.
STOP IT!
MAYBE WE DO.
HOW MUCH IS IT WORTH?
AMERICAN DOLLARS!
SERIOUSLY?! YOU DON'T KNOW?!
HAHAHAHA!
NO WAY, NO SPOILERS!
I AM ON VACATION.
AAARGH!
Oh YEAH, I KNOW MR. PATCH!

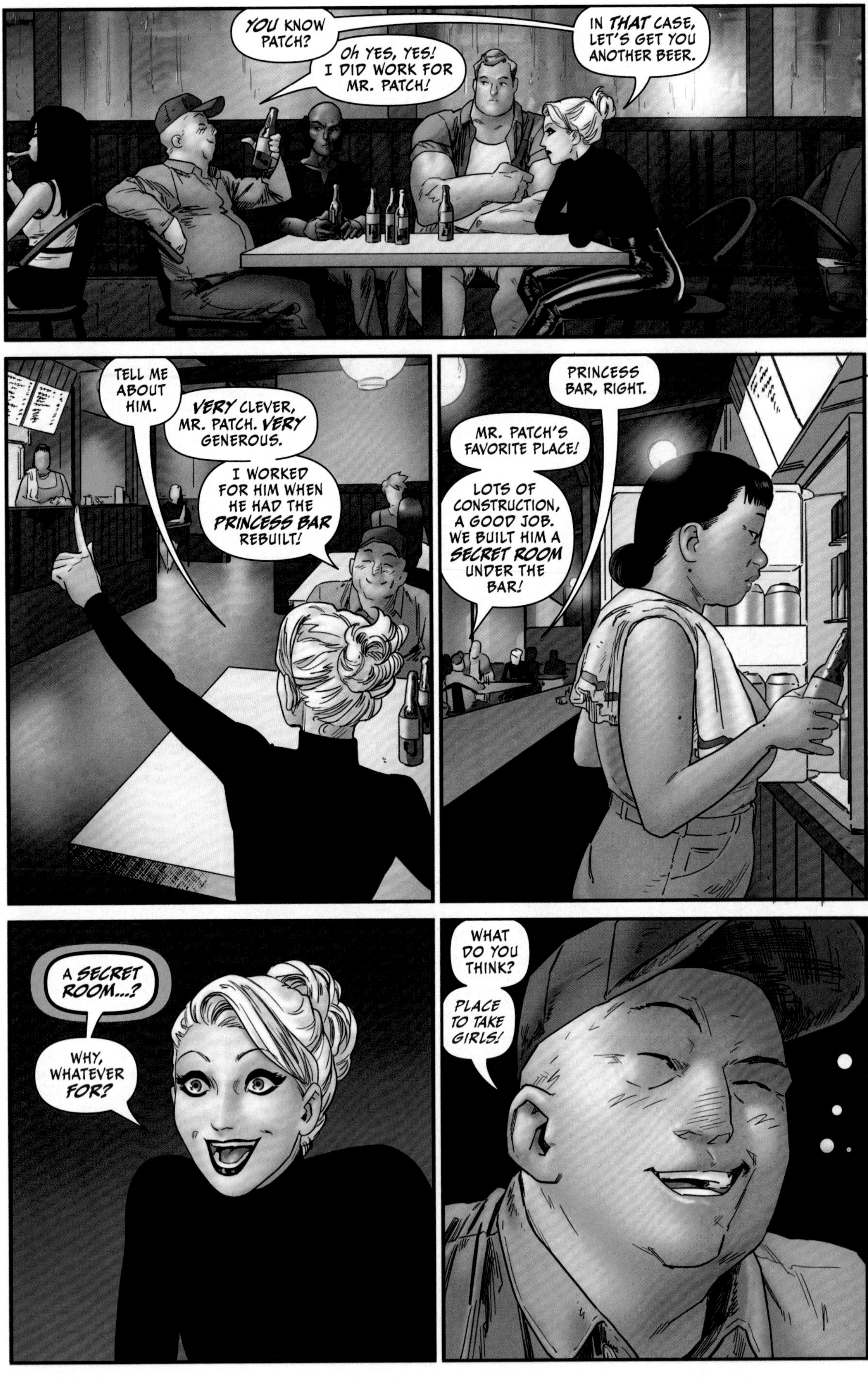
YOU KNOW PATCH?
Oh YES, YES! I DID WORK FOR MR. PATCH!
IN THAT CASE, LET'S GET YOU ANOTHER BEER.
TELL ME ABOUT HIM.
VERY CLEVER, MR. PATCH. VERY GENEROUS.
I WORKED FOR HIM WHEN HE HAD THE PRINCESS BAR REBUILT!
PRINCESS BAR, RIGHT.
MR. PATCH'S FAVORITE PLACE!
LOTS OF CONSTRUCTION, A GOOD JOB. WE BUILT HIM A SECRET ROOM UNDER THE BAR!
A SECRET ROOM...?
WHY, WHATEVER FOR?
WHAT DO YOU THINK?
PLACE TO TAKE GIRLS!

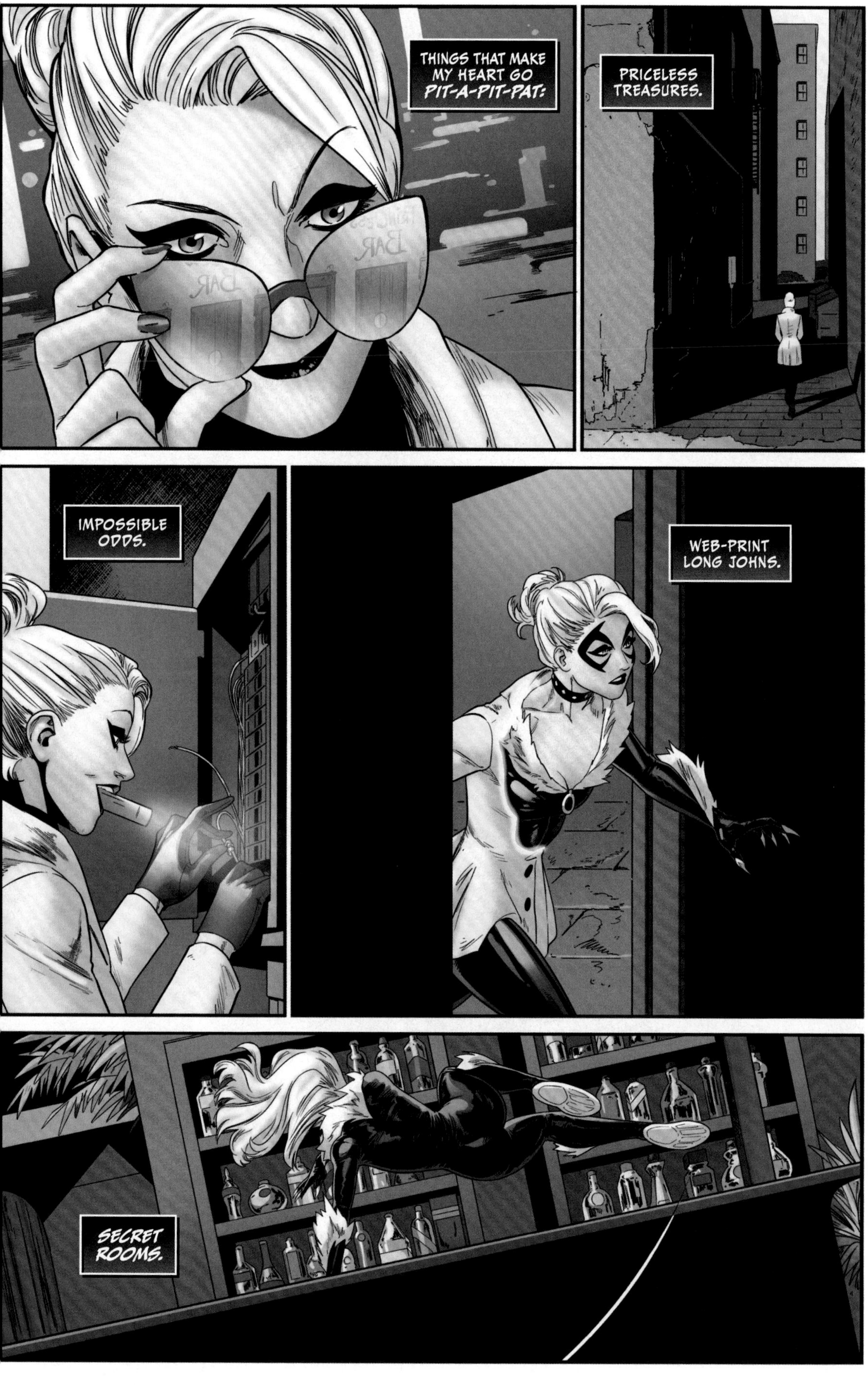
THINGS THAT MAKE MY HEART GO *PIT-A-PIT-PAT:*
PRICELESS TREASURES.
IMPOSSIBLE ODDS.
WEB-PRINT LONG JOHNS.
*SECRET ROOMS.*

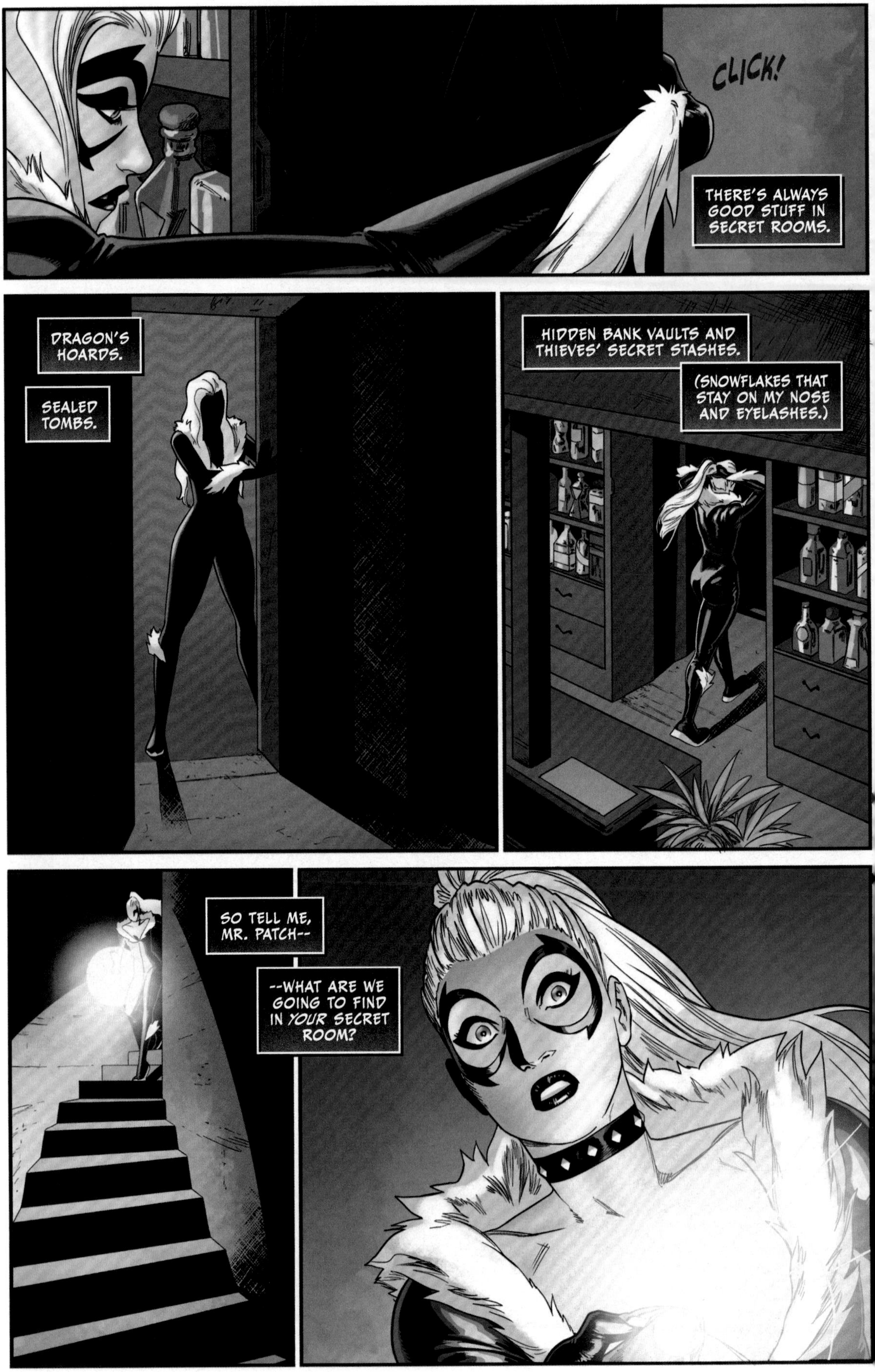
CLICK!
THERE'S ALWAYS GOOD STUFF IN SECRET ROOMS.
DRAGON'S HOARDS.
SEALED TOMBS.
HIDDEN BANK VAULTS AND THIEVES' SECRET STASHES.
(SNOWFLAKES THAT STAY ON MY NOSE AND EYELASHES.)
SO TELL ME, MR. PATCH--
--WHAT ARE WE GOING TO FIND IN *YOUR* SECRET ROOM?

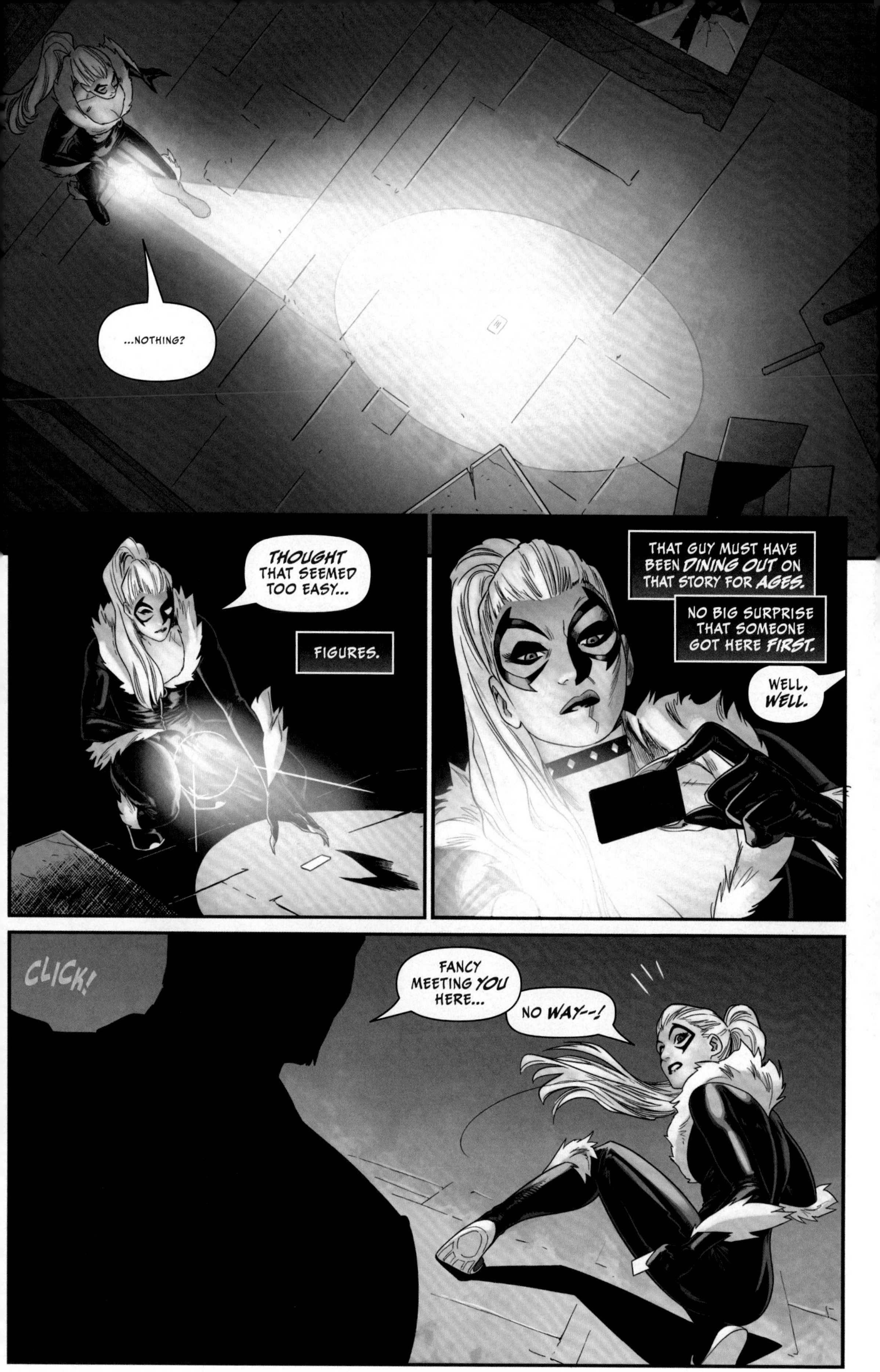
...NOTHING?
THOUGHT THAT SEEMED TOO EASY...
FIGURES.
THAT GUY MUST HAVE BEEN DINING OUT ON THAT STORY FOR AGES.
NO BIG SURPRISE THAT SOMEONE GOT HERE FIRST.
WELL, WELL.
CLICK!
FANCY MEETING YOU HERE...
NO WAY--!

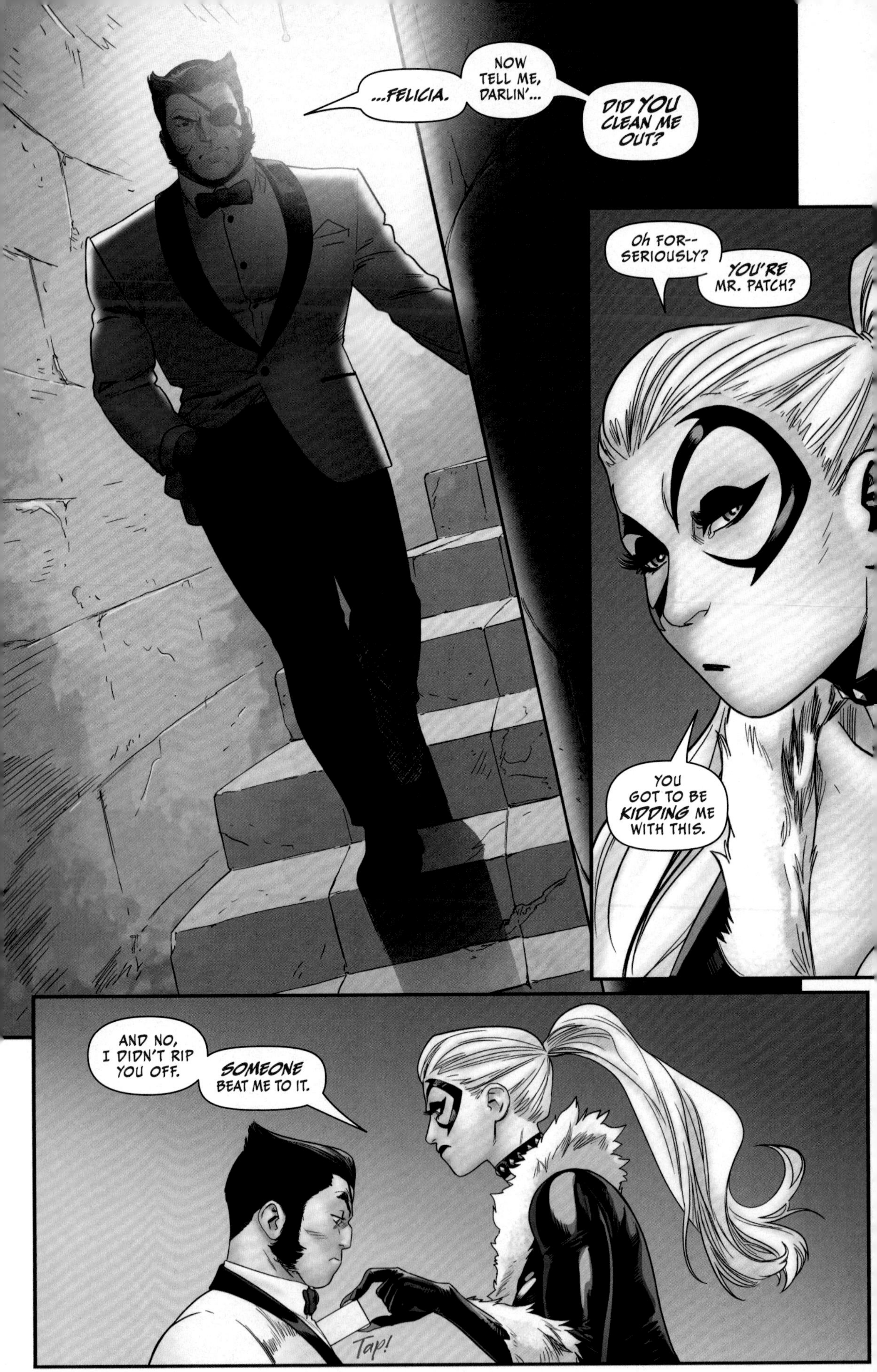
...FELICIA.
NOW TELL ME, DARLIN'...
DID YOU CLEAN ME OUT?
Oh FOR-- SERIOUSLY?
YOU'RE MR. PATCH?
YOU GOT TO BE KIDDING ME WITH THIS.
AND NO, I DIDN'T RIP YOU OFF.
SOMEONE BEAT ME TO IT.
Tap!

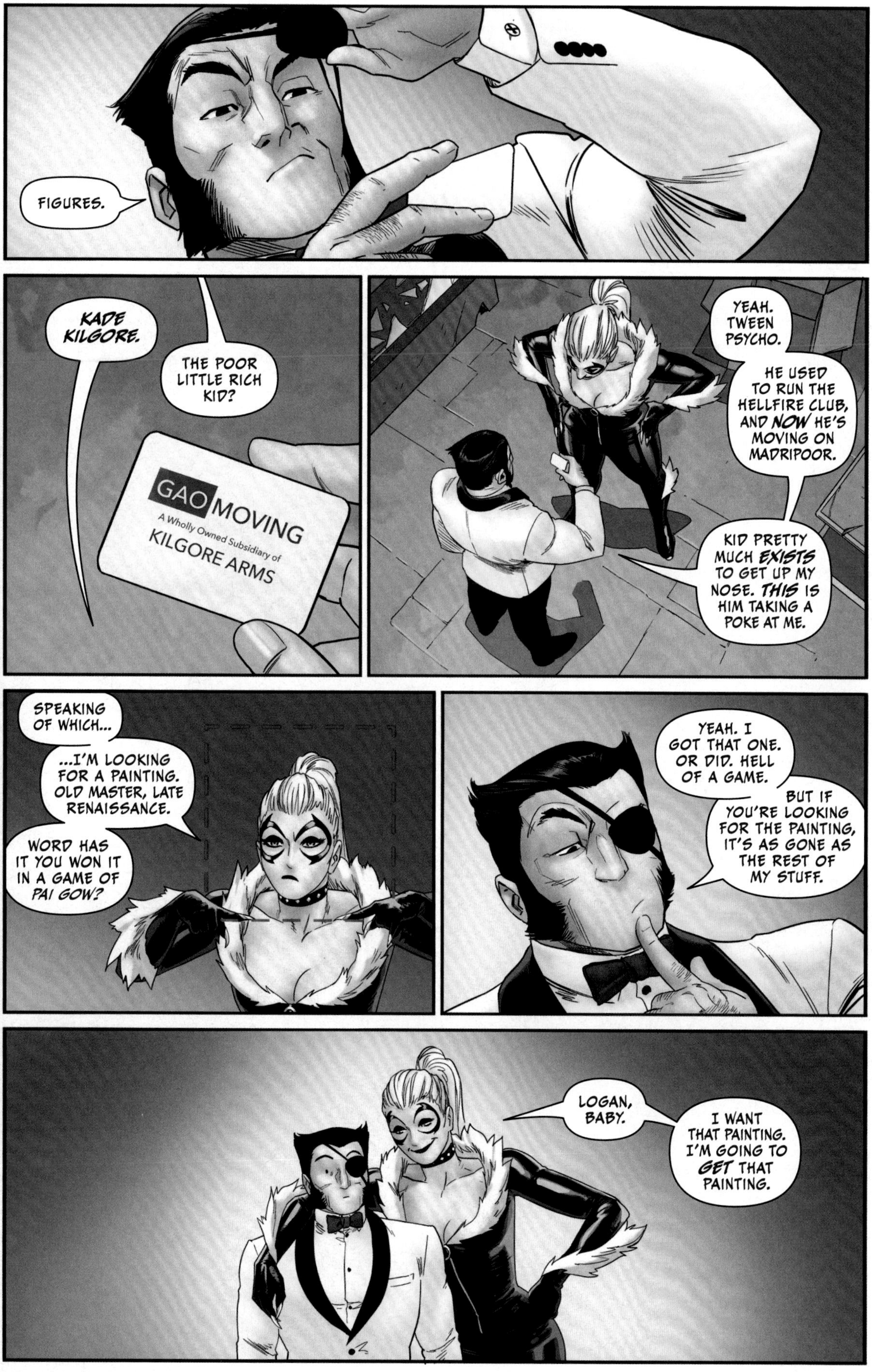

FIGURES.
KADE KILGORE.
THE POOR LITTLE RICH KID?
GAO MOVING
A Wholly Owned Subsidiary of
KILGORE ARMS
YEAH. TWEEN PSYCHO.
HE USED TO RUN THE HELLFIRE CLUB, AND NOW HE'S MOVING ON MADRIPOOR.
KID PRETTY MUCH EXISTS TO GET UP MY NOSE. THIS IS HIM TAKING A POKE AT ME.
SPEAKING OF WHICH...
...I'M LOOKING FOR A PAINTING. OLD MASTER, LATE RENAISSANCE.
WORD HAS IT YOU WON IT IN A GAME OF PAI GOW?
YEAH. I GOT THAT ONE. OR DID. HELL OF A GAME.
BUT IF YOU'RE LOOKING FOR THE PAINTING, IT'S AS GONE AS THE REST OF MY STUFF.
LOGAN, BABY.
I WANT THAT PAINTING. I'M GOING TO GET THAT PAINTING.

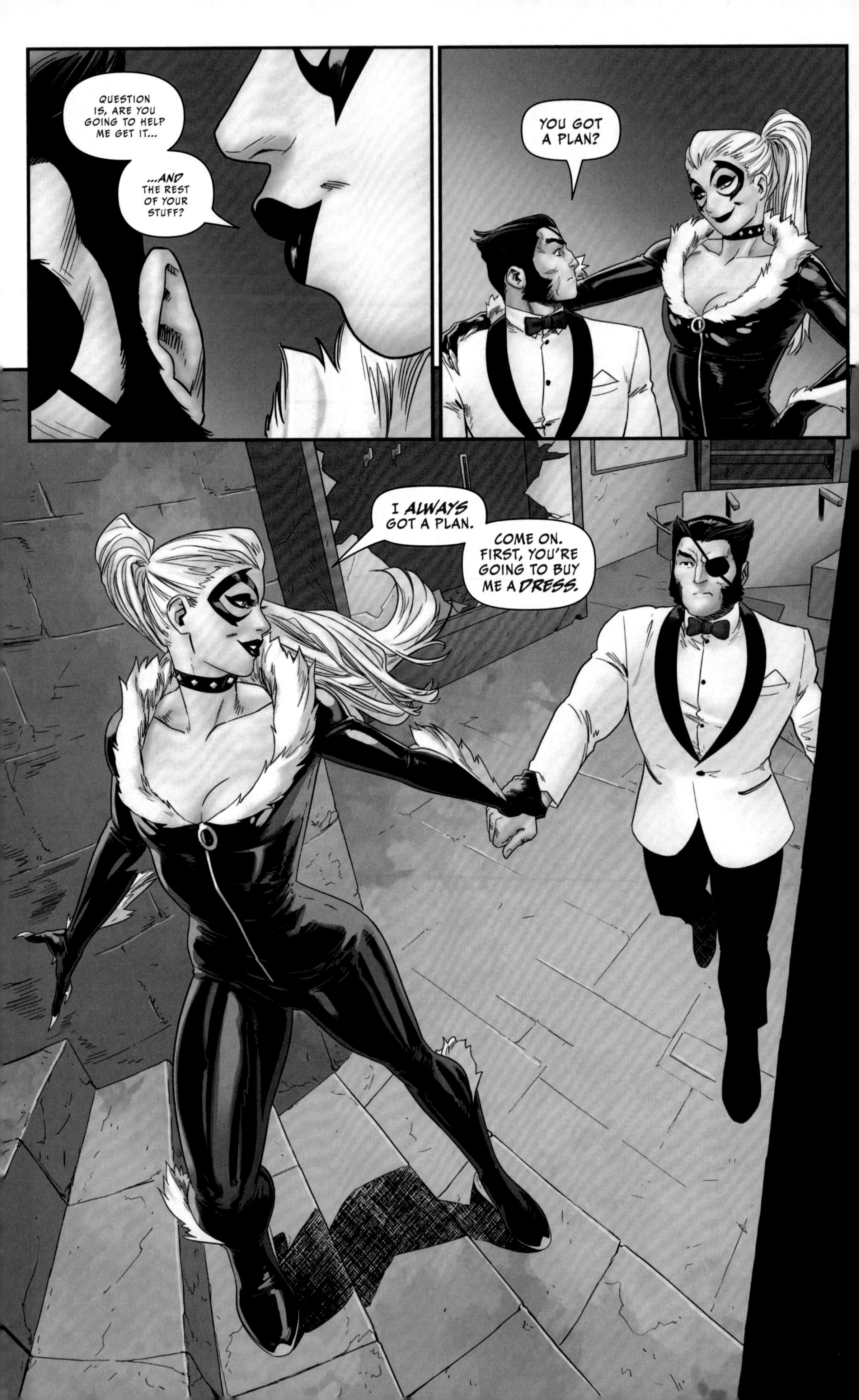
QUESTION IS, ARE YOU GOING TO HELP ME GET IT...
...AND THE REST OF YOUR STUFF?
YOU GOT A PLAN?
I ALWAYS GOT A PLAN.
COME ON. FIRST, YOU'RE GOING TO BUY ME A DRESS.

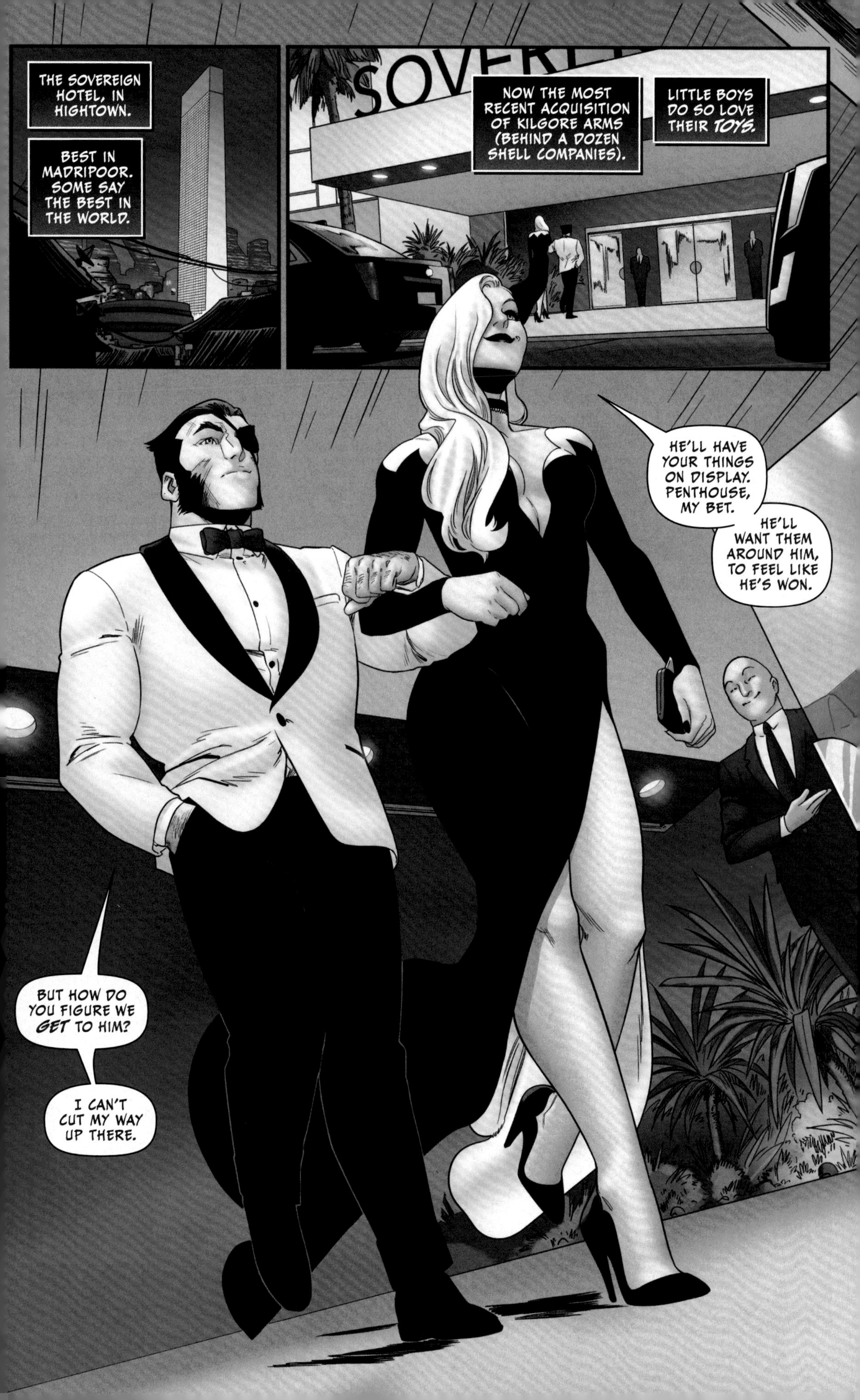
THE SOVEREIGN HOTEL, IN HIGHTOWN.
BEST IN MADRIPOOR. SOME SAY THE BEST IN THE WORLD.
SOVERE
NOW THE MOST RECENT ACQUISITION OF KILGORE ARMS (BEHIND A DOZEN SHELL COMPANIES).
LITTLE BOYS DO SO LOVE THEIR *TOYS.*
HE'LL HAVE YOUR THINGS ON DISPLAY. PENTHOUSE, MY BET.
HE'LL WANT THEM AROUND HIM, TO FEEL LIKE HE'S WON.
BUT HOW DO YOU FIGURE WE *GET* TO HIM?
I CAN'T CUT MY WAY UP THERE.

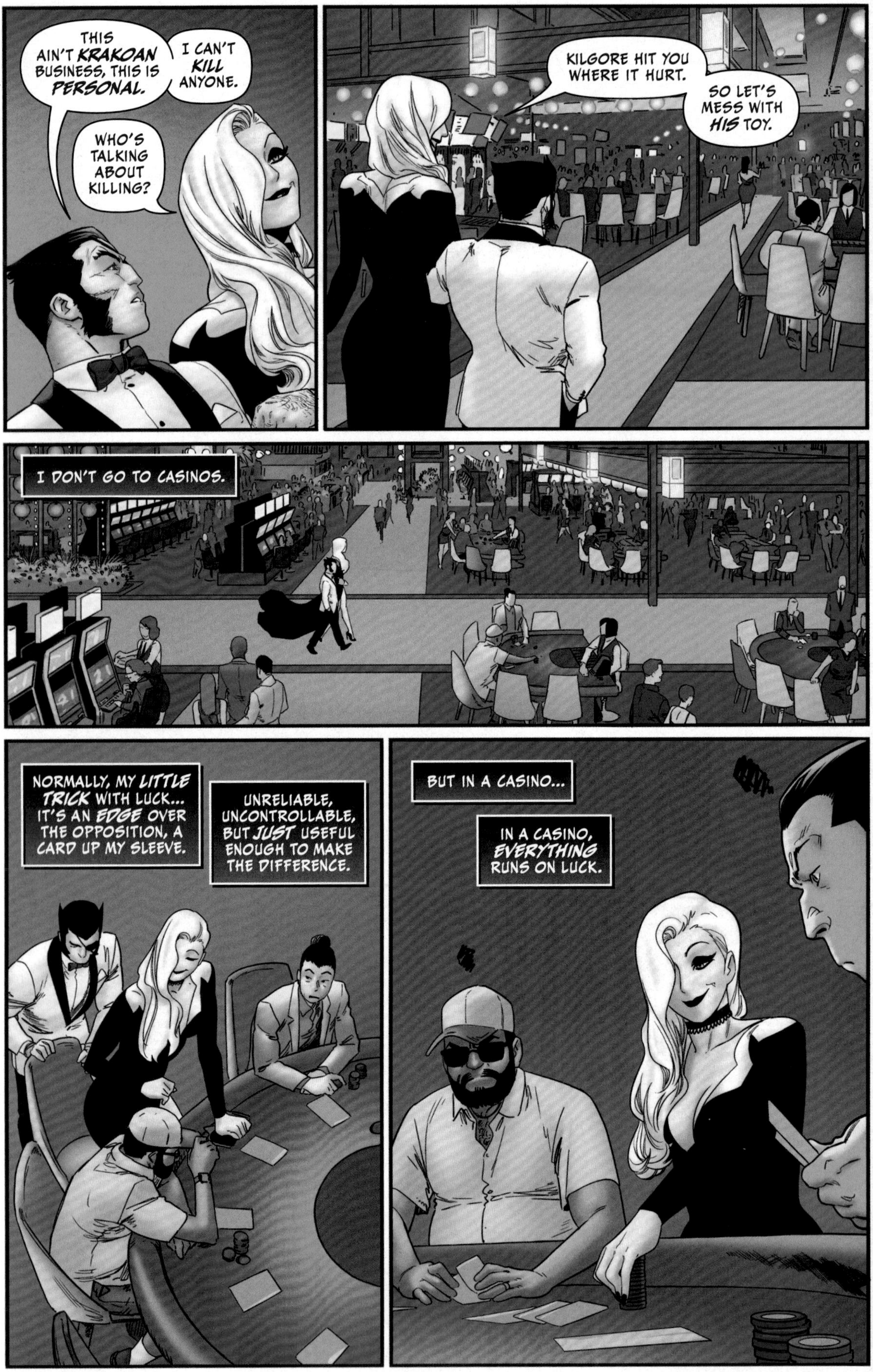
THIS AIN'T KRAKOAN BUSINESS, THIS IS PERSONAL.
I CAN'T KILL ANYONE.
WHO'S TALKING ABOUT KILLING?
KILGORE HIT YOU WHERE IT HURT.
SO LET'S MESS WITH HIS TOY.
I DON'T GO TO CASINOS.
NORMALLY, MY LITTLE TRICK WITH LUCK... IT'S AN EDGE OVER THE OPPOSITION, A CARD UP MY SLEEVE.
UNRELIABLE, UNCONTROLLABLE, BUT JUST USEFUL ENOUGH TO MAKE THE DIFFERENCE.
BUT IN A CASINO...
IN A CASINO, EVERYTHING RUNS ON LUCK.

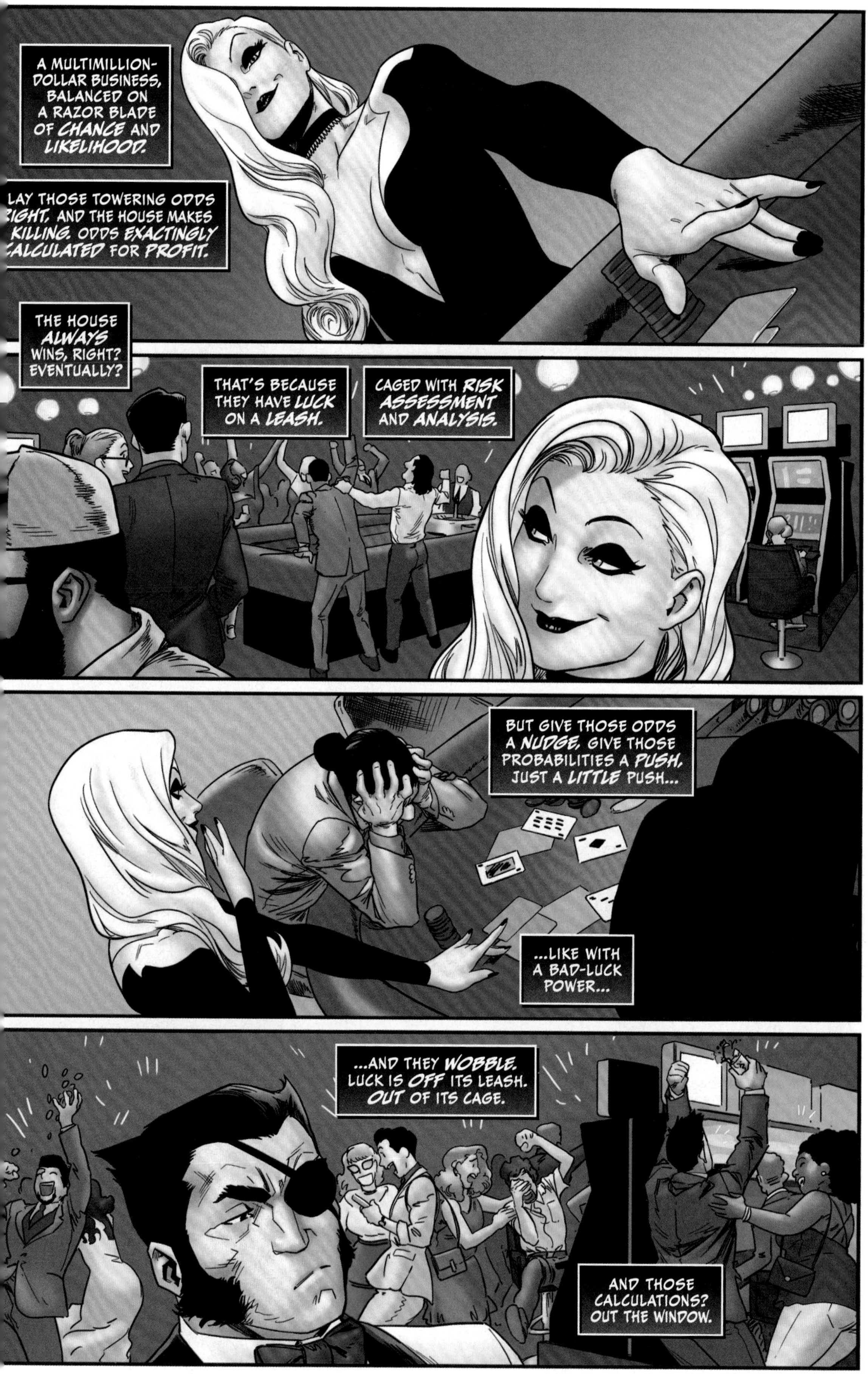
A MULTIMILLION-DOLLAR BUSINESS, BALANCED ON A RAZOR BLADE OF CHANCE AND LIKELIHOOD.
LAY THOSE TOWERING ODDS RIGHT, AND THE HOUSE MAKES KILLING. ODDS EXACTINGLY CALCULATED FOR PROFIT.
THE HOUSE ALWAYS WINS, RIGHT? EVENTUALLY?
THAT'S BECAUSE THEY HAVE LUCK ON A LEASH.
CAGED WITH RISK ASSESSMENT AND ANALYSIS.
BUT GIVE THOSE ODDS A NUDGE, GIVE THOSE PROBABILITIES A PUSH, JUST A LITTLE PUSH...
...LIKE WITH A BAD-LUCK POWER...
...AND THEY WOBBLE. LUCK IS OFF ITS LEASH. OUT OF ITS CAGE.
AND THOSE CALCULATIONS? OUT THE WINDOW.

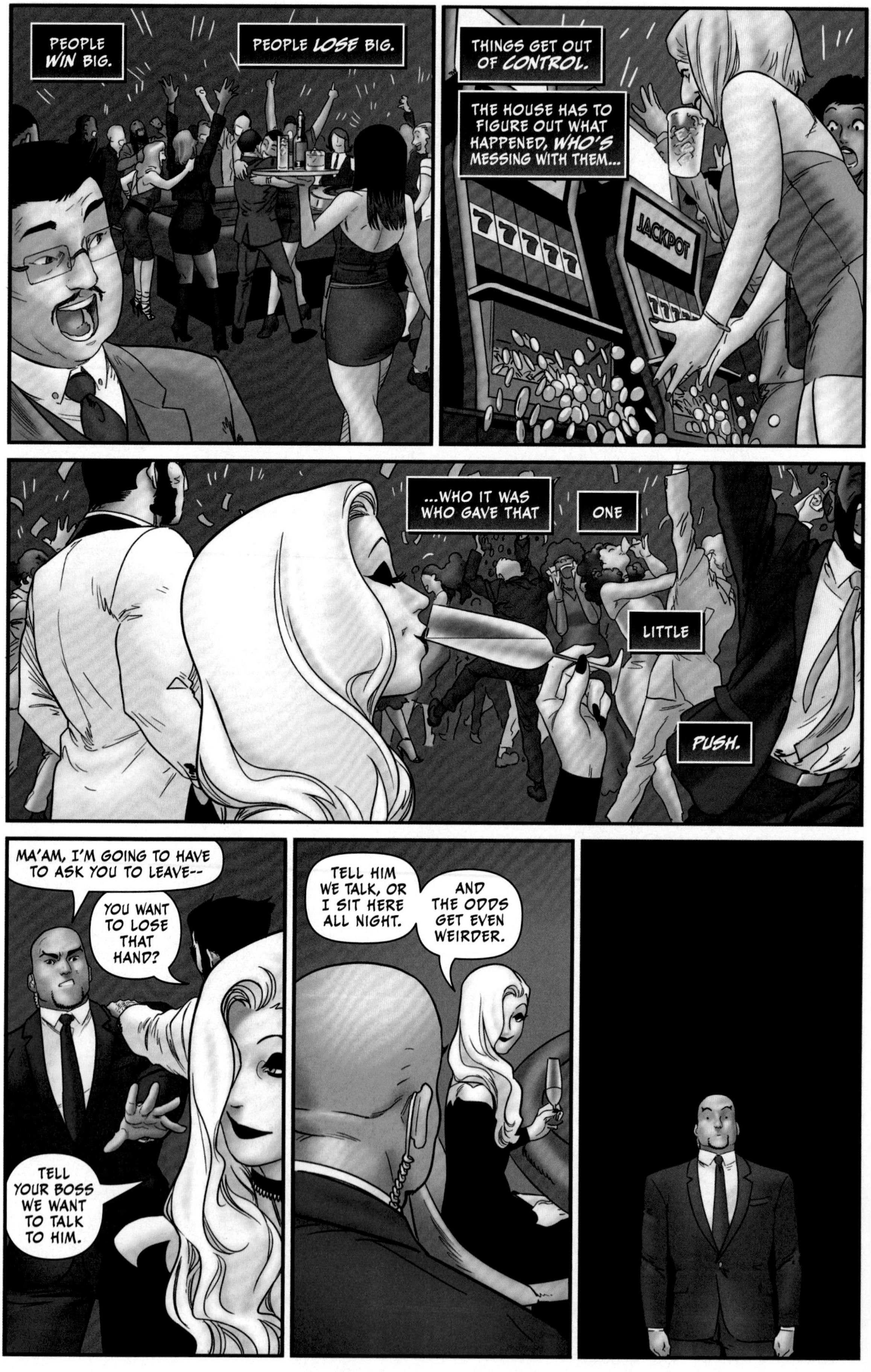
PEOPLE WIN BIG.
PEOPLE LOSE BIG.
THINGS GET OUT OF CONTROL.
THE HOUSE HAS TO FIGURE OUT WHAT HAPPENED, WHO'S MESSING WITH THEM...
JACKPOT
...WHO IT WAS WHO GAVE THAT
ONE
LITTLE
PUSH.
MA'AM, I'M GOING TO HAVE TO ASK YOU TO LEAVE--
YOU WANT TO LOSE THAT HAND?
TELL YOUR BOSS WE WANT TO TALK TO HIM.
TELL HIM WE TALK, OR I SIT HERE ALL NIGHT.
AND THE ODDS GET EVEN WEIRDER.

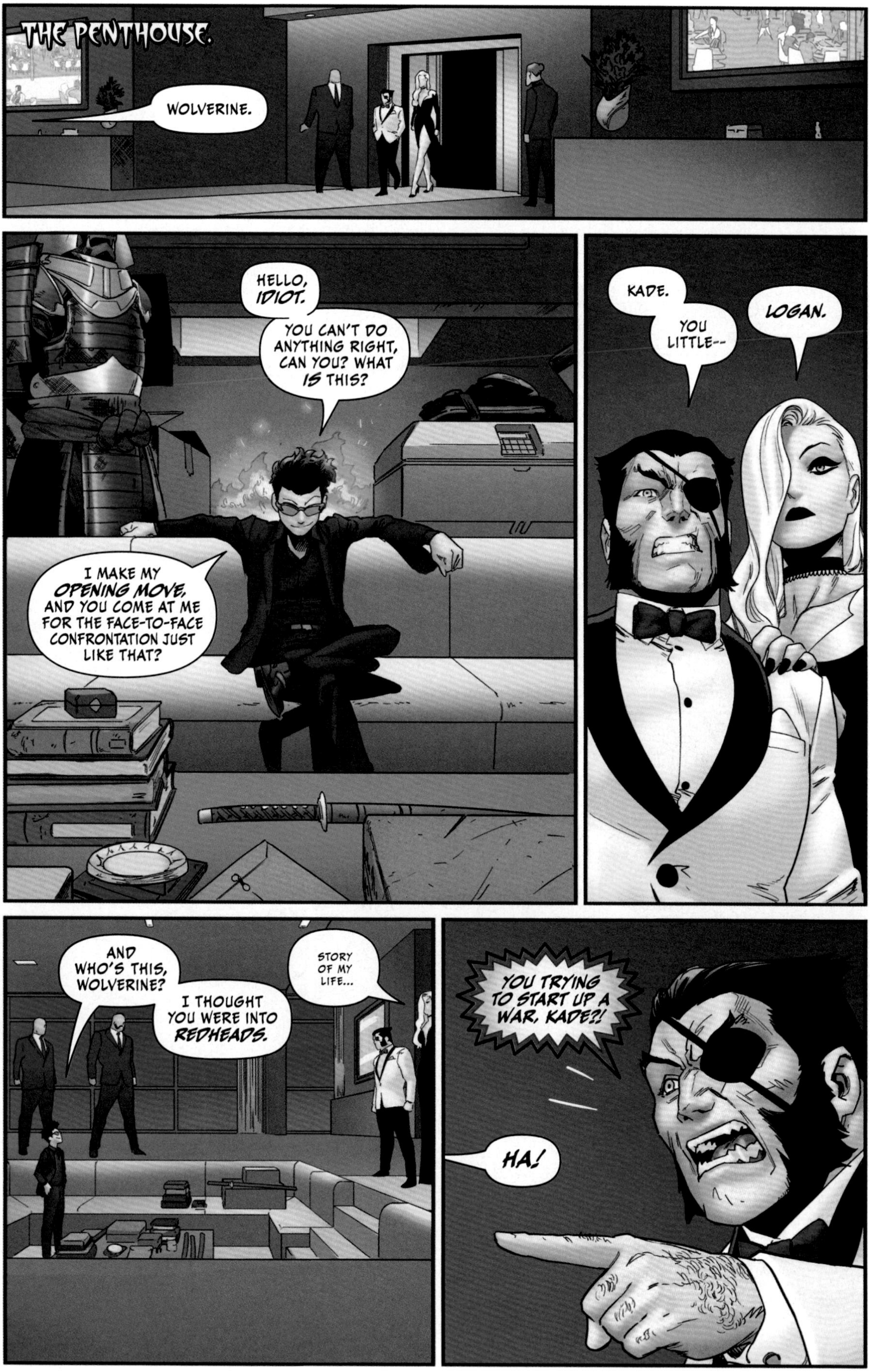
THE PENTHOUSE.
WOLVERINE.
HELLO, IDIOT.
YOU CAN'T DO ANYTHING RIGHT, CAN YOU? WHAT IS THIS?
I MAKE MY OPENING MOVE, AND YOU COME AT ME FOR THE FACE-TO-FACE CONFRONTATION JUST LIKE THAT?
KADE.
YOU LITTLE--
LOGAN.
AND WHO'S THIS, WOLVERINE?
I THOUGHT YOU WERE INTO REDHEADS.
STORY OF MY LIFE...
YOU TRYING TO START UP A WAR, KADE?!
HA!

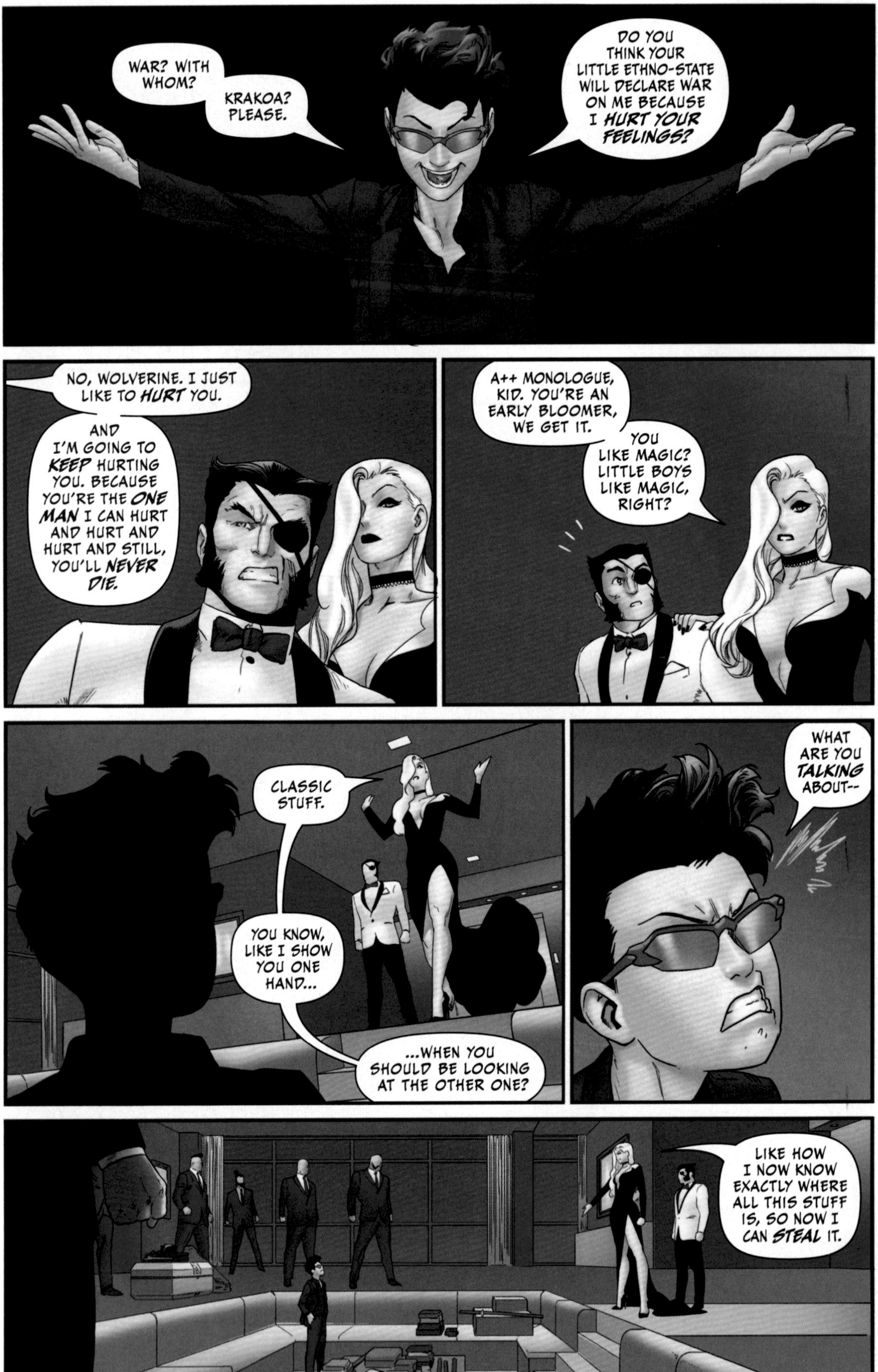
WAR? WITH WHOM?
KRAKOA? PLEASE.
DO YOU THINK YOUR LITTLE ETHNO-STATE WILL DECLARE WAR ON ME BECAUSE I HURT YOUR FEELINGS?
NO, WOLVERINE. I JUST LIKE TO HURT YOU.
AND I'M GOING TO KEEP HURTING YOU. BECAUSE YOU'RE THE ONE MAN I CAN HURT AND HURT AND HURT AND STILL, YOU'LL NEVER DIE.
A++ MONOLOGUE, KID. YOU'RE AN EARLY BLOOMER, WE GET IT.
YOU LIKE MAGIC? LITTLE BOYS LIKE MAGIC, RIGHT?
CLASSIC STUFF.
YOU KNOW, LIKE I SHOW YOU ONE HAND...
...WHEN YOU SHOULD BE LOOKING AT THE OTHER ONE?
WHAT ARE YOU TALKING ABOUT--
LIKE HOW I NOW KNOW EXACTLY WHERE ALL THIS STUFF IS, SO NOW I CAN STEAL IT.

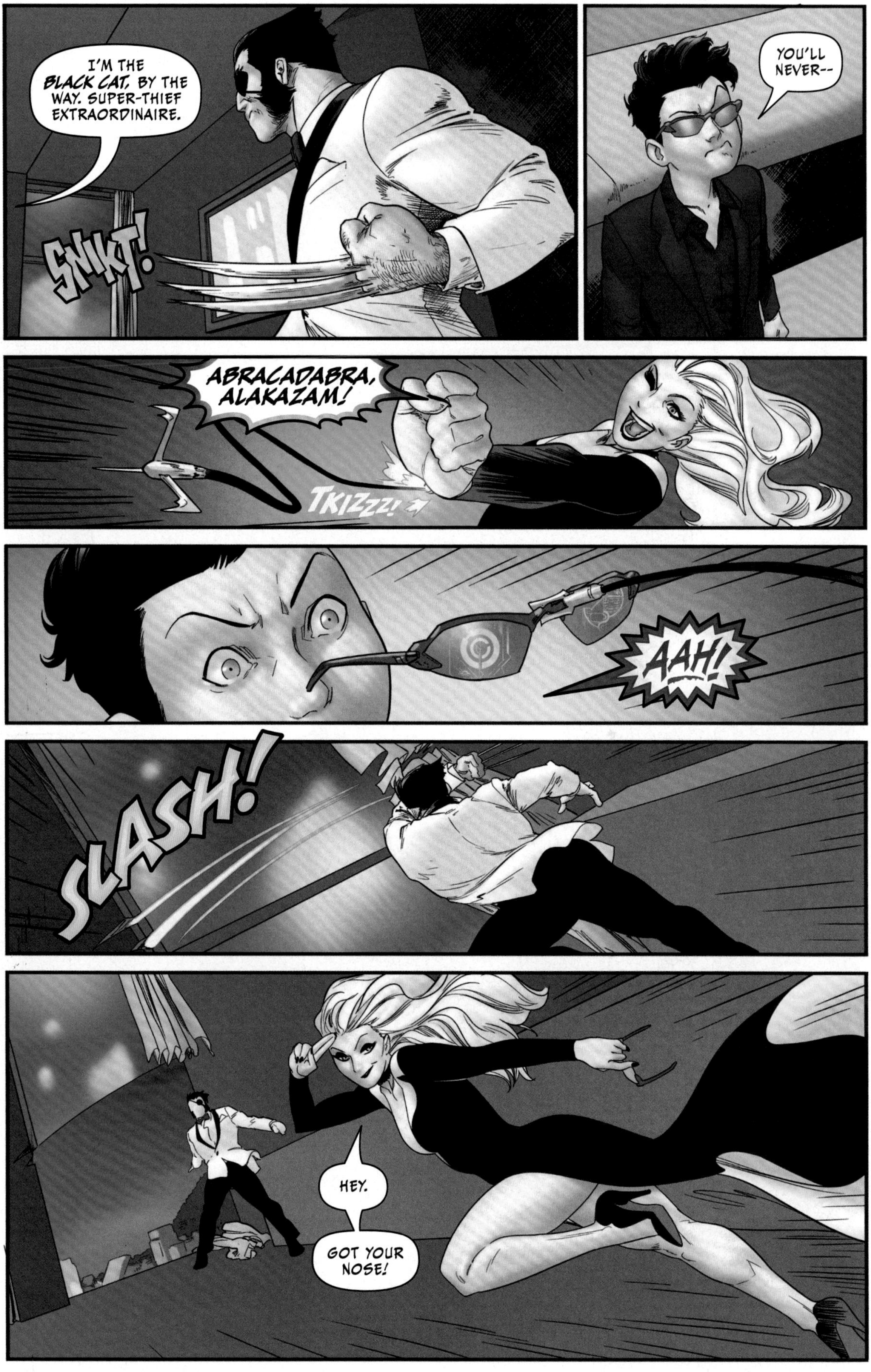

I'M THE BLACK CAT, BY THE WAY. SUPER-THIEF EXTRAORDINAIRE.
SNIKT!
YOU'LL NEVER--
ABRACADABRA, ALAKAZAM!
TKIZZZ!
AAH!
SLASH!
HEY.
GOT YOUR NOSE!

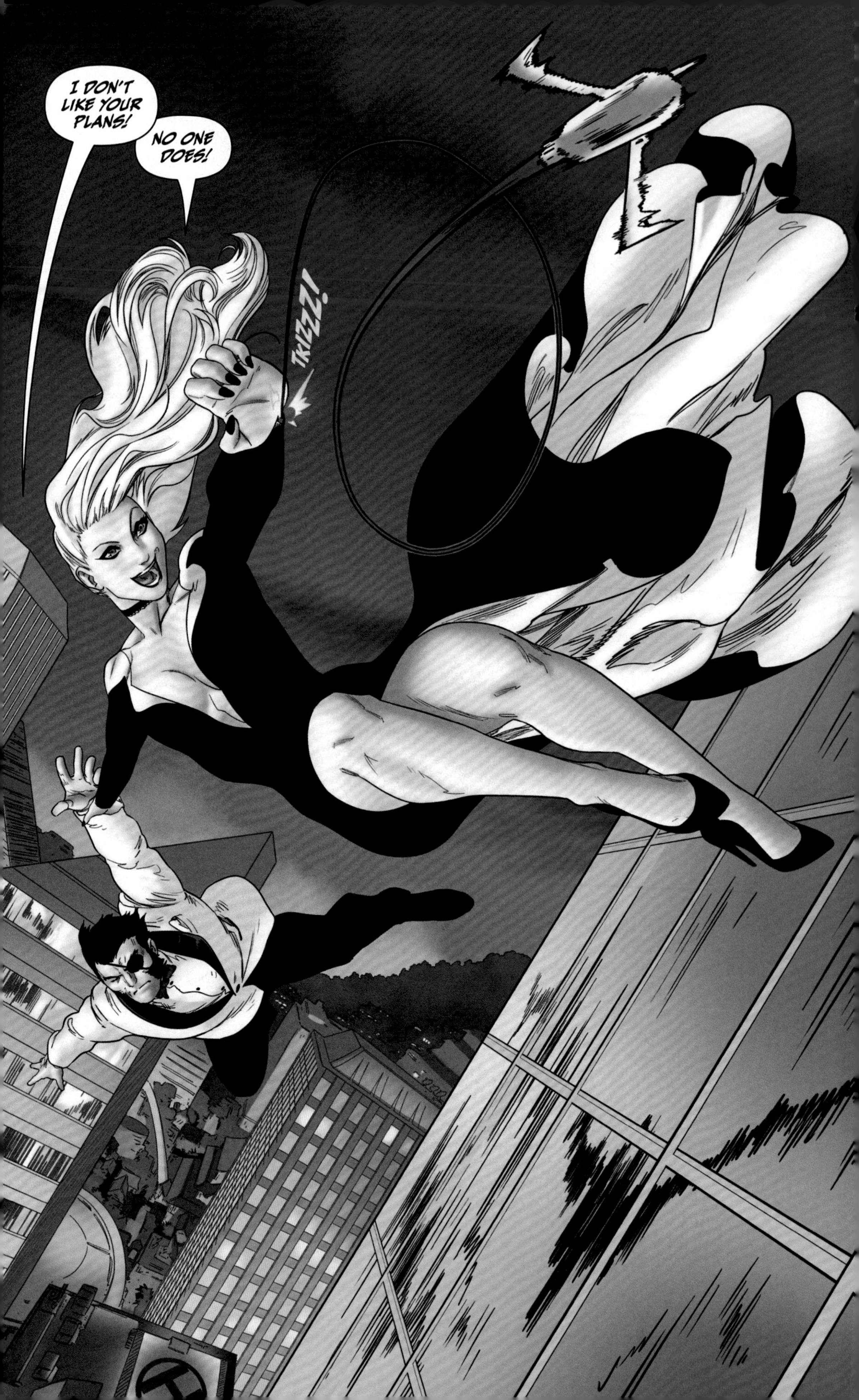
I DON'T LIKE YOUR PLANS!
NO ONE DOES!
TKIZZZ!

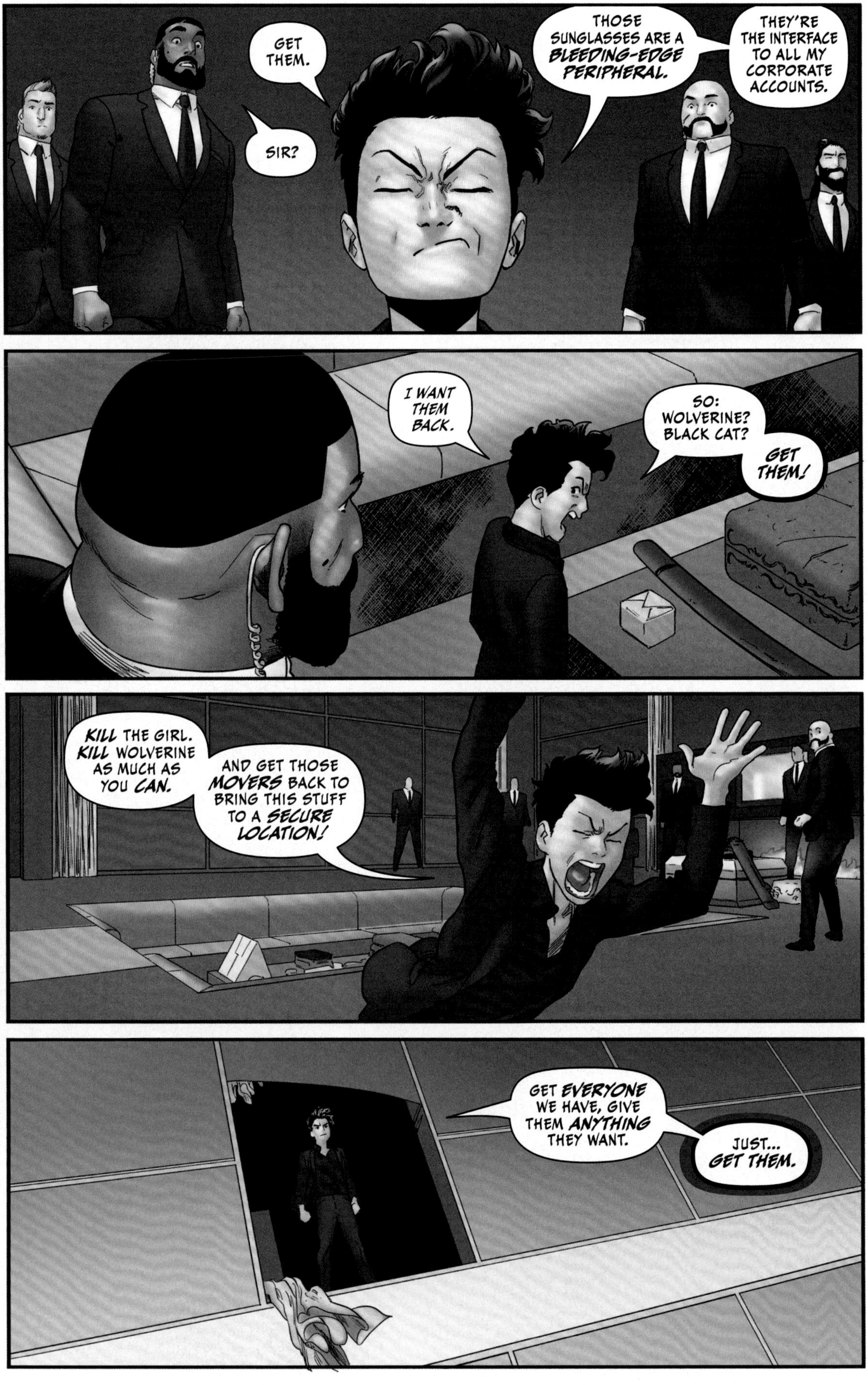
GET THEM.
SIR?
THOSE SUNGLASSES ARE A BLEEDING-EDGE PERIPHERAL.
THEY'RE THE INTERFACE TO ALL MY CORPORATE ACCOUNTS.
I WANT THEM BACK.
SO: WOLVERINE? BLACK CAT? GET THEM!
KILL THE GIRL. KILL WOLVERINE AS MUCH AS YOU CAN.
AND GET THOSE MOVERS BACK TO BRING THIS STUFF TO A SECURE LOCATION!
GET EVERYONE WE HAVE, GIVE THEM ANYTHING THEY WANT.
JUST... GET THEM.

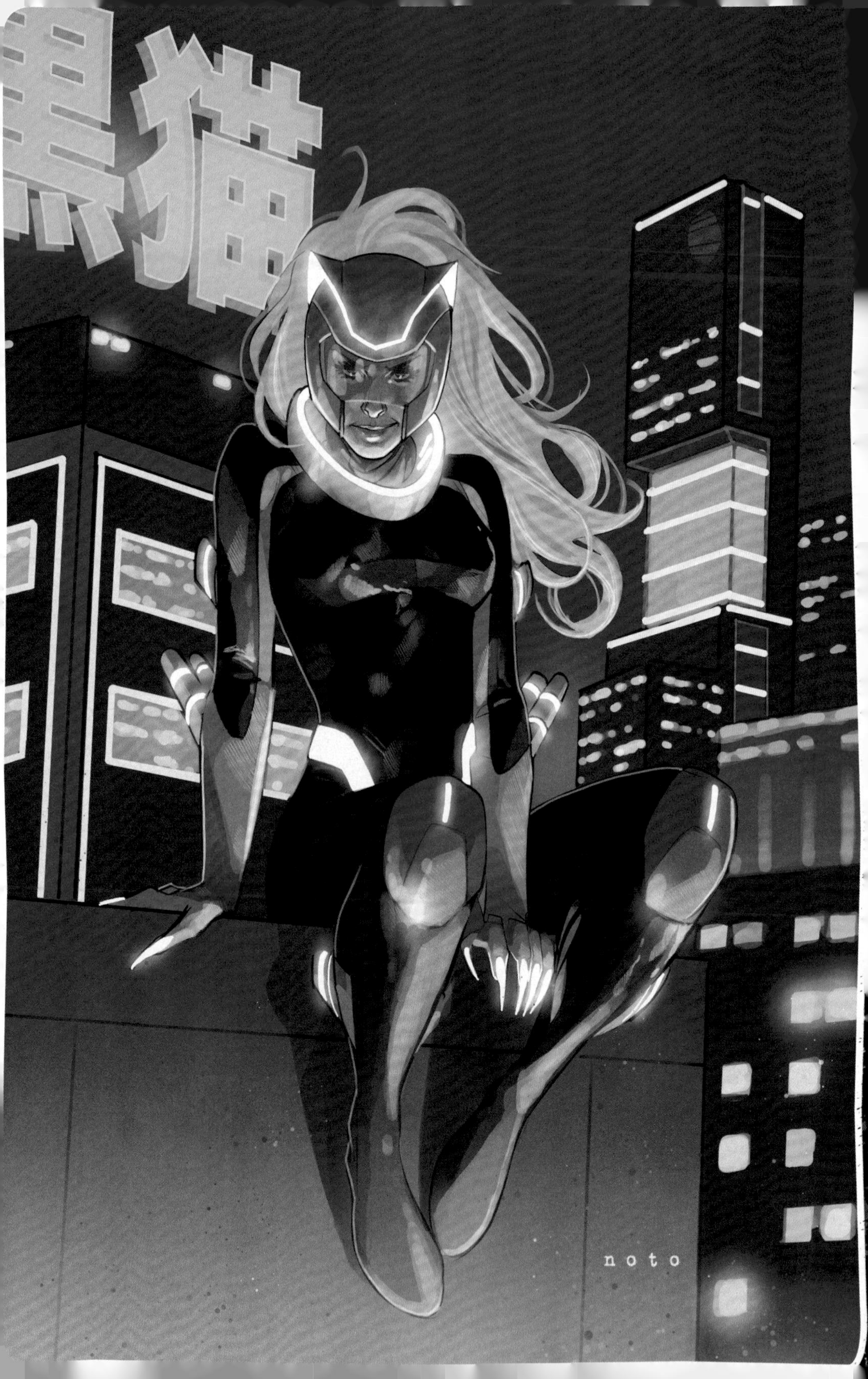
黒猫
noto

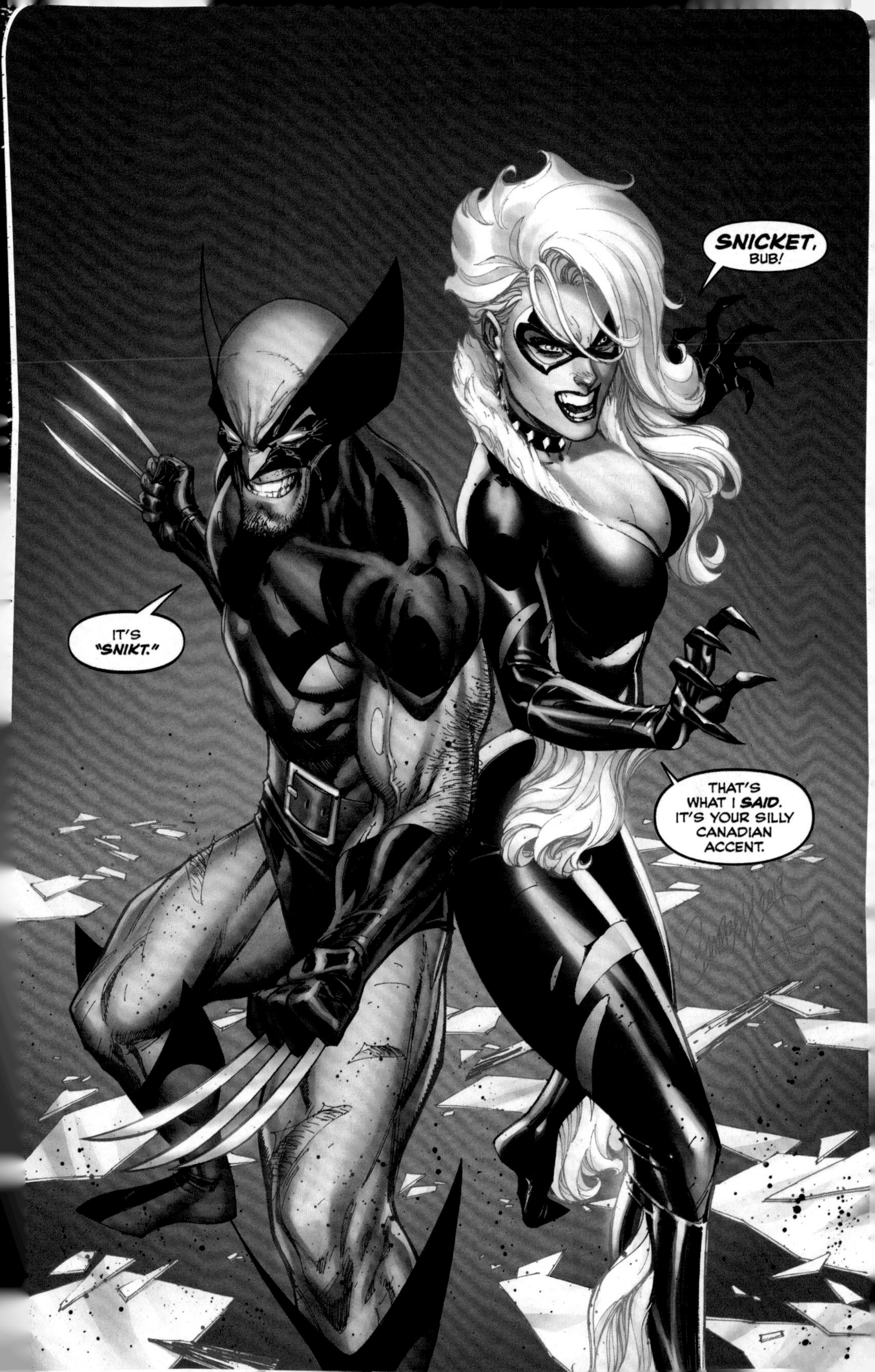

SNICKET, BUB!
IT'S "SNIKT."
THAT'S WHAT I SAID. IT'S YOUR SILLY CANADIAN ACCENT.

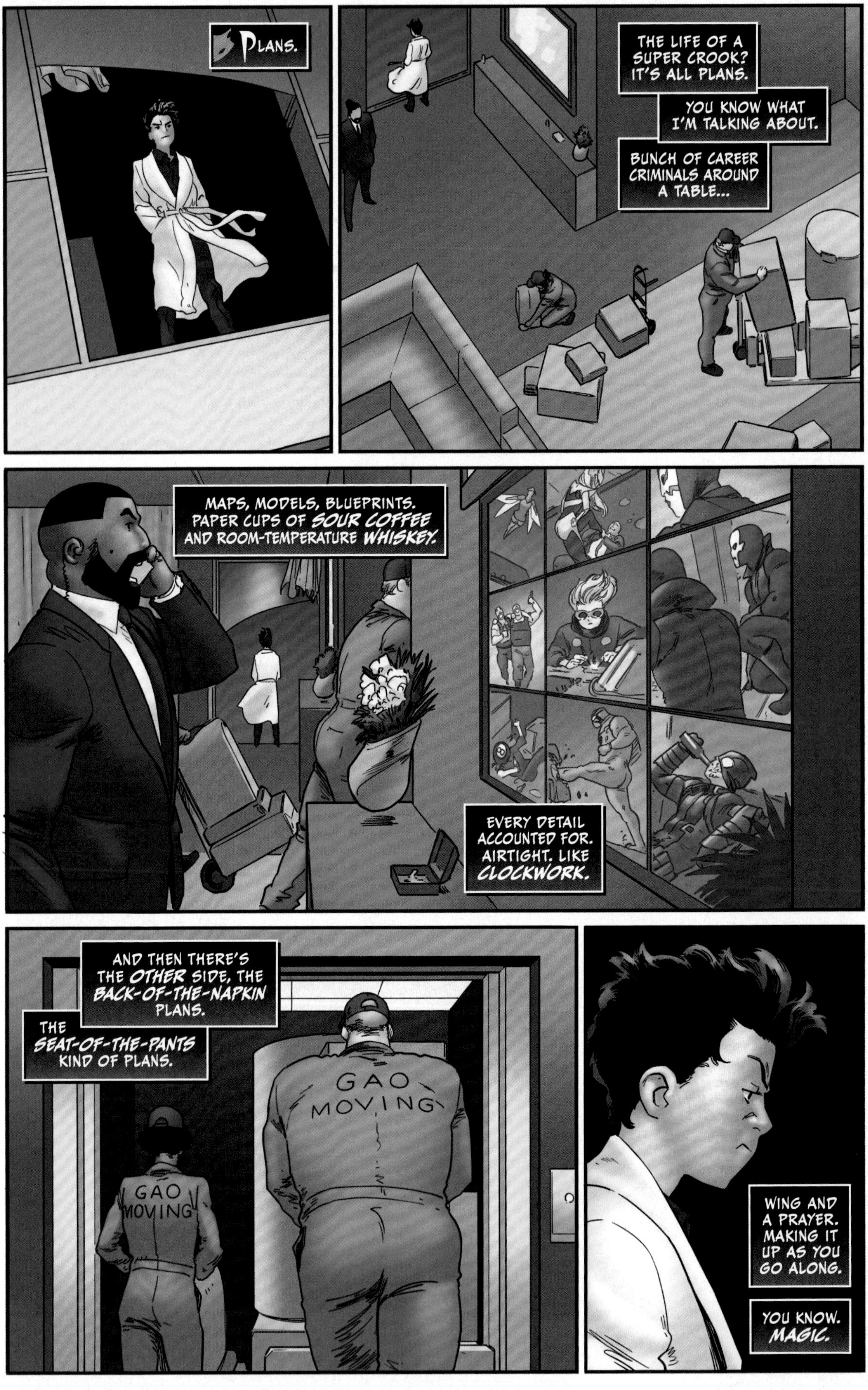
Plans.
The life of a super crook? It's all plans.
You know what I'm talking about.
Bunch of career criminals around a table...
Maps, models, blueprints. Paper cups of sour coffee and room-temperature whiskey.
Every detail accounted for. Airtight. Like clockwork.
And then there's the other side, the back-of-the-napkin plans.
The seat-of-the-pants kind of plans.
GAO MOVING
GAO MOVING
Wing and a prayer. Making it up as you go along.
You know. Magic.

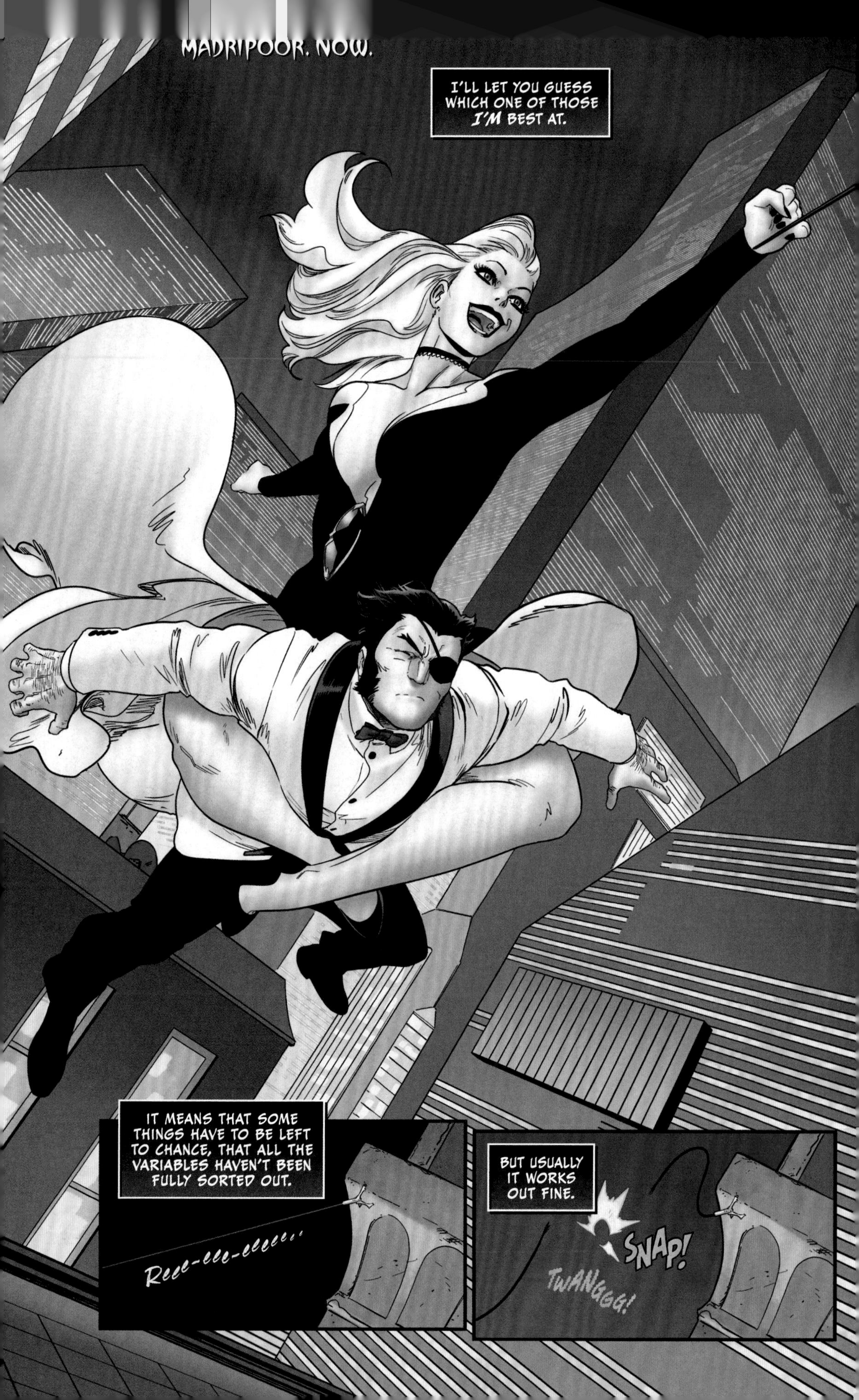
MADRIPOOR. NOW.
I'LL LET YOU GUESS WHICH ONE OF THOSE I'M BEST AT.
IT MEANS THAT SOME THINGS HAVE TO BE LEFT TO CHANCE, THAT ALL THE VARIABLES HAVEN'T BEEN FULLY SORTED OUT.
Reee-eee-eeeee...
BUT USUALLY IT WORKS OUT FINE.
SNAP!
TWANGGG!

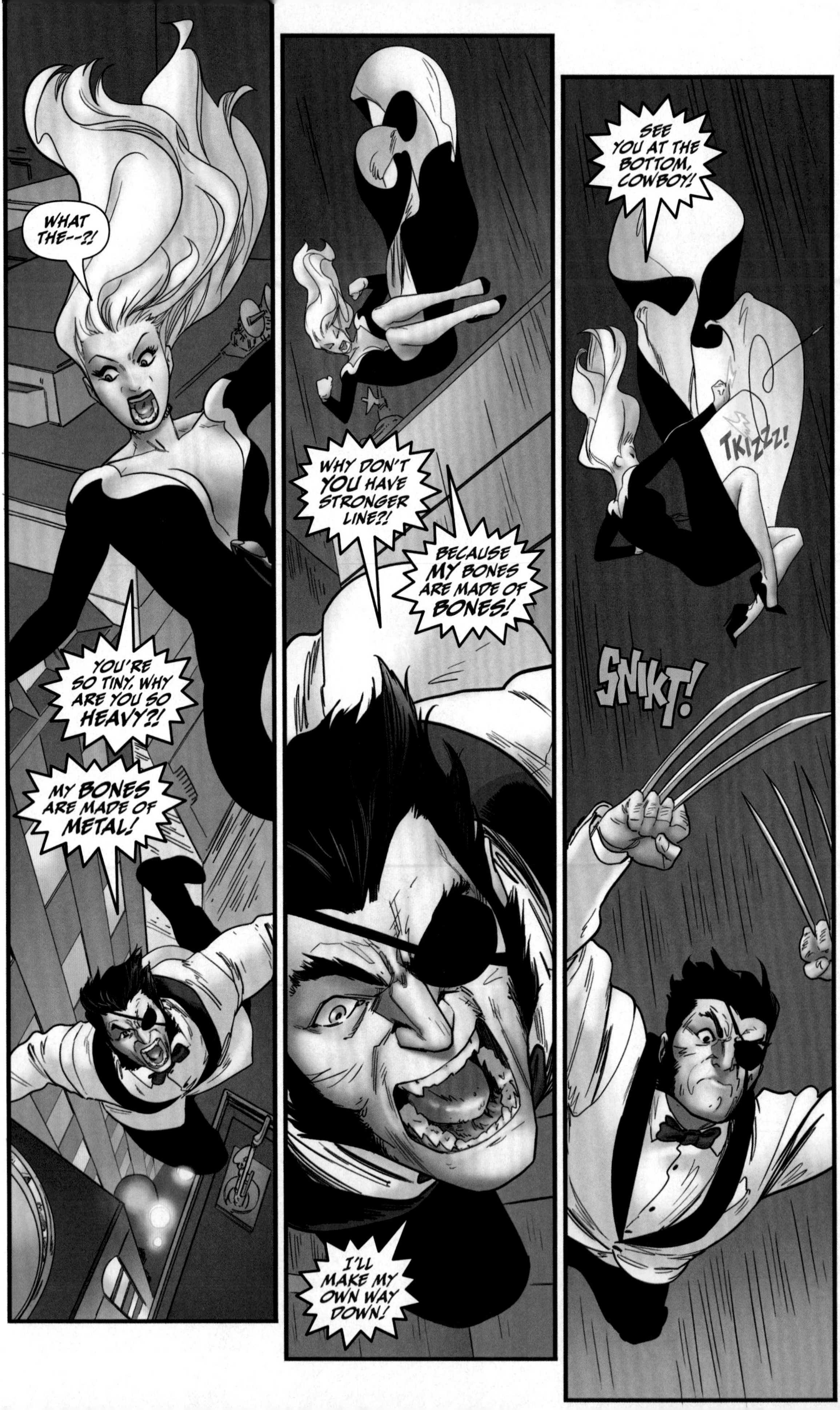
WHAT THE--?!
YOU'RE SO TINY, WHY ARE YOU SO HEAVY?!
MY BONES ARE MADE OF METAL!
WHY DON'T YOU HAVE STRONGER LINE?!
BECAUSE MY BONES ARE MADE OF BONES!
I'LL MAKE MY OWN WAY DOWN!
SEE YOU AT THE BOTTOM, COWBOY!
TKIZZZ!
SNIKT!

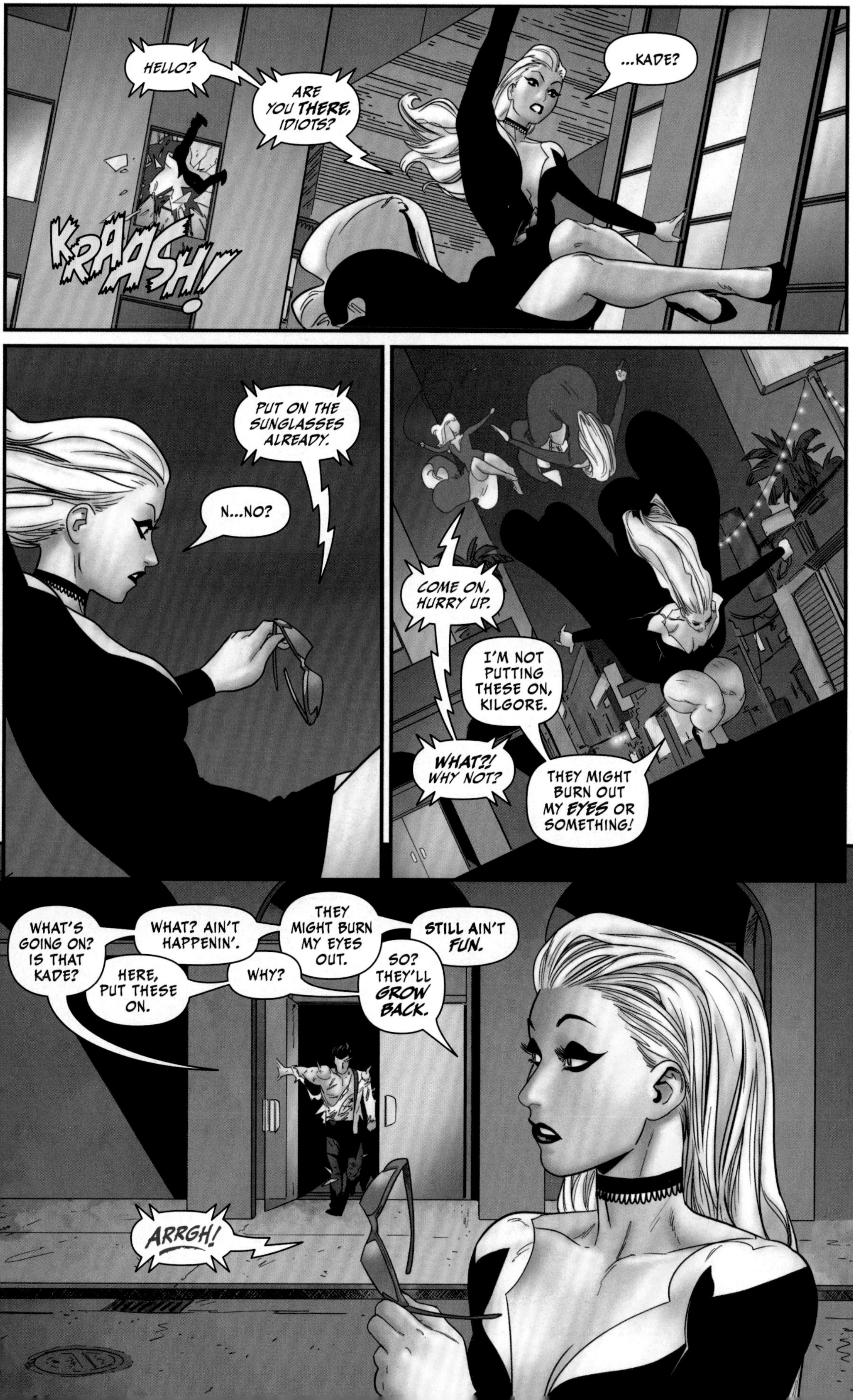
HELLO?
ARE YOU THERE, IDIOTS?
...KADE?
KRAASH!
PUT ON THE SUNGLASSES ALREADY.
N...NO?
COME ON, HURRY UP.
I'M NOT PUTTING THESE ON, KILGORE.
WHAT?! WHY NOT?
THEY MIGHT BURN OUT MY EYES OR SOMETHING!
WHAT'S GOING ON? IS THAT KADE?
HERE, PUT THESE ON.
WHAT? AIN'T HAPPENIN'.
WHY?
THEY MIGHT BURN MY EYES OUT.
SO? THEY'LL GROW BACK.
STILL AIN'T FUN.
ARRGH!

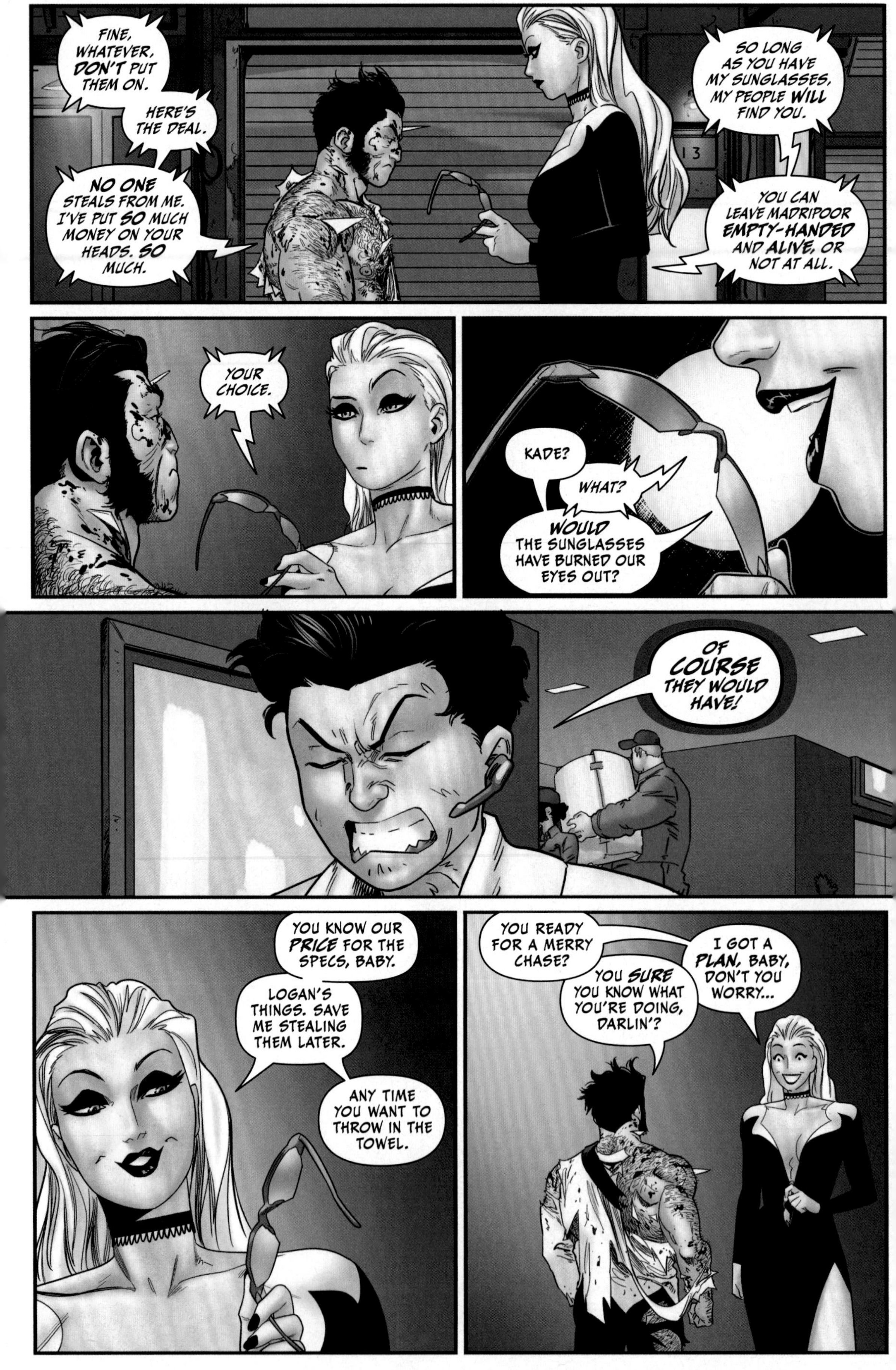
FINE, WHATEVER, DON'T PUT THEM ON.
HERE'S THE DEAL.
NO ONE STEALS FROM ME. I'VE PUT SO MUCH MONEY ON YOUR HEADS. SO MUCH.
SO LONG AS YOU HAVE MY SUNGLASSES, MY PEOPLE WILL FIND YOU.
YOU CAN LEAVE MADRIPOOR EMPTY-HANDED AND ALIVE, OR NOT AT ALL.
YOUR CHOICE.
KADE?
WHAT?
WOULD THE SUNGLASSES HAVE BURNED OUR EYES OUT?
OF COURSE THEY WOULD HAVE!
YOU KNOW OUR PRICE FOR THE SPECS, BABY.
LOGAN'S THINGS. SAVE ME STEALING THEM LATER.
ANY TIME YOU WANT TO THROW IN THE TOWEL.
YOU READY FOR A MERRY CHASE?
I GOT A PLAN, BABY, DON'T YOU WORRY...
YOU SURE YOU KNOW WHAT YOU'RE DOING, DARLIN'?

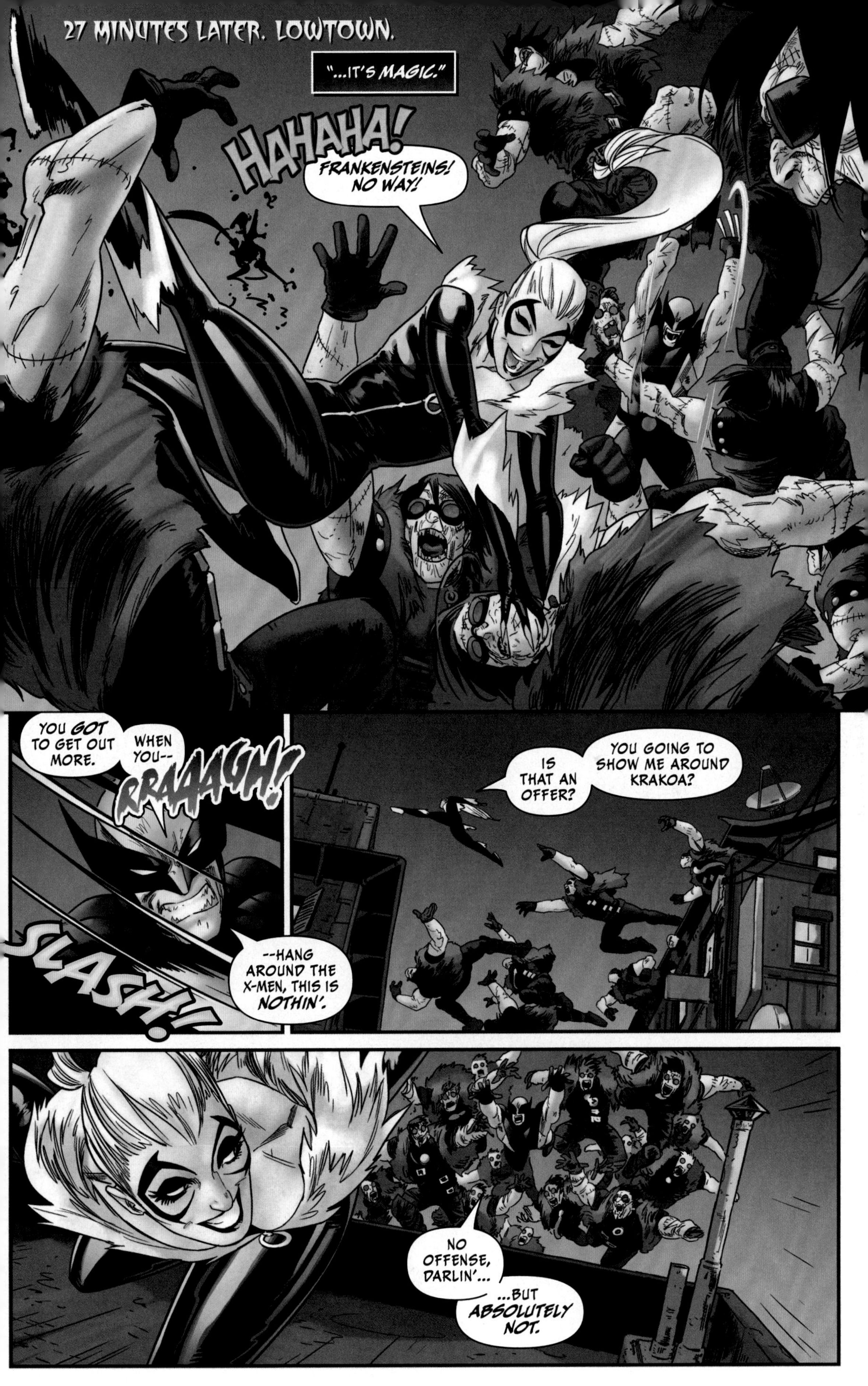
27 MINUTES LATER. LOWTOWN.
"...IT'S MAGIC."
HAHAHA!
FRANKENSTEINS! NO WAY!
YOU GOT TO GET OUT MORE.
WHEN YOU--
RRAAAGH!
SLASH!
--HANG AROUND THE X-MEN, THIS IS NOTHIN'.
YOU GOING TO SHOW ME AROUND KRAKOA?
IS THAT AN OFFER?
NO OFFENSE, DARLIN'...
...BUT ABSOLUTELY NOT.

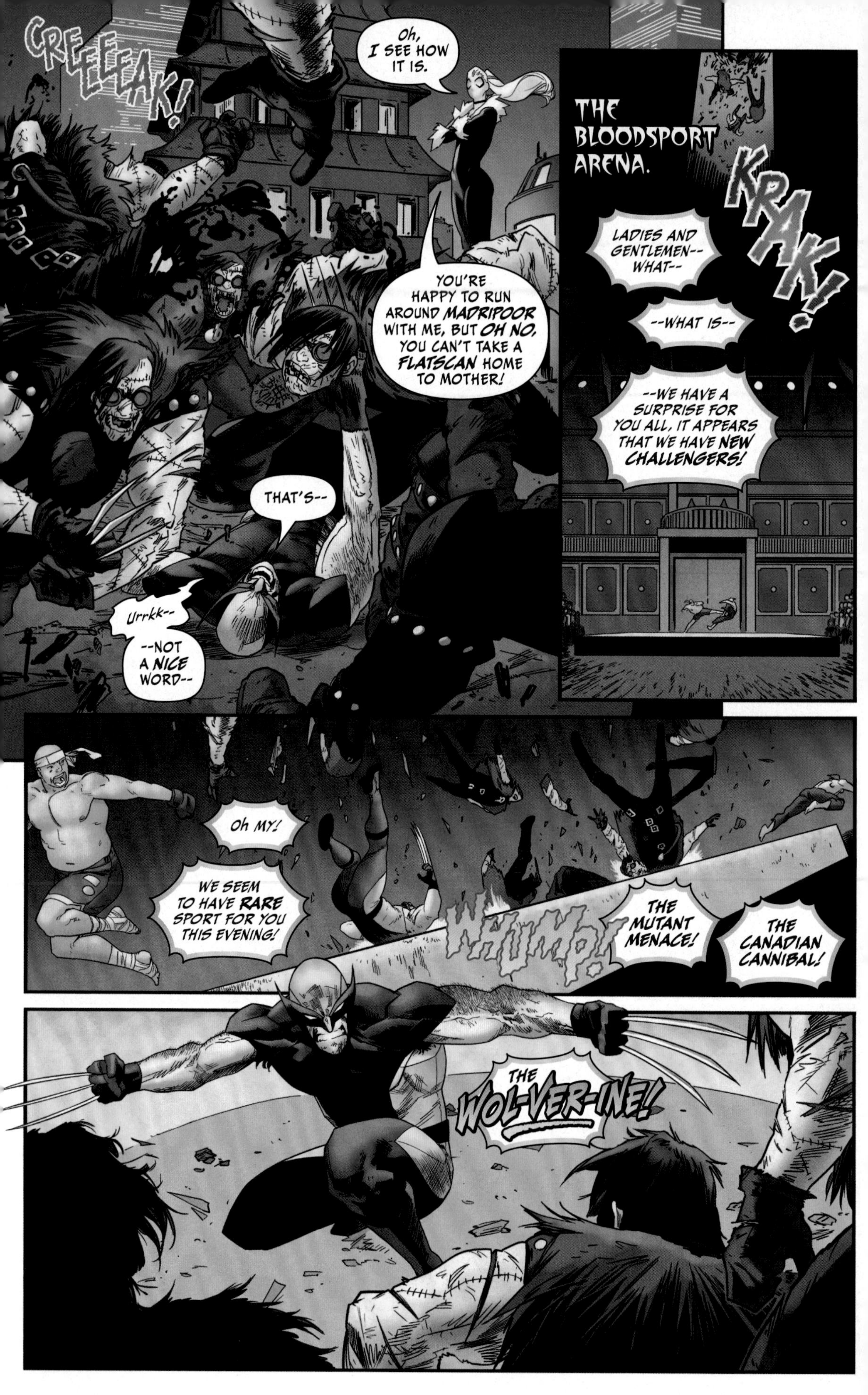
CREEEEAK!
Oh, I SEE HOW IT IS.
YOU'RE HAPPY TO RUN AROUND MADRIPOOR WITH ME, BUT OH NO, YOU CAN'T TAKE A FLATSCAN HOME TO MOTHER!
THAT'S--
Urrkk--
--NOT A NICE WORD--
THE BLOODSPORT ARENA.
KRAK!
LADIES AND GENTLEMEN-- WHAT--
--WHAT IS--
--WE HAVE A SURPRISE FOR YOU ALL, IT APPEARS THAT WE HAVE NEW CHALLENGERS!
Oh MY!
WE SEEM TO HAVE RARE SPORT FOR YOU THIS EVENING!
WHUMP!
THE MUTANT MENACE!
THE CANADIAN CANNIBAL!
THE WOL-VER-INE!

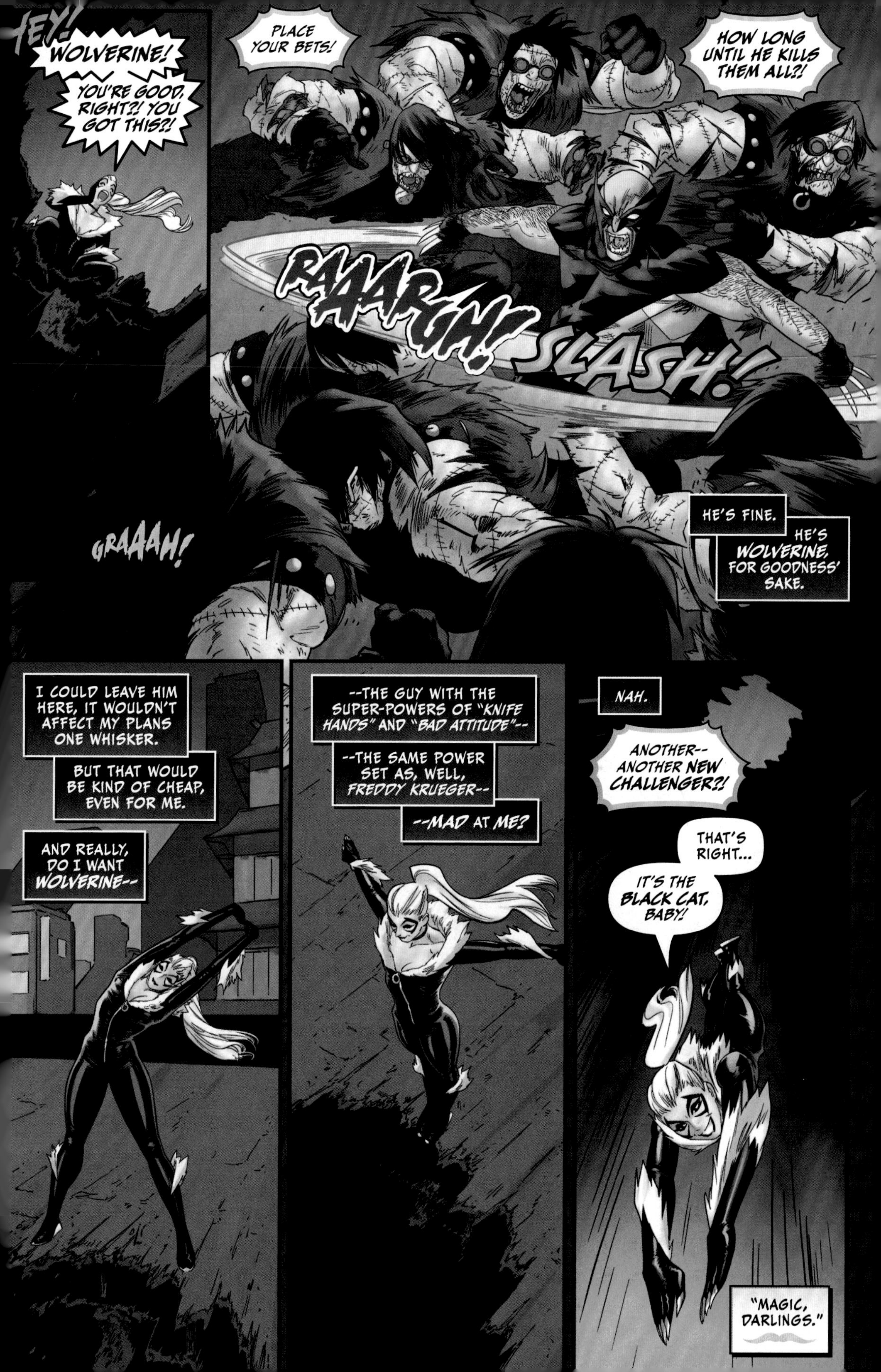
HEY!
WOLVERINE!
YOU'RE GOOD, RIGHT?! YOU GOT THIS?!
PLACE YOUR BETS!
HOW LONG UNTIL HE KILLS THEM ALL?!
RAAARGH!
SLASH!
GRAAAH!
HE'S FINE.
HE'S WOLVERINE, FOR GOODNESS' SAKE.
I COULD LEAVE HIM HERE, IT WOULDN'T AFFECT MY PLANS ONE WHISKER.
BUT THAT WOULD BE KIND OF CHEAP, EVEN FOR ME.
AND REALLY, DO I WANT WOLVERINE--
--THE GUY WITH THE SUPER-POWERS OF "KNIFE HANDS" AND "BAD ATTITUDE"--
--THE SAME POWER SET AS, WELL, FREDDY KRUEGER--
--MAD AT ME?
NAH.
ANOTHER-- ANOTHER NEW CHALLENGER?!
THAT'S RIGHT...
IT'S THE BLACK CAT, BABY!
"MAGIC, DARLINGS."

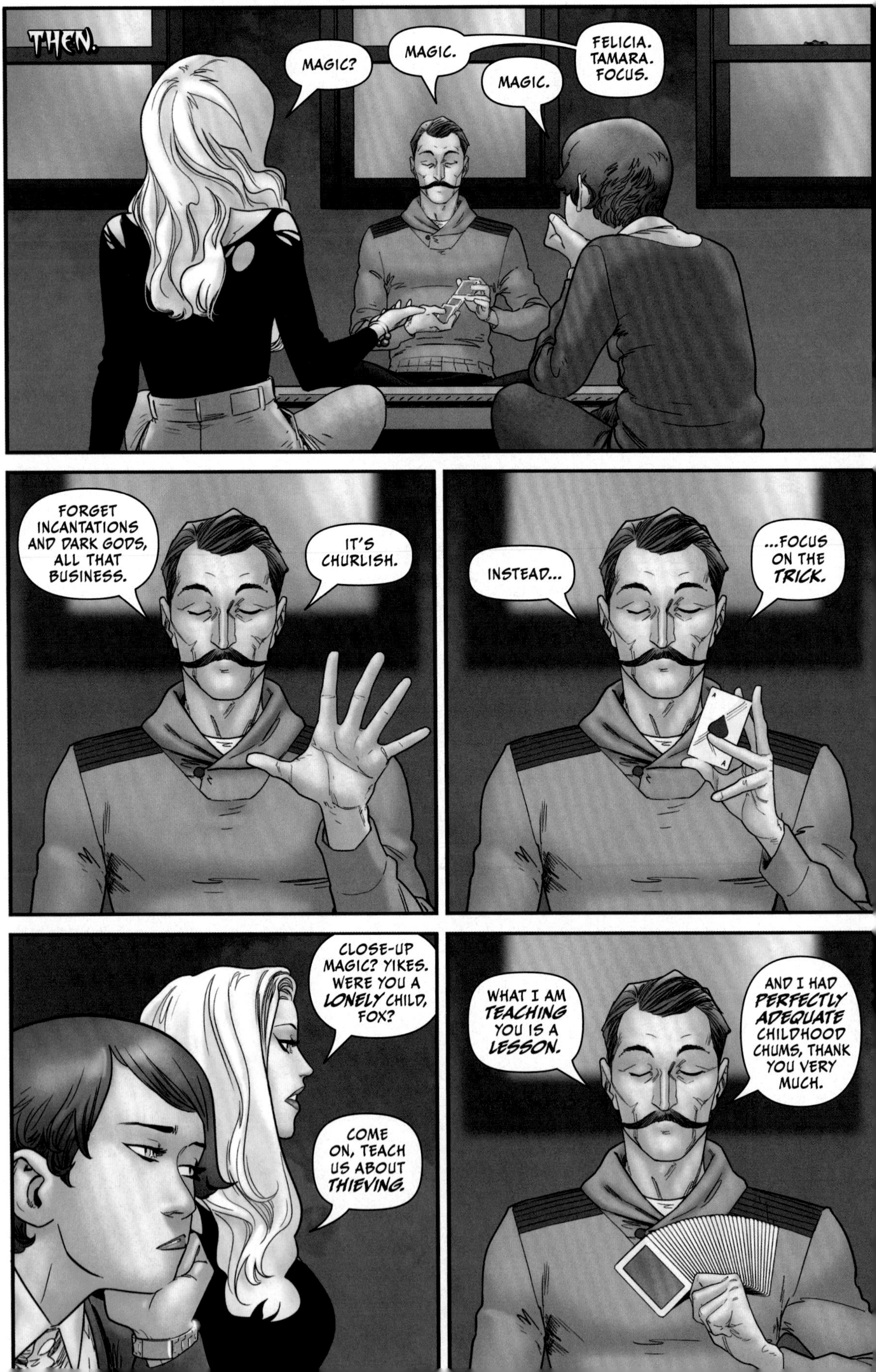
THEN.
MAGIC?
MAGIC.
MAGIC.
FELICIA. TAMARA. FOCUS.
FORGET INCANTATIONS AND DARK GODS, ALL THAT BUSINESS.
IT'S CHURLISH.
INSTEAD...
...FOCUS ON THE TRICK.
CLOSE-UP MAGIC? YIKES. WERE YOU A LONELY CHILD, FOX?
COME ON, TEACH US ABOUT THIEVING.
WHAT I AM TEACHING YOU IS A LESSON.
AND I HAD PERFECTLY ADEQUATE CHILDHOOD CHUMS, THANK YOU VERY MUCH.

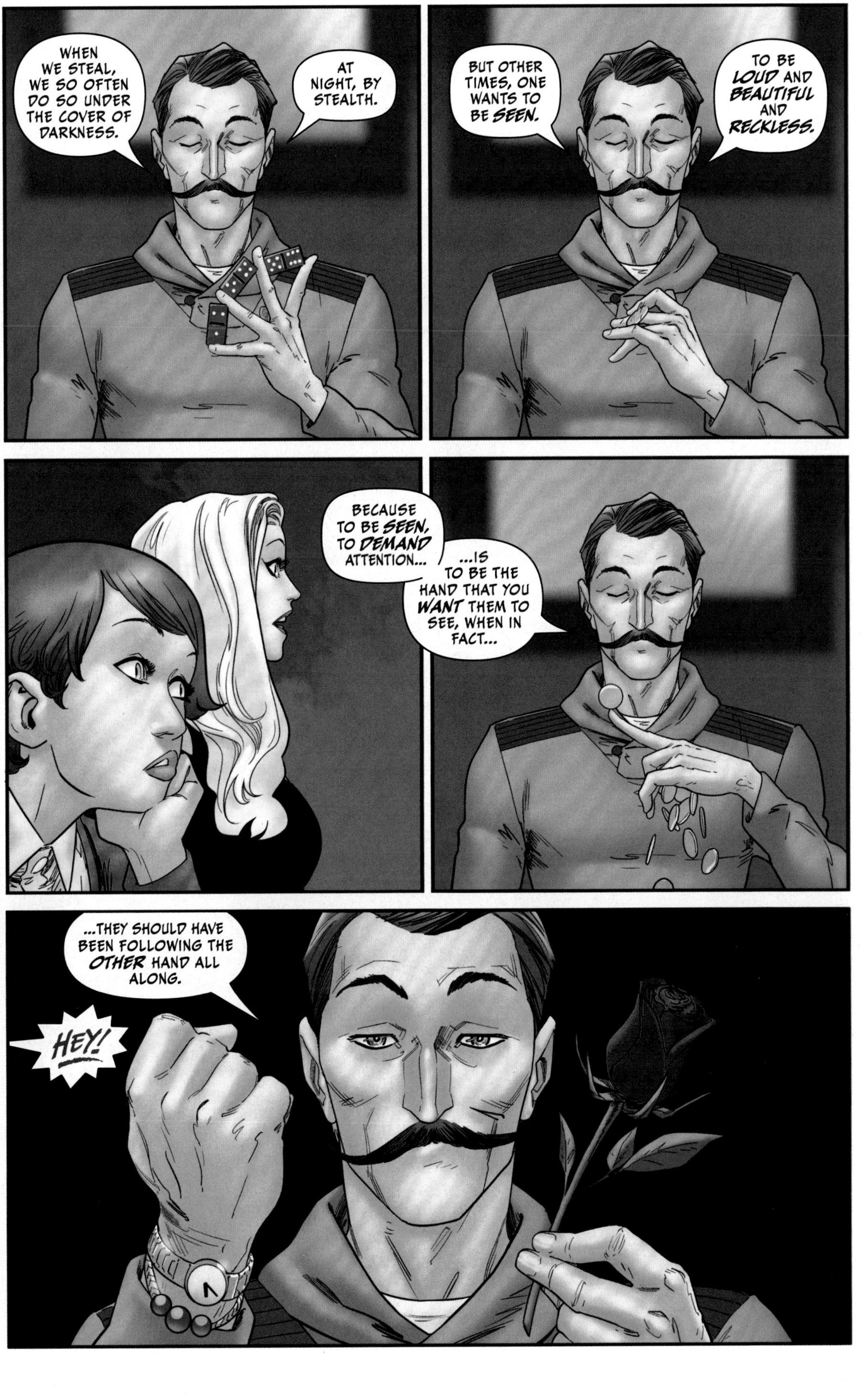
WHEN WE STEAL, WE SO OFTEN DO SO UNDER THE COVER OF DARKNESS.
AT NIGHT, BY STEALTH.
BUT OTHER TIMES, ONE WANTS TO BE SEEN.
TO BE LOUD AND BEAUTIFUL AND RECKLESS.
BECAUSE TO BE SEEN, TO DEMAND ATTENTION...
...IS TO BE THE HAND THAT YOU WANT THEM TO SEE, WHEN IN FACT...
...THEY SHOULD HAVE BEEN FOLLOWING THE OTHER HAND ALL ALONG.
HEY!

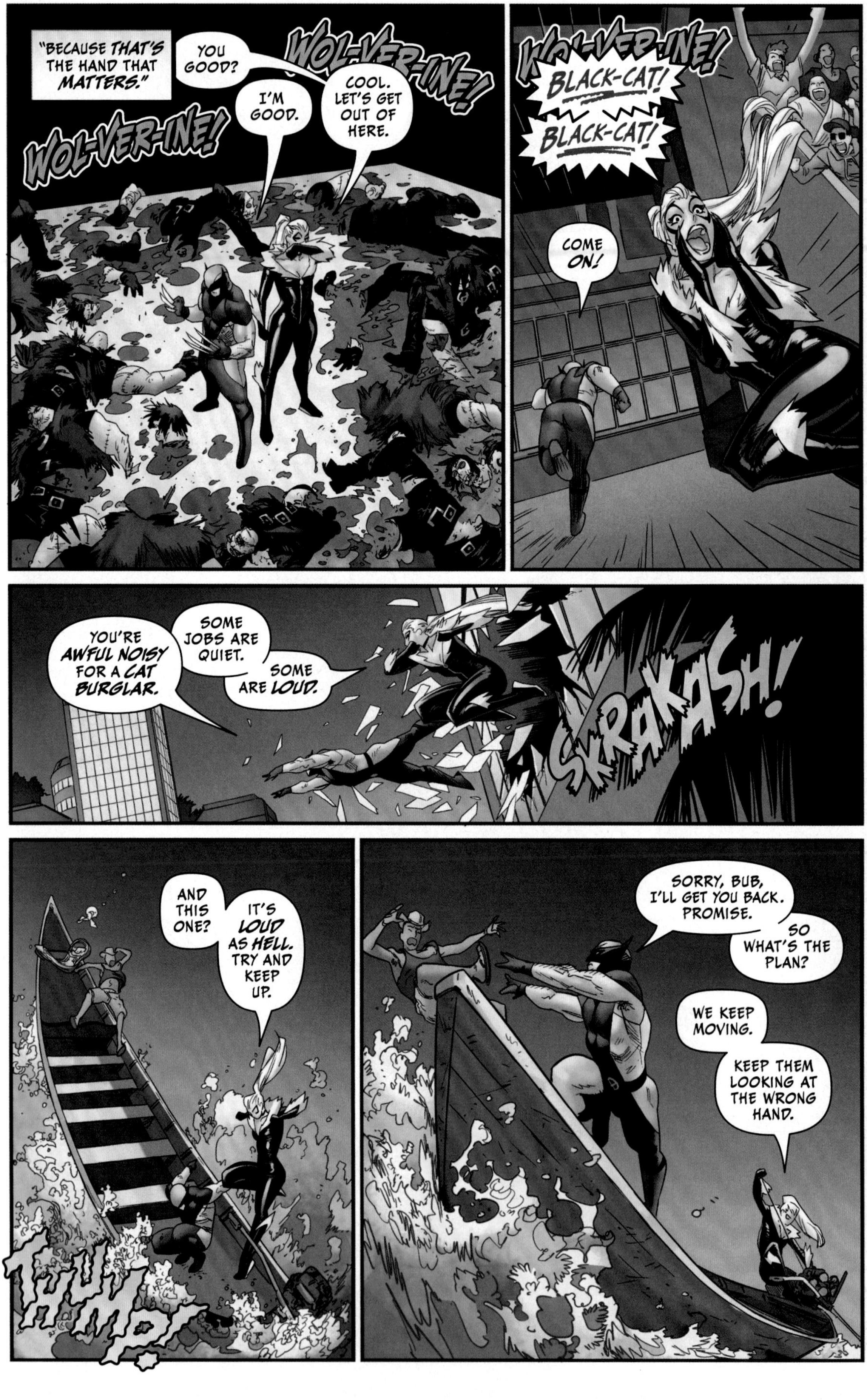
"BECAUSE THAT'S THE HAND THAT MATTERS."
YOU GOOD?
WOL-VER-INE!
I'M GOOD.
COOL. LET'S GET OUT OF HERE.
WOL-VER-INE!
WOL-VER-INE!
BLACK-CAT!
BLACK-CAT!
COME ON!
YOU'RE AWFUL NOISY FOR A CAT BURGLAR.
SOME JOBS ARE QUIET.
SOME ARE LOUD.
SKRAKASH!
AND THIS ONE?
IT'S LOUD AS HELL. TRY AND KEEP UP.
THUMP!
SORRY, BUB, I'LL GET YOU BACK. PROMISE.
SO WHAT'S THE PLAN?
WE KEEP MOVING.
KEEP THEM LOOKING AT THE WRONG HAND.

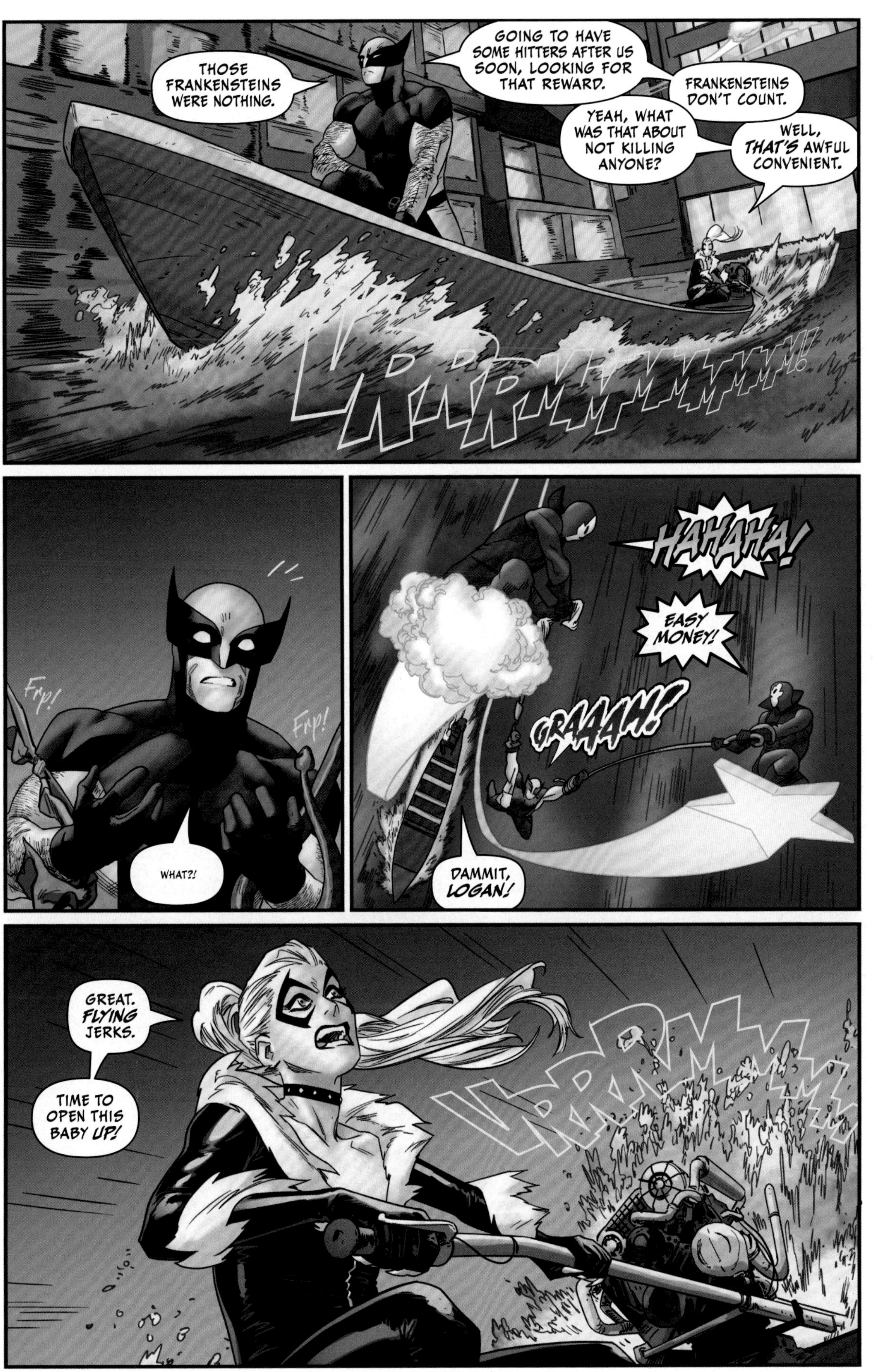
THOSE FRANKENSTEINS WERE NOTHING.
GOING TO HAVE SOME HITTERS AFTER US SOON, LOOKING FOR THAT REWARD.
FRANKENSTEINS DON'T COUNT.
YEAH, WHAT WAS THAT ABOUT NOT KILLING ANYONE?
WELL, THAT'S AWFUL CONVENIENT.
Frp!
Frp!
WHAT?!
HAHAHA!
EASY MONEY!
GRAAAH!
DAMMIT, LOGAN!
GREAT. FLYING JERKS.
TIME TO OPEN THIS BABY UP!

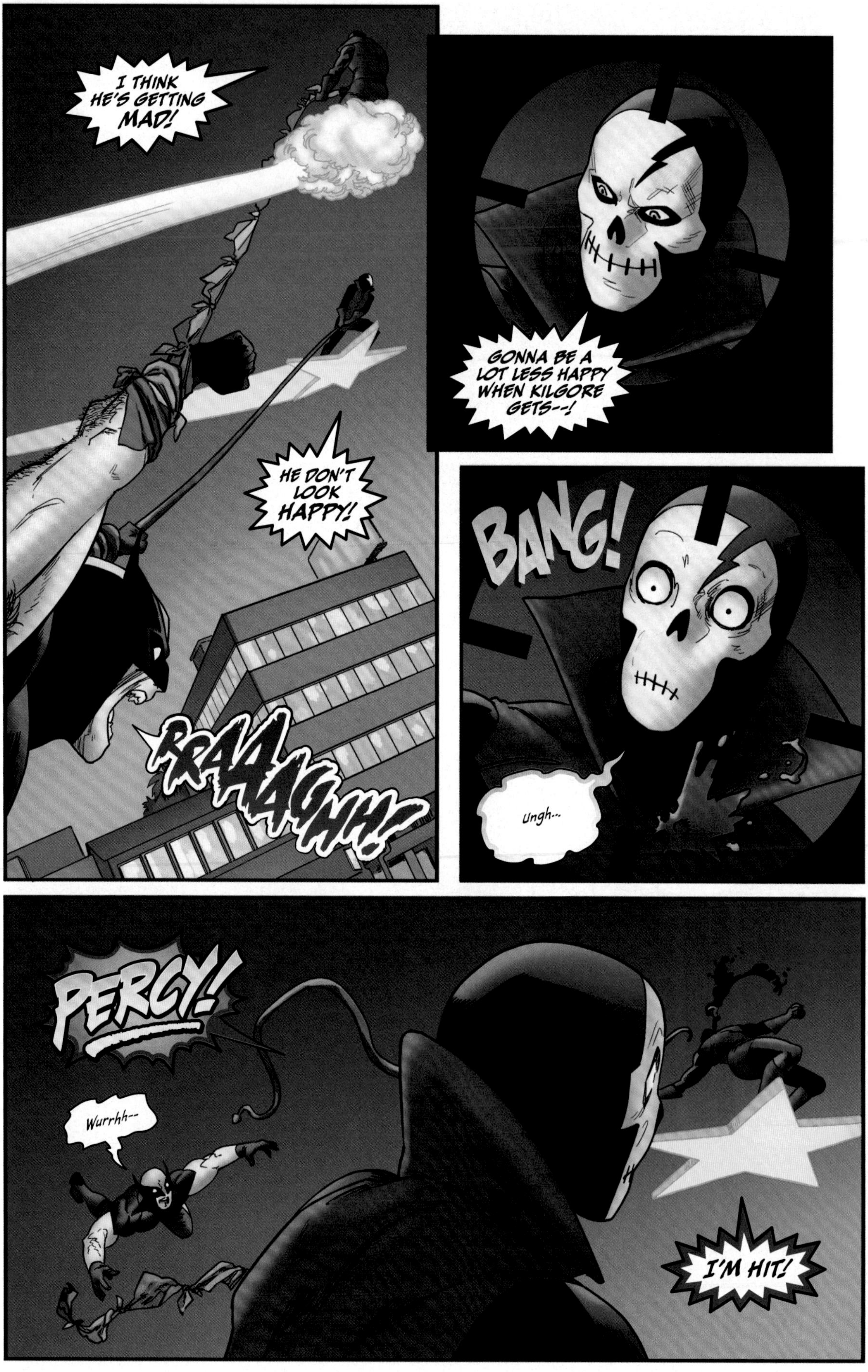
I THINK HE'S GETTING MAD!
HE DON'T LOOK HAPPY!
RRAAAAGHH!
GONNA BE A LOT LESS HAPPY WHEN KILGORE GETS--!
BANG!
Ungh...
PERCY!
Wurrhh--
I'M HIT!

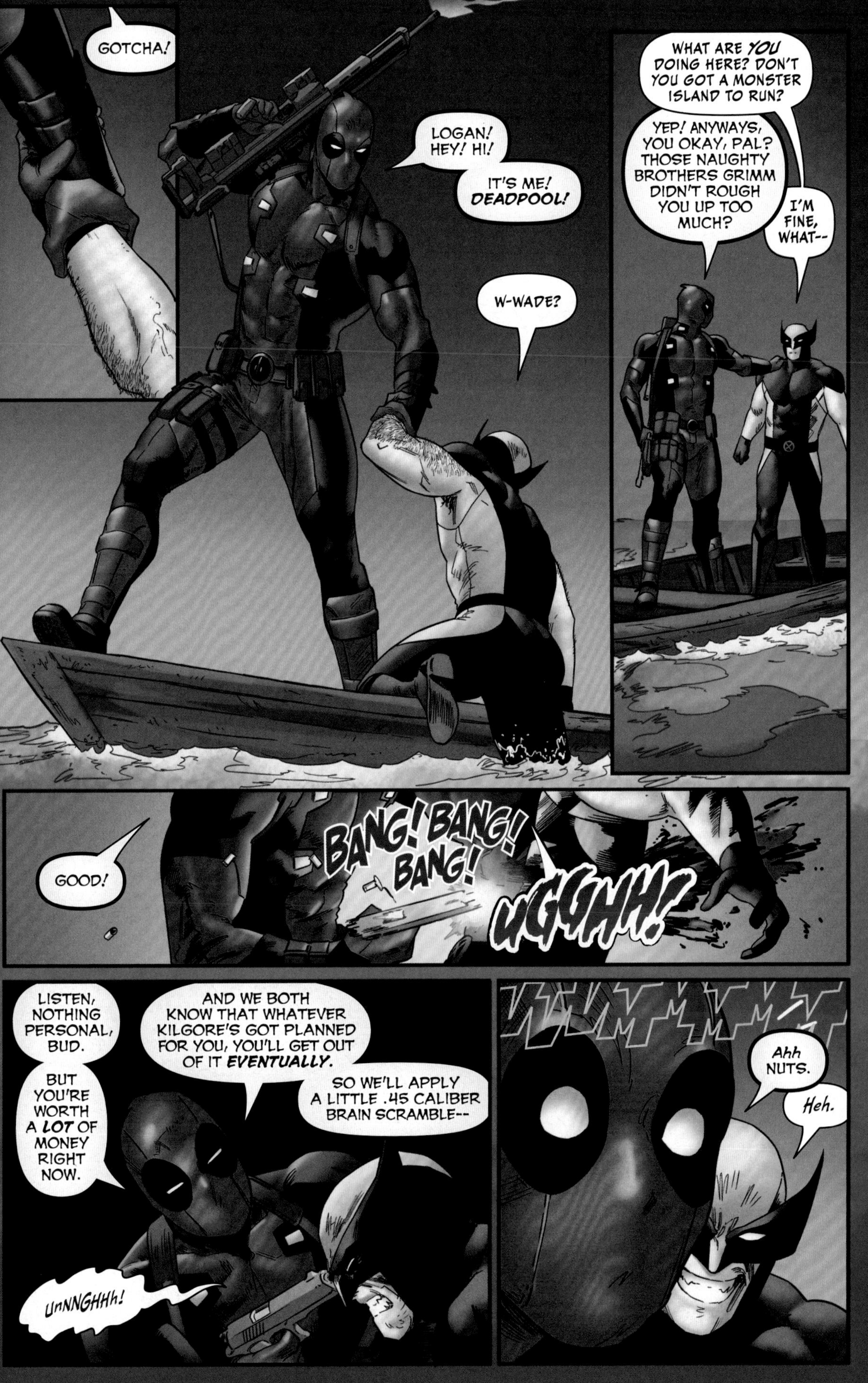
GOTCHA!
LOGAN! HEY! HI!
IT'S ME! DEADPOOL!
W-WADE?
WHAT ARE YOU DOING HERE? DON'T YOU GOT A MONSTER ISLAND TO RUN?
YEP! ANYWAYS, YOU OKAY, PAL? THOSE NAUGHTY BROTHERS GRIMM DIDN'T ROUGH YOU UP TOO MUCH?
I'M FINE, WHAT--
GOOD!
BANG! BANG! BANG!
UGGHH!
LISTEN, NOTHING PERSONAL, BUD.
BUT YOU'RE WORTH A LOT OF MONEY RIGHT NOW.
AND WE BOTH KNOW THAT WHATEVER KILGORE'S GOT PLANNED FOR YOU, YOU'LL GET OUT OF IT EVENTUALLY.
SO WE'LL APPLY A LITTLE .45 CALIBER BRAIN SCRAMBLE--
UnNNGHHh!
Ahh NUTS.
Heh.

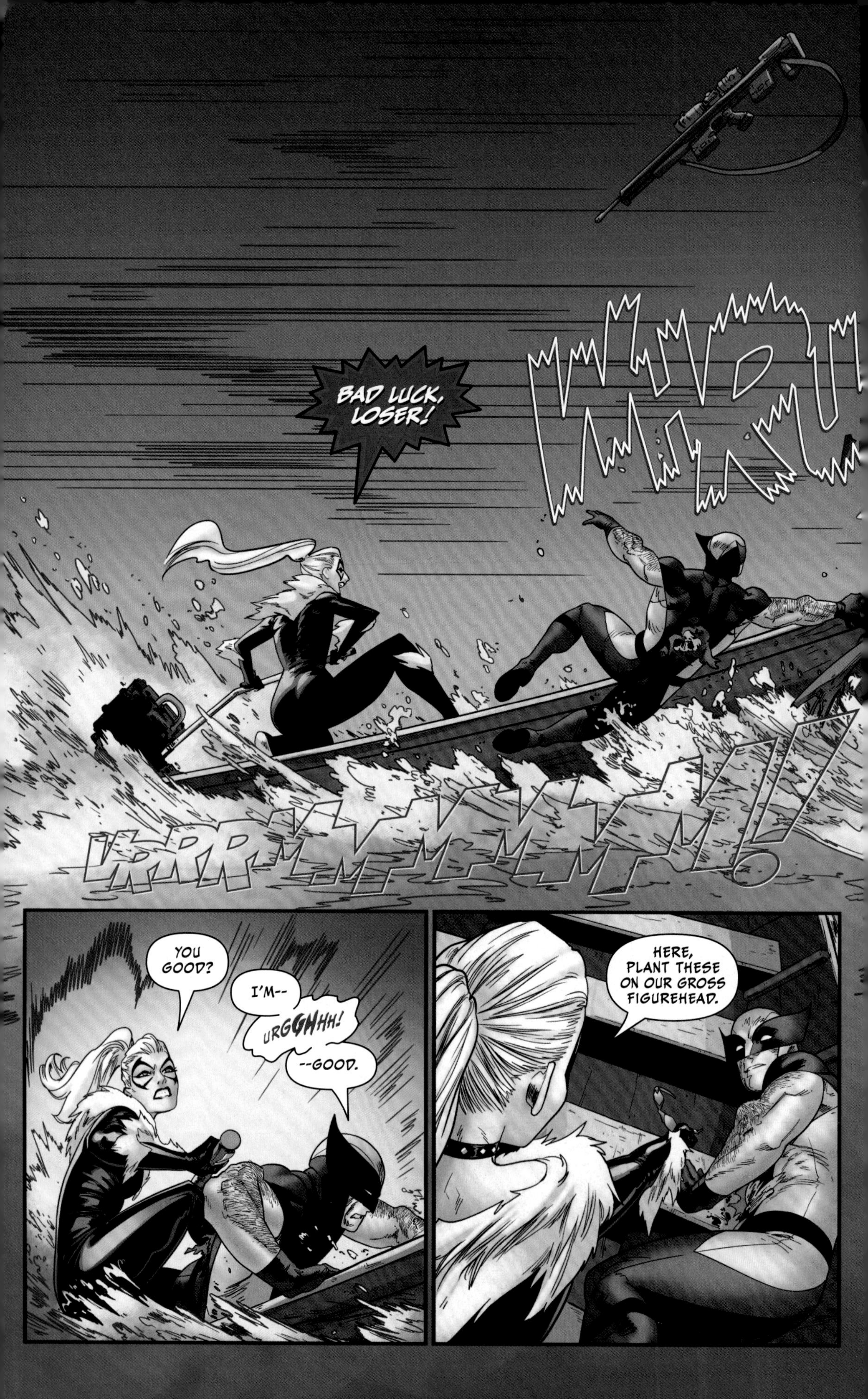
BAD LUCK, LOSER!
YOU GOOD?
I'M--
URGGHHH!
--GOOD.
HERE, PLANT THESE ON OUR GROSS FIGUREHEAD.

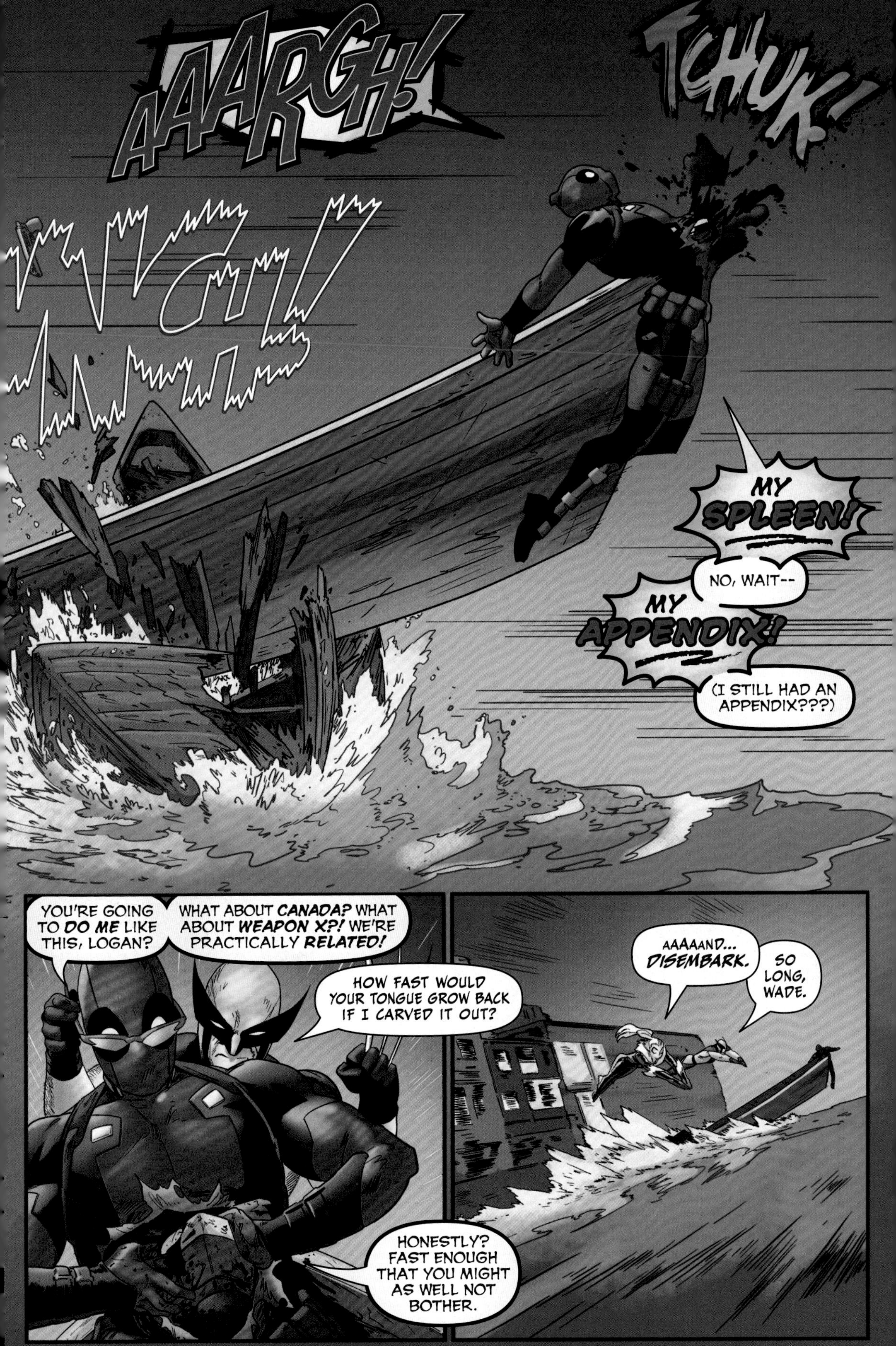

AAARGH!
TCHUK!
MY SPLEEN!
NO, WAIT--
MY APPENDIX!
(I STILL HAD AN APPENDIX???)
YOU'RE GOING TO DO ME LIKE THIS, LOGAN?
WHAT ABOUT CANADA? WHAT ABOUT WEAPON X?! WE'RE PRACTICALLY RELATED!
HOW FAST WOULD YOUR TONGUE GROW BACK IF I CARVED IT OUT?
HONESTLY? FAST ENOUGH THAT YOU MIGHT AS WELL NOT BOTHER.
AAAAAND... DISEMBARK.
SO LONG, WADE.

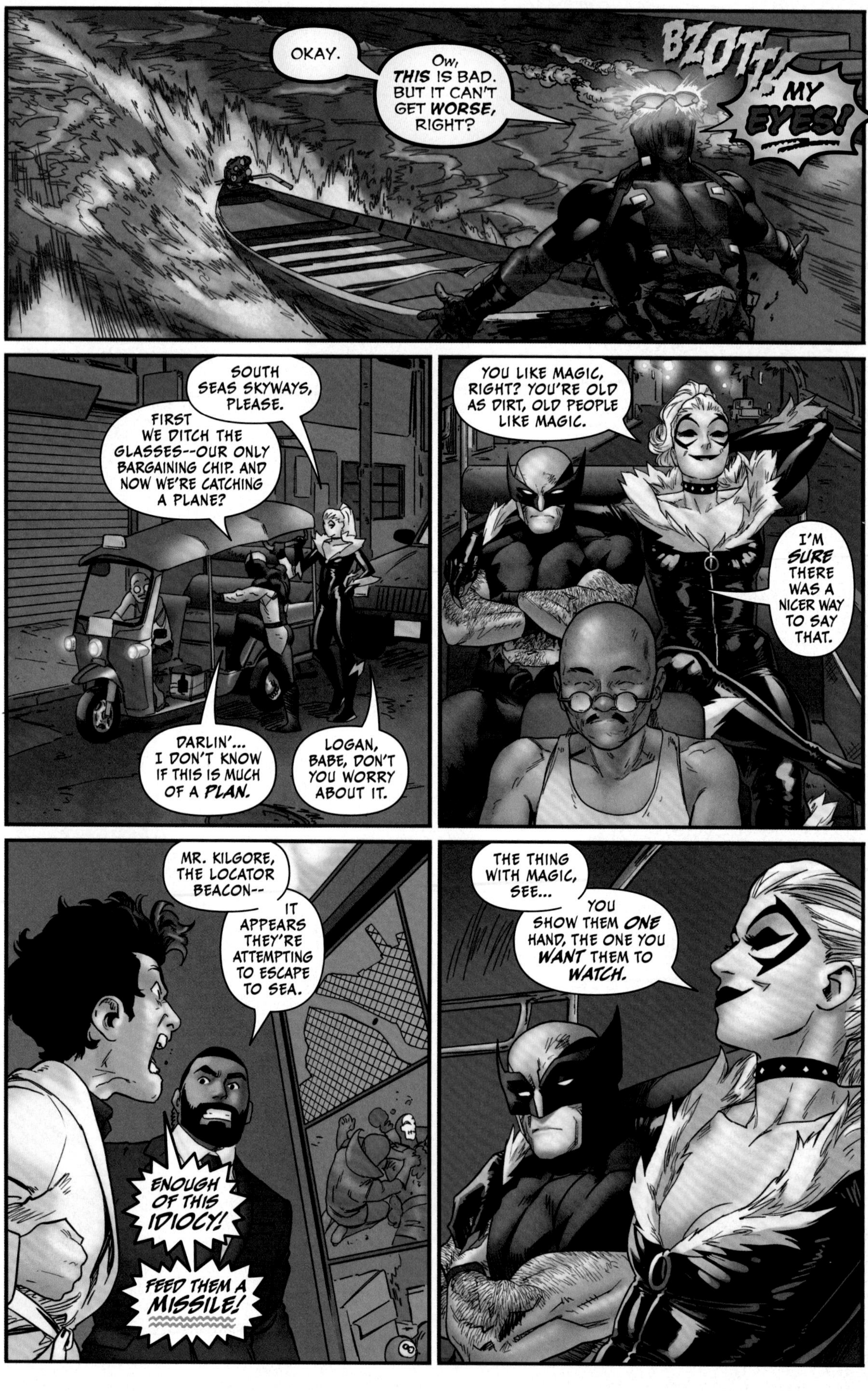

BZOTT!
MY EYES!
OKAY.
OW, THIS IS BAD. BUT IT CAN'T GET WORSE, RIGHT?
SOUTH SEAS SKYWAYS, PLEASE.
FIRST WE DITCH THE GLASSES--OUR ONLY BARGAINING CHIP. AND NOW WE'RE CATCHING A PLANE?
DARLIN'... I DON'T KNOW IF THIS IS MUCH OF A PLAN.
LOGAN, BABE, DON'T YOU WORRY ABOUT IT.
YOU LIKE MAGIC, RIGHT? YOU'RE OLD AS DIRT, OLD PEOPLE LIKE MAGIC.
I'M SURE THERE WAS A NICER WAY TO SAY THAT.
MR. KILGORE, THE LOCATOR BEACON--
IT APPEARS THEY'RE ATTEMPTING TO ESCAPE TO SEA.
ENOUGH OF THIS IDIOCY!
FEED THEM A MISSILE!
THE THING WITH MAGIC, SEE...
YOU SHOW THEM ONE HAND, THE ONE YOU WANT THEM TO WATCH.

"YOU MAKE IT SO THEY CAN'T TAKE THEIR EYES OFF IT, THAT HAND.

"YOU TAKE POSSESSION OF THEIR ATTENTION.

KILGORE

WHOOSH!

"YOU *STEAL* IT.

BZOTT!

Ow.

Ow.

Ow.

OKAY, *NOW* IT CAN'T GET ANY WORSE, RIGHT?

...RIGHT?

"BECAUSE WHILE THEY'RE WATCHING *THAT* HAND..."

...THEY'RE NOT WATCHING THE *OTHER* HAND.

BOYS.

BOSS.

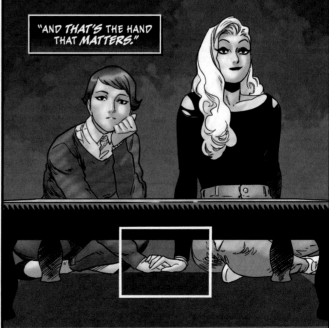

"AND *THAT'S* THE HAND THAT *MATTERS*."

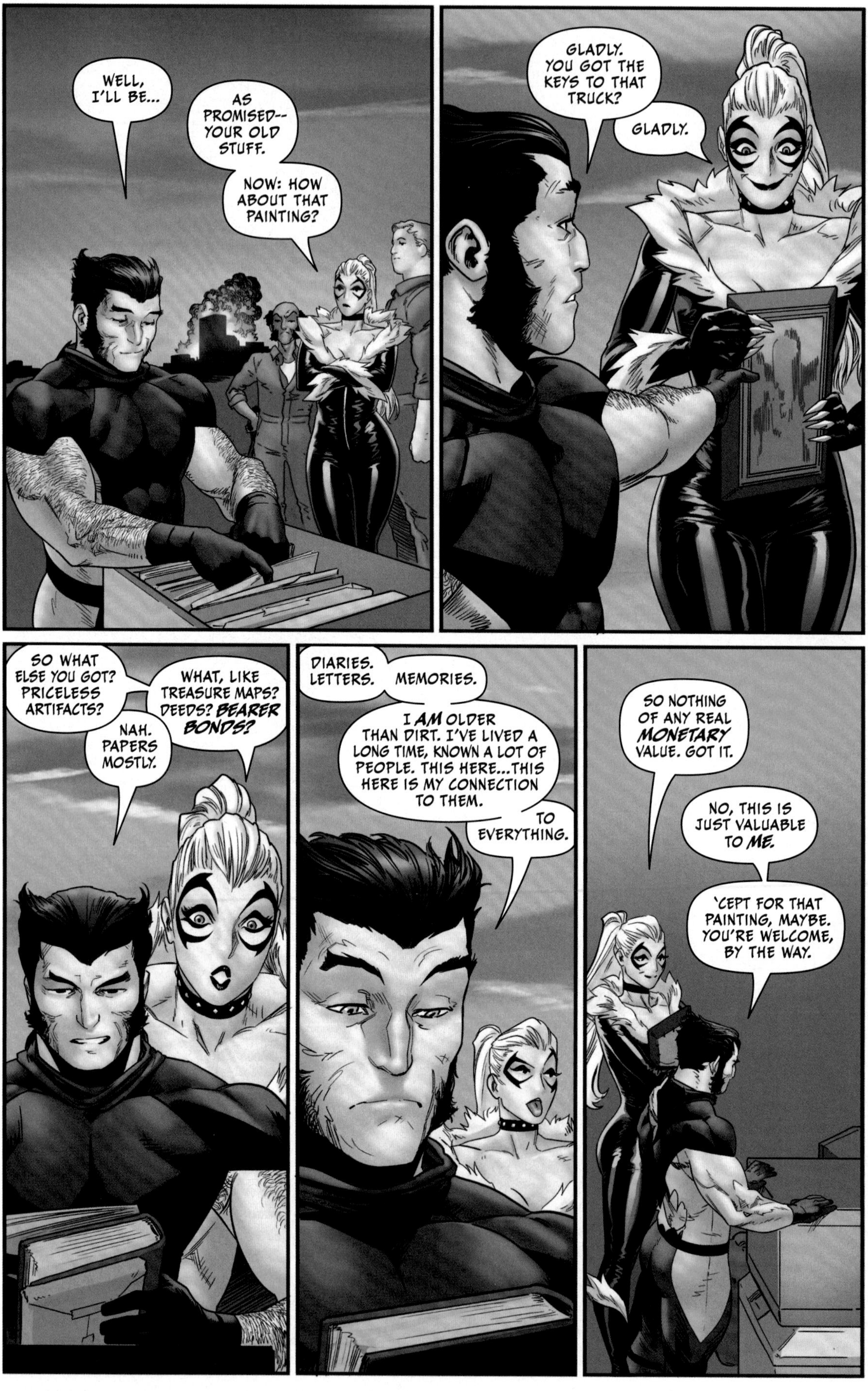
WELL, I'LL BE...
AS PROMISED--YOUR OLD STUFF.
NOW: HOW ABOUT THAT PAINTING?
GLADLY. YOU GOT THE KEYS TO THAT TRUCK?
GLADLY.
SO WHAT ELSE YOU GOT? PRICELESS ARTIFACTS?
WHAT, LIKE TREASURE MAPS? DEEDS? BEARER BONDS?
NAH. PAPERS MOSTLY.
DIARIES. LETTERS.
MEMORIES.
I AM OLDER THAN DIRT. I'VE LIVED A LONG TIME, KNOWN A LOT OF PEOPLE. THIS HERE...THIS HERE IS MY CONNECTION TO THEM.
TO EVERYTHING.
SO NOTHING OF ANY REAL MONETARY VALUE. GOT IT.
NO, THIS IS JUST VALUABLE TO ME.
'CEPT FOR THAT PAINTING, MAYBE. YOU'RE WELCOME, BY THE WAY.

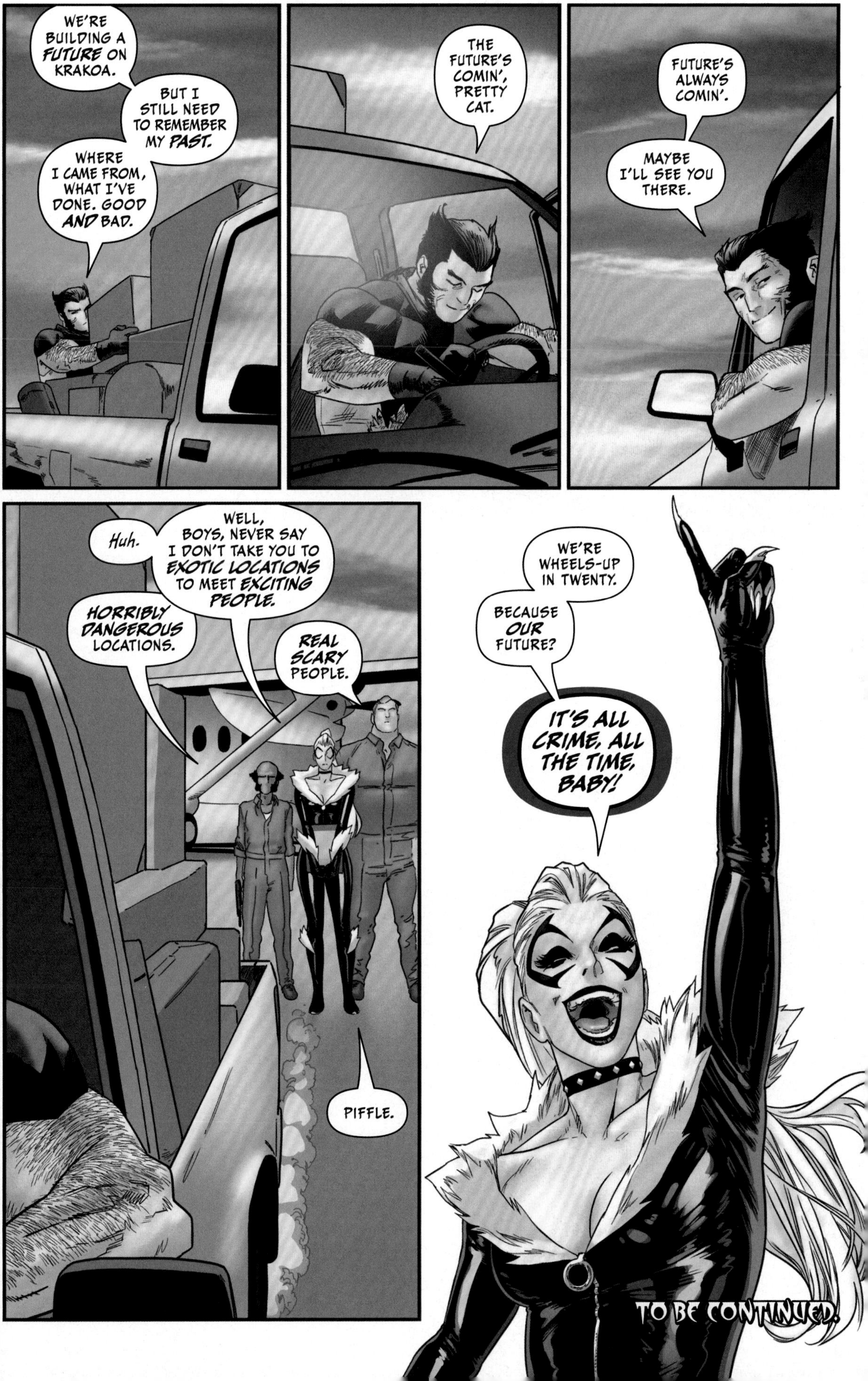
WE'RE BUILDING A FUTURE ON KRAKOA.
BUT I STILL NEED TO REMEMBER MY PAST.
WHERE I CAME FROM, WHAT I'VE DONE. GOOD AND BAD.
THE FUTURE'S COMIN', PRETTY CAT.
FUTURE'S ALWAYS COMIN'.
MAYBE I'LL SEE YOU THERE.
Huh.
WELL, BOYS, NEVER SAY I DON'T TAKE YOU TO EXOTIC LOCATIONS TO MEET EXCITING PEOPLE.
HORRIBLY DANGEROUS LOCATIONS.
REAL SCARY PEOPLE.
PIFFLE.
WE'RE WHEELS-UP IN TWENTY.
BECAUSE OUR FUTURE?
IT'S ALL CRIME, ALL THE TIME, BABY!
TO BE CONTINUED.

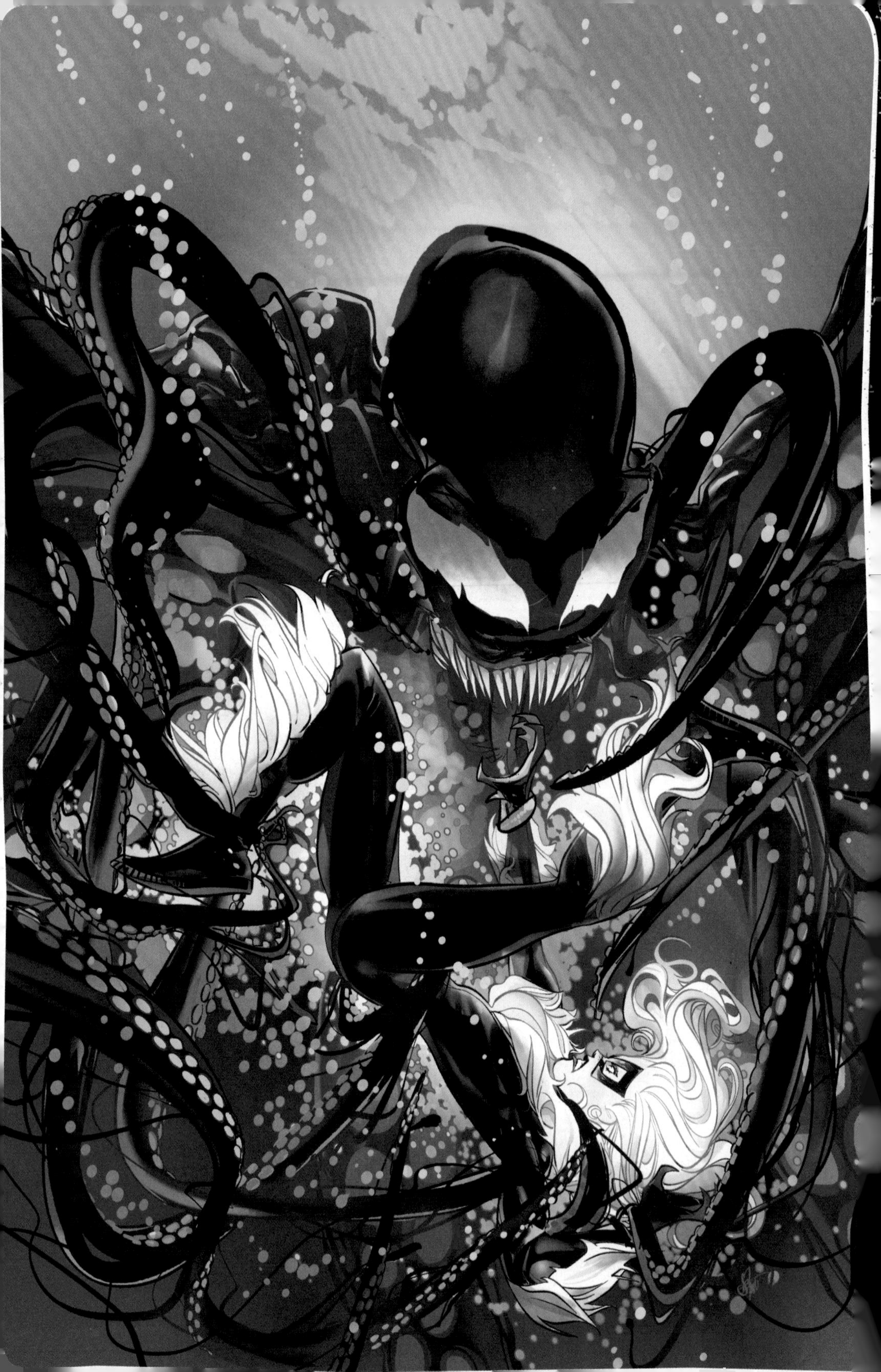

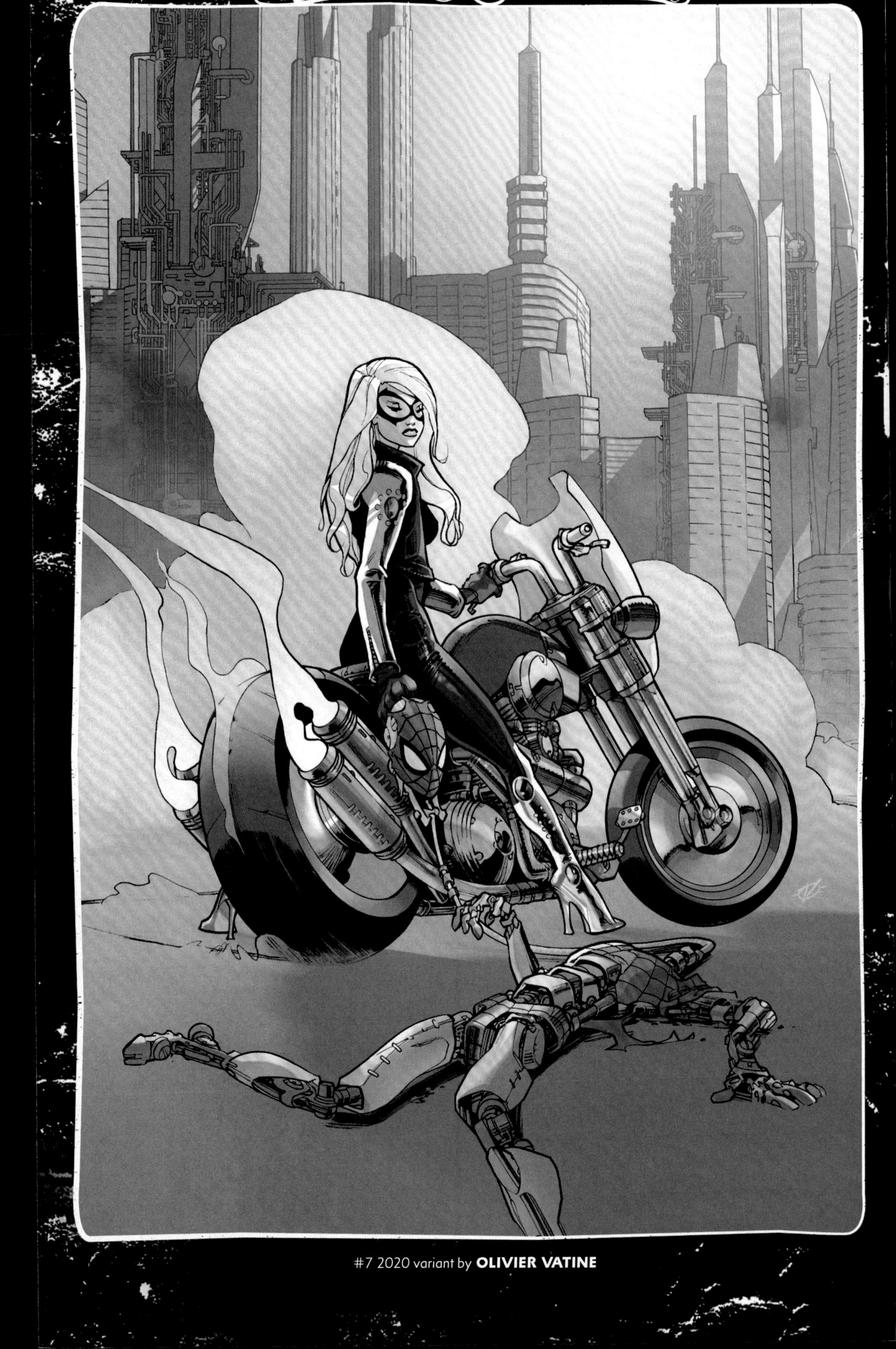

#7 2020 variant by **OLIVIER VATINE**

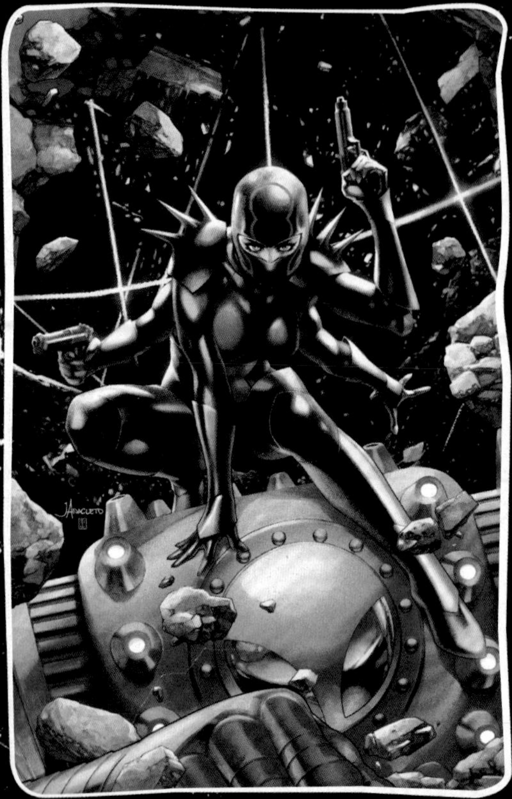

#8 Marvels X variant
by **JAY ANACLETO** & **NEERAJ MENON**

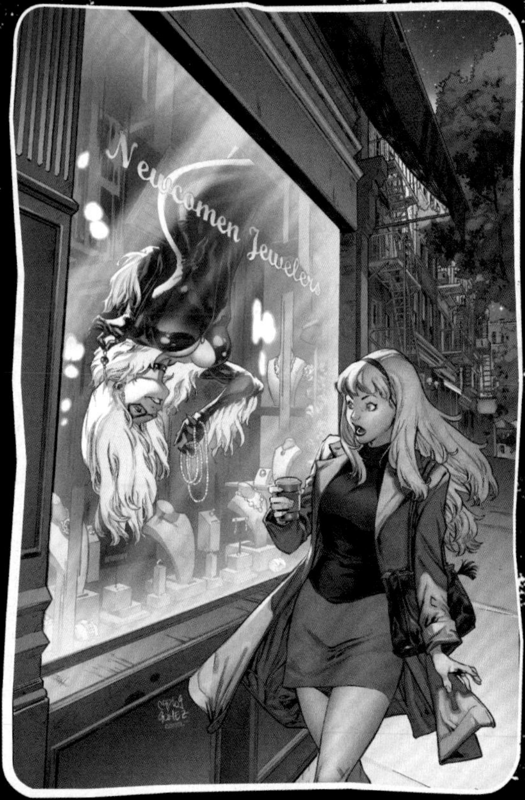
Newcomen Jewelers

#9 Gwen Stacy variant
by **CARLOS GÓMEZ** & **DAVID CURIEL**

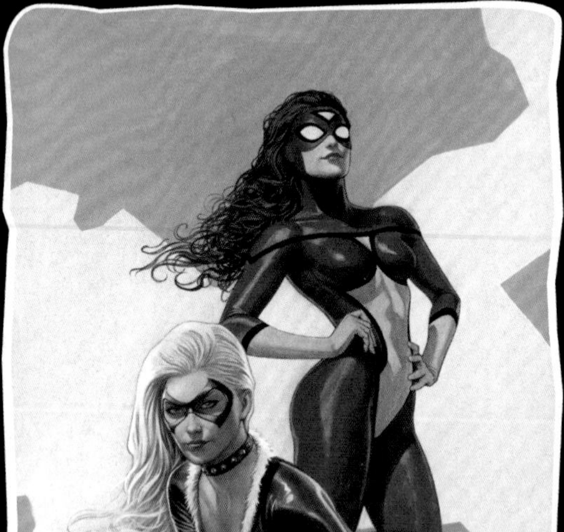

#10 Spider-Woman variant by **ADI GRANOV**